Graphic Standards Field Guide to Softscape

Graphic Standards Field Guide to Softscape

LEONARD J. HOPPER, RLA FASLA

John Wiley & Sons, Inc.

Library of Congress Cataloging-in-Publication Data

Hopper, Leonard J.
   Graphic standards field guide to softscape / Leonard J. Hopper.
      p. cm.—(Graphic standards field guide series)
   Includes index.
    ISBN 978-0-470-42964-8 (pbk.); 978-0-470-95132-3 (ebk); 978-0-470-95151-4 (ebk);
   978-1-118-10570-2 (ebk); 978-1-118-10571-9 (ebk); 978-1-118-10572-6 (ebk)
   1. Landscape design. 2. Landscape architectural drawing. 3. Landscape architecture—
Graphic methods. I. Title.
   SB472.45.H66 2011
   624—dc22

                                                              2011012206

Printed in the United States of America
10 9 8 7 6 5 4 3 2 1

Contents

Introduction

Welcome to Wiley's Graphic Standards Field Guides!

We know that when you're on a job site or in a meeting, questions come up. Even the most seasoned professionals may wish they could look up just that one piece of information that is just outside their instant recall or just beyond their current experience. There is a real need to make immediate on-site decisions—to access information on the spot, no matter where you are.

Graphic Standards Field Guide to Softscape is designed to be a quick and portable reference for busy professionals like you. It focuses on just the information you need away from the design desk, no matter where you are.

Who This Book Is For

The connection between what happens in the design office and on the project site (before, during, and after construction) is critical. Yet there is a trend toward creating a separation between office and site. This book attempts to bridge that gap and provide a handy field reference that will be a valuable resource on site visits.

If you're a landscape architect, designer, construction inspector, or facilities manager involved in site work, this book is for you. This book contains the critical core information you'll need when working away from the office. It's like having the job site knowledge of your firm's most experienced professional in your pocket.

How This Book Is Organized

The content of this book is organized to follow a logical topic sequence from site assessment of existing conditions through site maintenance. Each chapter covers a specific division, and includes topics appropriate to softscape site design and construction. Use the chapter's opening pages to find a specific topic within a division, or refer to the index to find exactly what you need.

Some of the material is geared toward preliminary site visits, assessment of existing conditions, and factors to consider during design development. Some information will be valuable as the project moves into the preparation of contract documents. Other information on how the contractor executes the information provided on the contract drawings will be helpful during the construction phase. Some information is geared toward project aftercare and maintenance.

Information on specific topics is presented in lists and tables, making it easy to find and reference quickly. Construction details and drawings, coupled with photographs, demonstrate standards and help you evaluate what you may encounter on-site.

Each topic contains the following sections:

Description: A brief overview of the topic, to provide some context.

Assessing Site Conditions: Key things to look for when you're in the field that will help guide your decisions.

Acceptable Practices: Keys to what constitutes good-quality work and references to industry standards.

Practices to Avoid: A quick list of what to look out for.

Resources: This section tells you where to find more information about the topic within this book or in other sources.

This symbol ▶ indicates information you may need in the field that are good rules of thumb or acceptable practices.

How to Use This Book

The Field Guides are meant to go anywhere you go. Take them to meetings and site visits, or keep one in the glove compartment just in case—the book is a handy reference to have on hand whenever you are away from the design desk and out of the office.

Use the Field Guide to:

- Help a client evaluate a prospective property or site.
- Develop an existing conditions inventory and analysis.
- Define a project scope with site opportunities and constraints.
- Find information on unexpected on-site conditions.
- Remind yourself of possibilities and alternatives.

- Create a checklist to make sure you asked all the right questions during a site visit.
- Expand your expertise on construction practices.

Ultimately, a good design professional must have an understanding of the relationship that the existing conditions of the site and construction materials and practices have with every phase of the design process. This book attempts to strengthen that understanding.

About the Author

Leonard J. Hopper, FASLA, is a former project administrator for site improvements for the New York City Housing Authority. Currently, Hopper is a senior associate with Mark K. Morrison Landscape Architecture, PC, in New York City. In the thirty years with NYCHA and the past four with Mark K. Morrison, Len has been responsible for all phases of design development, project management, and construction administration across a broad spectrum of the profession. As a participant in the Sustainable Sites Initiative, Len served on a technical subcommittee that established guidelines and performance benchmarks for documenting how sites can use natural elements in designs that provide human benefits as well as benefits to the environment. He continues to serve as a technical advisor to that group's ongoing efforts.

As a faculty member at The City College Spitzer School of Architecture, Masters in Landscape Architecture Program; at Columbia University's Masters of Science in Landscape Design Program; and at SUNY Farmingdale's Horticultural Technology Management Program, Len teaches the technology course sequence that includes site inventory and analysis, grading, soil science, storm water management, soil erosion and sediment control, and construction materials and details.

Len served as Editor-in-Chief of *Landscape Architectural Graphic Standards* and *Landscape Architectural Graphic Standards, Student Edition*, and author of *Security and Site Design* and *Graphic Standards Field Guide to Hardscape* (all from Wiley).

Len Hopper is an active member of the American Society of Landscape Architects (ASLA), serving as national president for 2000–2001. He served as president of the Landscape Architecture Foundation for 2005–2006. In recognition of his accomplishments and contributions, Len received an award for "Outstanding Leadership on Issues Affecting Urban Design, Rehabilitation and Policy" from the Landscape Architecture Foundation in 1993; he was elected to ASLA's Council of Fellows in 1994, and was the recipient of the ASLA President's Medal in 2005.

About Graphic Standards

First Published in 1932, *Architectural Graphic Standards* (AGS) is a comprehensive source of architectural and building design data and construction details.

Now in its eleventh edition, AGS has sold more than one million copies and has become one of the most influential and indispensable tools of the trade for architects, builders, draftsmen, engineers and students, interior designers, real estate professionals, and many others. The entire family of Graphic Standards resources is ready to help you in your work. In recent years, the franchise has expanded to include Interior Graphic Standards, Planning and Urban Design Standards, and the most recent publication, *Landscape Architectural Graphic Standards*. Each of these major references follows in the tradition of Architectural Graphic Standards and is the first source of comprehensive design data for any design or construction project. Explore what these products have to offer, and see how quickly they become an essential part of your practice.

Visit www.graphicstandards.com for more information.

Acknowledgments

This book would never have been completed without the patience, support, and gentle prodding of my Editor, Kathryn Malm Bourgoine; the help whenever I needed it from her Editorial Assistant, Lauren Poplawski; and the technical guidance of my Production Editor, Doug Salvemini. My thanks and appreciation to these great people and all the staff at John Wiley & Sons who contribute to making these books possible.

Many thanks to my family who had to share vacation time and holidays with me typing away on the computer to meet (or nearly meet) a deadline. And especially to my wife, Cindy, who kept the music playing and the beer cold in the most hectic of times. I could not have written this book without their constant support and generous sharing of my time.

PART I

SOILS AND EARTH

Chapter 1

Soils

Soil Overview

Description

Soil as a growing medium may be defined as a natural system, composed of mineral particles, organic matter, water, and air, all supporting growing plants. The "soil profile" consists of horizons, and there exist important interrelationships among the horizons, as they are interdependent and necessary for the entire profile to fulfill its function as a rooting medium, both in nature and in the designed landscape project (Craul and Craul 2006). The ideal soil has about 45 percent mineral solids, 5 percent organic matter solids, and 25 percent each water and air.

Understanding the functional relationships within the general form of the natural soil profile (Craul 1992, 1999) is necessary to make a reasonable estimate of the degree of limitations present in the existing project soil materials, which is essential to formulating a soil design plan.

Assessing Site Conditions

As shown in Figure 1.1, the major horizons of the ideal natural soil profile include:

- *O horizon (organic)* — This horizon functions as a mulch that reduces evaporative water losses, lowers daytime and maintains nighttime surface soil temperatures, and contributes organic matter for soil tilth and acts as a source of energy for soil organisms.
- *A horizon (topsoil)* — This horizon contains incorporated organic matter and a large and diverse organism population, and serves as the major rooting medium for most of the plant roots.
- *B horizon (subsoil)* — This horizon provides added necessary rooting volume for plant stability and nutrient and water storage, to supplement the topsoil.
- *C horizon (substratum or parent material)* — The C horizon contributes deep rooting and drainage volume. It becomes more important to good plant growth in relatively shallow soils.

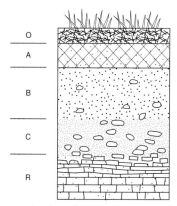

Figure 1.1 Ideal natural soil profile.
Source: Hopper, *Landscape Architecture Graphic Standards.* Copyright John Wiley & Sons, Inc., 2007.

- *R horizon (bedrock)* — The R horizon comprises the consolidated material from which the soil profile may or may not have been derived. Some soil materials have been transported by various agents of erosion and deposited on other existing bedrock.

In the context of urban soils and those on most landscape projects, it is useful to distinguish soils that have been intensively altered from those that retain most of their natural characteristics (with perhaps alteration only to the surface), appearing nearly like the soil profile shown in Figure 1.2. In contrast, the profile of a highly disturbed soil would appear as shown in the figure "Complex Urban Soil," with characteristics that would decrease its capability to sustain the plant palette. In this case, typically, alteration or replacement is required, and installation of a specially designed soil becomes a viable alternative on many projects.

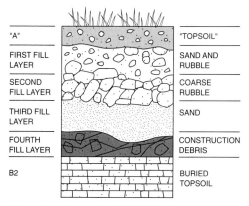

Figure 1.2 Complex urban soil.
Source: Hopper, *Landscape Architecture Graphic Standards.* Copyright John Wiley & Sons, Inc., 2007.

Acceptable Practices

Particle Size Distribution (Texture)

The soil texture or particle size distribution is the most influential physical characteristics of many other soil characteristics, including density and susceptibility to compaction, structure formation, drainage and aeration, and relative fertility. Its overall effects are modified by the presence of organic matter. Therefore, it is the first property of concern in examining existing soils.

Texture is defined and described by the proportion of sand (2 to 0.05 mm), silt (0.05 to 0.002 mm), and clay (< 0.002 mm) particles in the soil. The complete particle size classes are given in Table 1.1, and these form the basis of texture description.

These different soil particles in varying percentages join together to form small clumps of soil called peds. The arrangement of these peds contributes to the soil's structure.

Sand is the largest particle size in soil. Sand is broken down into subcategories from very coarse to very fine. Sand has an impact on the drainage quality of soils and its resistance to compaction. Soils that contain mostly very fine sands may not drain well, whereas soils that contain mostly very coarse sand may drain so quickly that they can't support the development of a healthy root system. Although sand particles do not bond together, they do combine with silt and clay to

Table 1.1 USDA Size Classes of Soil Mineral Particles

Size Class (Separate)	Diameter Range (mm)	U.S. Standard Sieve Size (No.)
Coarse fragments	> 2.00	—
Very coarse sand	2.00 to 1.00	10
Coarse sand	1.00 to 0.50	18
Medium sand	0.50 to 0.25	35
Fine sand	0.25 to 0.10	60
Very fine sand	0.10 to 0.05	140
Silt	0.05 to 0.002	300
Clay	< 0.002	—*

NOTE
*Determined by sedimentation test rather than sieving.
Source: Craul 1999.

form the soil's structure as well as improve water and nutrient retention important for root development.

Silt particles are the next-largest size particles in soil. Their primary role is to hold water and, to a lesser extent, nutrients and to make them available to plant roots. Silt particles do not bond easily.

Clay particles are the smallest particle size in soils. Clay particles bond easily with nutrients that are made available to the roots and promote plant growth. They also bond with sand and silt to form larger soil particles that together provide good drainage, as well as good water and nutrient retention. Although clay particles alone can retain a significant amount of water, it is not readily accessible to plant roots. Soils that contain 10–30 percent clay are considered desirable for plant growth. The bond between clay peds is not very strong and is easily broken when wet, which can increase the soil's bulk density. Therefore, grading or any moving with heavy equipment of soils containing a significant percentage of clay should not be permitted when the soil is wet.

The USDA-NRCS classification system (see Figure 1.3) categorizes different soil textures according to the percentages of clay, silt, and

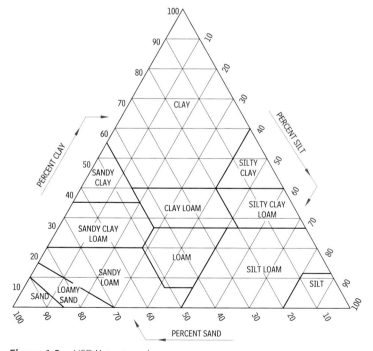

Figure 1.3   USDA's texture classes.
Source: Hopper, *Landscape Architecture Graphic Standards.* Copyright John Wiley & Sons, Inc., 2007.

sand. The name and texture of a specific soil are based on the USDA Soil Texture Classification Triangle. Soils are named based on their texture, such as "sandy loam," "silty clay," or "silt loam." Soils made up of 20 percent or more clay often have "clay" in their names, soils that have 50 percent or more sand have "sand" in their names, and soils that have 40 percent or more silt have "silt" in the their names. Soils that contain all three textures are described as "loam."

▶ The designation "loam" is a texture description and does not necessarily reflect the quality of the soil, as is sometimes thought.

Soils in the lower central area of the triangle are generally considered better agronomic soils. Soils that fall closer to the corners or edges of the triangle have less proportional mixture of all three types of soil textures and are considered less desirable as a growing medium.

Soil Structure

Aided by microorganisms and insects within the soil, the clay, silt, and sand soil particles bond together into larger aggregate particles called peds. The arrangement of the peds and the spaces between them contributes to a soil's structure.

There are five primary types of soil structure:

- *Granular* — Less than 0.5 cm in diameter, these particles resemble cookie crumbs. Generally found in the surface horizons of the soil. These soils provide good drainage and aeration. See Figure 1.4.
- *Blocky* — Between 1.5 and 5.0 cm in diameter, these particles are generally found in subsoil but can sometimes be found in the surface horizons. See Figure 1.5.
- *Prismatic* — Vertical columns several cm long, typically found in the B horizon. The vertical cracks are caused by water and roots moving downward as well as by freeze/thaw and wet/dry conditions. See Figure 1.6.
- *Columnar* — Vertical columns similar to prismatic, but with a distinct cap at the top of the column. These caps, caused by sodium-affected soils or swelling clays, are very dense and are not conducive to root system development. Columnar soils can often be found in the subsoils of arid climates. See Figure 1.7.
- *Platy* — Thin, flat plates that are generally oriented horizontally. Generally found in subsurface soils that have been subject to compaction. This type of soil structure does not allow water to move through easily, and is not conducive to root system development. See Figure 1.8.

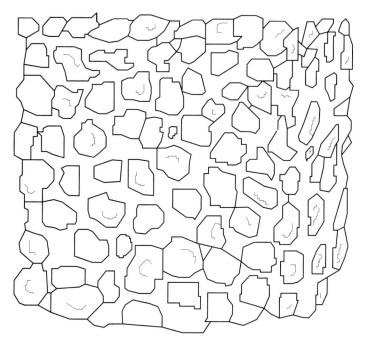

Figure 1.4   Granular Soil Structure.

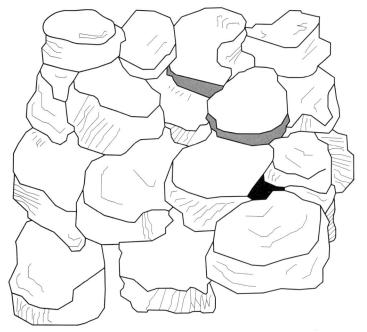

Figure 1.5   Blocky Soil Structure.

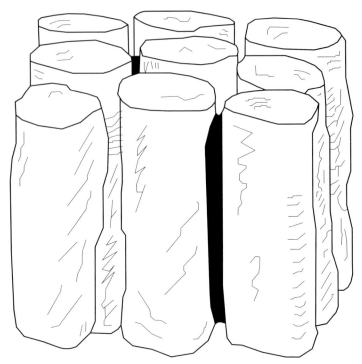

Figure 1.6 *Prismatic Soil Structure.*

▶ Peds occur naturally in the soil and maintain their structure through cycles of wetting and drying. Soil clods are soil aggregates that are broken into shapes on the surface by actions such as tilling or frost action, and are not considered peds.

There are two soil types that are described as lacking structure. They are:

- *Single grained* — The individual soil particles do not bond together and have a very loose consistency. Most common in sandy soils. See Figure 1.9.
- *Massive* — Soil with no visible structure. One blocklike mass with no aggregation of smaller peds. Often caused by overcompaction that has destroyed the original soil's structure. See Figure 1.10.

Soil Texture and Structure

The combination of texture and structure contributes to soil characteristics that are important to good root system development and plant growth.

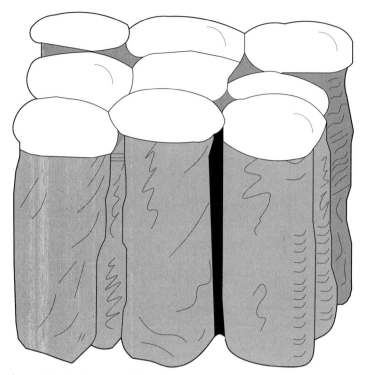

Figure 1.7   Columnar Soil Structure.

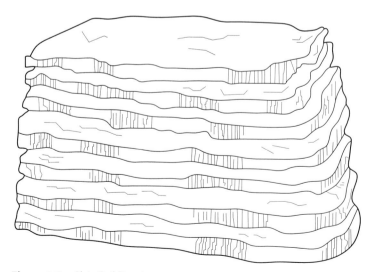

Figure 1.8   Platy Soil Structure.

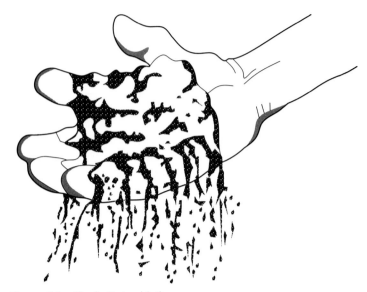

Figure 1.9 Single-Grained Soil.

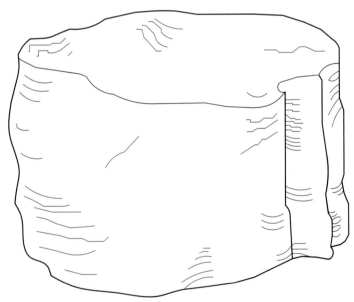

Figure 1.10 Massive Soil.

- Granular soil structures with a loamy texture provide good drainage and aeration, hold water and nutrients, and make them available to a plant's root system.
- Single-grained soils allow water to drain through quickly and lack the ability to hold nutrients necessary for plant growth.
- Dense soil structures, such as platy soils, impede the flow of water and air through the soil and make root system development difficult.

Soils can be amended to improve drainage, aeration, and water- and nutrient-retaining characteristics that would be desirable for root system development and plant growth. (Refer to the "Soil Amendments" section in Chapter 4.)

Macropores and Micropores

In good-quality soil, the peds combine to create void space that accounts for approximately 50 percent of a soil's volume. These voids are classified as either macropores or micropores.

- Macropores are the relatively large interconnected spaces between the peds that allow excess water to drain through freely, with air being drawn in to fill these voids after water has passed through. Soils with large macropores are well drained and have good aeration.
- Micropores are the smaller spaces within the peds that hold water through the forces of adhesion (attraction of water to a solid surface) and cohesion (attraction of water to itself), offsetting the force of gravity that would pull it away.

As pores increase in size, the force of adhesion is weakened and gravity exerts a greater force, drawing the water downward. As pores decrease in size, the force of adhesion becomes greater than the force of gravity, and the water is held within the ped and made available to a plant's root system. When little water remains on the surface of the soil particles, the force of adhesion can be strong enough to prevent the plant roots from drawing the water away.

▶ Ideally, the system of macropores and micropores is balanced so that soil is well drained and aerated as well as retaining water necessary for the plant's root system.

When soils become *saturated*, as in a heavy or extended period of rain, their macropores and micropores are entirely filled with water. As the water drains from the macropores, the remaining water in the micropores makes up the maximum amount of water the soil can hold, which is referred to as the soil's *field capacity*. With the soil at field capacity, water is taken up by the roots through osmosis, and some water at the surface is lost to the atmosphere by evaporation. At the point where the surface tension or adhesion is stronger than the ability of the water to pass through to the roots, the soil has reached its *wilting point*. After the wilting point, no water is made available to the plant's root system, and if this condition remains for an extended period of time, the plant will begin to show signs of drought stress.

▶ **The water held between field capacity and wilting point is referred to as *plant available water*.**

Different types of soil structures hold different amounts of water at field capacity and wilting point. Larger-particle sandy soils contain a large number of macropores but few micropores, making their ability to provide plant available water very small. Smaller-particle clay soils have few macropores and many micropores. Having fewer macropores results in poor drainage and less oxygen available to the plant roots. The micropores are very small and adhesion force very great, and even when a clay soil contains a significant amount of water, the water is not plant available.

Practices to Avoid

- Do not ignore the importance of soil texture and structure during site assessment. (Refer to the "Soil Assessment" section.)
- Do not allow soil structure to be destroyed during construction. (Refer to the section "Construction Damage to Existing Trees" in Chapter 3.)
- Do not lose the opportunity to improve a soil's ability to sustain healthy plant growth and root system development. (Refer to "Soil Amendments" section in Chapter 4.)

Soil Assessment

Description

It is widely held that the majority of a plant's problems come from the soil where it is planted, and indeed there is a strong consensus among urban horticulturists that soil largely determines the success of a landscape planting. Soil assessment is the most critical part of the site assessment process and is the part that requires the most time.

It is important to understand the physical properties of the soil because they are key to allowing roots to grow and to that all-important balance between air and water in the soil. We also need to understand the depth and usable volume of the soil that is present, as well as its chemical properties. The focus for soils is, then, on volume, physical properties, and chemical properties. The importance of understanding soil, the medium in which all landscape plants grow, even in wetlands, cannot be overestimated.

Assessing Site Conditions

A soil site assessment should include:

- Identifying good soil and integrating approaches to save it for use or reuse. Areas with good soil will be naturally suitable areas for planting. In areas that will be paved, the good soil should be stripped, preserved, and redistributed to planted areas after construction. Do not allow valuable topsoil to be mixed with poor soil or be buried.
- Preventing soil compaction in areas that will be planted. If construction has not yet taken place, planted areas should be marked off and protected from compaction by heavy equipment.
- Identification of other vegetation growing on the site. Every plant has specific soil requirements for good growth. Plants that are thriving can be a good indicator of subsurface soil conditions.
- Collecting soil samples for testing. Soil samples should be taken from different areas of the site to test for soil properties. Samples

15

should be taken wherever there is reason to believe soil properties are different. More locations should be taken in urban areas, as the soil properties can differ greatly over a site depending on previous development.

Acceptable Practices

Texture

It is possible to test for soil texture in the field. There are a couple of approaches, both that involve taking a soil sample, adding some water, forming the soil into a ball, and then pressing forward between the thumb and forefinger to create a soil ribbon. See Figures 1.11 through 1.16. These field tests are predicated on the fact that soils that contain more silt and clay can be made into a longer, more flexible ribbon than soils with a higher percentage of sand. Soils with a higher percentage of sand will tend to flake rather than form a ribbon.

▶ These tests are relatively easy to perform but do require a bit of practice to master, particularly the squeezing of the soil into a ribbon.

Clayey soils tend to drain poorly; particular attention should be paid to drainage, and generally wet-tolerant plants should be chosen for these types of soils. Sandy soils tend to drain quickly, and if irrigation will not be provided, more drought-tolerant plants should be considered, especially for trees planted within paved areas. Water-soluble nutrients leach quickly in sandy soils; if a fertilization program is not likely to be included in the management of the landscape, species more tolerant of lower nutrient levels and sandy soils should be considered.

Percolation

The tree roots require oxygen to develop and grow. In poorly drained soils, pooling water fills the voids in the soil structure, preventing oxygen from reaching the roots. If information on percolation is not otherwise available, an informal percolation test can be performed as follows:

- Dig a 12" diameter hole, 12" deep. Scarify the sides and bottom. See Figure 1.17.
- Cover the bottom of the hole with an inch or two of fine gravel to prevent clogging of the bottom soil.

- If possible, fill the hole with water 24 hours before the test, to saturate the soil (if the soil is dry and that is not possible, fill the hole several times with water before the test).

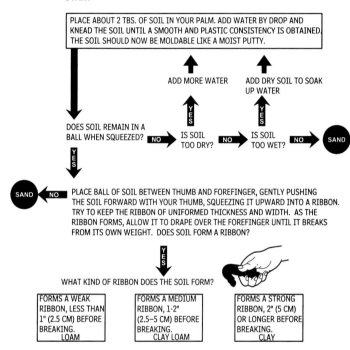

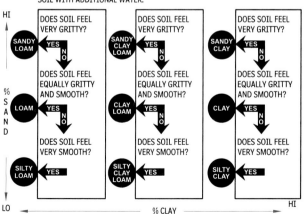

Figure 1.11 Guide to soil texture by feel.
Source: Trowbridge and Bassuk, *Trees in the Urban Landscape.* Copyright John Wiley & Sons, Inc., 2004.

- Wet the area around the hole.
- Fill the hole to the top with water. See Figure 1.18.
- For the test, fill the hole with water and measure the change in level on an hourly basis to determine the percolation rate. See Figure 1.19.

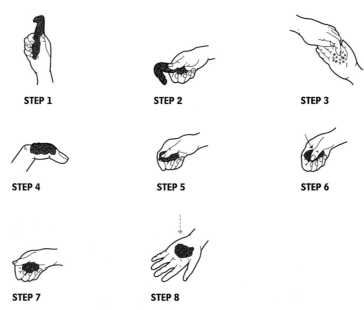

STEP 1 **STEP 2** **STEP 3**

STEP 4 **STEP 5** **STEP 6**

STEP 7 **STEP 8**

Figure 1.12   Step 1 – After preparing a baseball-sized handful of soil by moistening similar to Figure 1.11, make the thickest ribbon possible straight up in the air (about 1/2 to 3/4 inch thick). Measure length when it falls over.

Step 2 – Make a thick ribbon with your hand pointed sideways. Measure the length when it falls. Take the average of both lengths. For every inch of ribbon assume an 8% clay content.

Step 3 – Feel for sand percentage by smearing a thin layer in your palm and rubbing hard. Estimate sand content to be 10% or less; about 25%; about 50%; about 75%; or about 90%. Reference the textural triangle to identify the texture of the soil.

Step 4 – Examine the ribbon. A smooth shiny surface with no skips or gaps means about 30 percent clay or more.

Steps 5 and 6 – If you can push your thumb into the ball and it feels like pizza dough, it is probably a silty loam.

Steps 7 and 8 – If it is very sandy, make a ball and drop it into your other hand. If it breaks, it is a loamy sand. If it holds together, it is a sandy loam.
Source: Trowbridge and Bassuk, *Trees in the Urban Landscape.* Copyright John Wiley & Sons, Inc., 2004.

Figure 1.13 To start the soil ribbon test, first grab a hand full of soil. Moisten the soil enough so that it will hold together, but not so much that it becomes muddy or runny.

Figure 1.14 Squeeze the soil tightly so that it forms an egg-sized ball.

Figure 1.15   Begin to squeeze the soil out between your thumb and fore-finger, forming a ribbon.

Figure 1.16   Try to make a ribbon as long as possible, and check the length at the point where it breaks. Compare the length to the chart.

Figure 1.17 A hole is dug 12 inches in diameter by 12 inches deep, and the sides are scarified.

Figure 1.18 After covering the bottom of the hole with an inch or so of fine gravel, add water to the top of the hole.

Figure 1.19 Check the depth of the water in the hole on an hourly basis, and record the drop in level in inches.

As a general rule of thumb, adequate drainage should register a minimum of a 2-inch drop in water level per hour; a drop of 2–8 inches per hour represents moderate drainage, and a drop of over 8 inches per hour is excessive drainage. If the rate is less than 2 inches, the soil should be amended to improve its drainage characteristics, or a sub-surface drainage system will need to be considered. Excessively draining soils should be amended to improve drainage characteristics.

Trees generally do well when planted in well-drained loamy soil. Although some tree species will tolerate wet conditions, trees will not survive in tree pits filled with standing water.

▶ Poorly draining soils often have a foul smell and gray color that can be very noticeable while digging the hole for the percolation test.

In urban or suburban areas, site disruption and the tendency for construction to mix debris, different subsoil types, and good topsoil all together in various compacted layers on the site can impact percolation. These various layers can sometimes be made visible by digging test pits and looking for distinctly different soil layer colors or textures. The separate layer boundaries should be broken down by tilling deep enough to integrate the different layers.

A more formal percolation test can be conducted by using a double-ring infiltrometer (see Figure 1.20). It consists of two open-ended

Figure 1.20   Double-Ring Infiltrometer.

metal cylinders that are driven concentrically into the ground and then filled with water (the outside ring should be filled first). The outer ring is 24 inches in diameter, and the inner ring is 12 inches in diameter. The outer ring prevents horizontal flow and encourages only vertical flow from the inner ring. As water drains into the soils, water is added to the cylinders to keep the liquid level constant. Measuring the amounts of water added to the center cylinder over a specified time period allows the infiltration rate of the soil to be calculated. The data collected are plotted on a graph to identify the steady state infiltration rate reached after the soil has become saturated.

Bulk Density

The bulk density of soil is a good indicator of the level of soil compaction. An easy method to determine bulk density is to:

- Weigh a bucket or container large enough to hold a cubic foot of soil.
- Dig an 8-10"-deep by 8-10" diameter hole with a shovel, placing all the excavated soil in the container. Take care to keep the sides relatively smooth and not disturb the adjacent soil.
- Line the hole with a plastic bag and fill the hole level to the top with water. Measure the volume of water in the bag. See Figure 1.21.
- Completely dry the excavated soil in an oven for a minimum of 8 hours at 200–220 degrees F (or for a quicker result, dry in a microwave for about 4 minutes, then let cool for a minute).

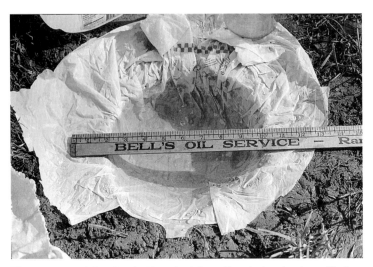

Figure 1.21   Hole is lined with a plastic bag. After the bag has been filled to the top with water, the volume of the water is measured and compared with the weight of the dried soil.

Source: Trowbridge and Bassuk, *Trees in the Urban Landscape.* Copyright John Wiley & Sons, Inc., 2004.

- Calculate the weight of the dried soil by weighing the soil and container together and then subtracting the weight of the container alone.
- Soil Bulk Density = Soil Dry Weight (g)/Soil Volume (cubic cm or ml) Note: The volume of 1 cubic centimeter equals the volume of one milliliter.

Table 1.2 can be used to determine if bulk density indicates that soil compaction levels are too high to promote proper root development and tree growth.

If bulk densities exceed the values in the table, the soil should be amended. See "Soil Amendments."

Soil pH Testing

A pH test is very simple and inexpensive. Kits are available that allow quick tests in the field to be made, providing preliminary pH level data. See Figure 1.22.

Samples should be taken by digging a small hole or using a soil-coring device to about a depth of 12 inches. Mix the soil sample in a clean container before testing or taking it to a lab.

▶ Soil-testing laboratories will often include measures for adjusting pH levels with the test results.

Table 1.2 Critical Bulk Density Values for Different Soil Textures

Soil Texture	Critical Bulk Density[1] Range g/cc[2]
Clay, silt loam	1.4–1.55
Silty clay, silty clay loam, silt	1.4–1.45
Clay loam	1.45–1.55
Loam	1.55–1.65
Sandy clay loam	1.55–1.75
Sandy loam	1.55–1.75
Loamy sand, sand	> 1.75

Notes

1. Bulk densities greater than these values could restrict root growth.
2. Grams per cubic centimeter
* This technique can underestimate bulk density by 3 to 9 percent.

Source: Adapted from Trowbridge and Bassuk, *Trees in the Urban Landscape.* Copyright John Wiley & Sons, Inc., 2004.

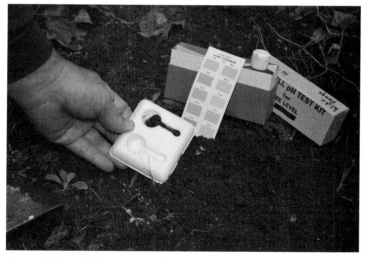

Figure 1.22 A field pH test kit allows preliminary data to be determined.

A critical component of the testing is to take enough samples from areas where trees will be planted to account for any differences in soil types. Results can vary over a site, especially where soil color or texture appears different and in developed areas that have been disturbed by construction.

▶ Construction debris can affect pH levels (e.g., concrete left in the soil raises pH levels) and should be removed from the planting site.

Soil Elements

There are three categories of soil elements found in soils:

- Basic nonmineral elements
- Macronutrients
- Micronutrients

These are the three basic nonmineral elements:

- Oxygen (O)
- Hydrogen (H)
- Carbon (C)

Carbon and oxygen are extracted from the air by the breaking down of carbon dioxide (CO_2), and hydrogen is found in the water (H_2O) in the soil. Through photosynthesis, these basic elements are used in large quantities to make starches and sugars for plant structure (most of a tree's weight is made up of carbon atoms).

Macronutrients are dissolved in water and absorbed by the roots to be used for general plant functions. They include the elements most often found in fertilizers (nitrogen, phosphorus, potassium), and they are the first to get the call to correct soil deficiencies, because the plants use large amounts for growth. The application of a fertilizer might provide some short-term benefits, but longer term, adding organic material will address these nutrient deficiencies and improve other qualities of the soil as well. The macronutrients required by plants are:

- *Nitrogen (N)* — Necessary part of all proteins, enzymes, and metabolic processes involved in the synthesis and transfer of energy; part of chlorophyll, the green pigment of the plant that is responsible for photosynthesis; helps with plant growth.
- *Phosphorus (P)* — Essential component in the process of photosynthesis; helps formation of all oils, sugars, starches; helps transform solar energy into chemical energy; encourages blooming and root growth.
- *Potassium (K)* — Absorbed by plants in larger amounts than any other mineral except nitrogen, and sometimes calcium; helps build protein; helps in photosynthesis, fruit quality, and reduction of diseases.
- *Calcium (Ca)* — Essential part of plant cell wall structure; provides for normal transport and retention of other elements, and strengthens the plant as well; mitigates the effects of alkali salts and organic acids.
- *Magnesium (Mg)* — Part of chlorophyll in all green plants and essential for photosynthesis; activates plant enzymes needed for growth.

- *Sulfur (S)* — Essential for protein production; promotes activity and development of enzymes and vitamins; helps in chlorophyll formation; improves root growth; improves plant's resistance to cold.

Micronutrients are used by plants for specialized functions. They are required in relatively small quantities, and therefore are not usually added to soils. Some of these elements can be present in high enough concentrations to be detrimental in urban areas, where there are remnants of previous industrial activity on the site. If previous industrial activity is known or suspected, the soil should be tested to ensure that this is not the case (and that no other hazardous materials are present). Micronutrients required by plants are:

- *Boron (B)* — Aids in the use and regulation of other nutrients; helps in production of sugar and carbohydrates; essential for seed and fruit development.
- *Chlorine (Cl)* — Helps in metabolism.
- *Cobalt (Co)* — Aids in shoot development and growth.
- *Copper (Cu)* — Important for reproductive growth; helps root metabolism and utilization of proteins.
- *Iron (Fe)* — Essential for formation of chlorophyll.
- *Manganese (Mn)* — Functions with enzyme systems involved in breakdown of carbohydrates and in nitrogen metabolism.
- *Molybdenum (Mo)* — Helps in the use of nitrogen.

Fertility

Fertility is the soil's ability to store nutrients and make them available to the plant's root system. Soils hold elements and nutrients by a process called cation exchange. Cation exchange is the attraction of positively charged elements to the negatively charged soil particles. The number of these soil particles and their ability to attract and hold these elements is referred to as cation exchange capacity (CEC).

The quantity of positively charged elements the soil can hold is based on the surface area of the soil particle. Clay particles are the smallest soil particles with the greatest surface area compared to their volume. Therefore, clay soils provide the best nutrient-holding capacity. Well-decayed organic matter particles, with their irregular, complex surface characteristics, provide good nutrient-holding capacity. The larger, smoother silt particles hold less, and sand particles have very little nutrient-holding capacity.

Clay and organic matter have the highest CEC and are therefore considered good components of a fertile soil. Soils with large percentages of sand, which have a low CEC, are considered less fertile. Because it is difficult to mix clay into a soil, mixing organic material into a soil to improve fertility is the preferred approach. Soil should be tested for percentages of clay and humus—the more of each, the more fertile the soil.

▶ Organic material should be replenished regularly, to keep the fertility level high.

Plants are sensitive to changes in soil nutrient levels. Even small changes can affect plant health and manifest themselves in visible distortions of leaves, color, and branches. If fertilization or other regular amending of the soil is discontinued, soils have a tendency to revert back to their original nutrient levels. Therefore, it is always best to choose plants that are matched to the original soil characteristics.

The soil's pH level also affects a plant's ability to absorb nutrients (see Figure 1.23). Soil tests may show that nutrients are present in the soil, but that the plants are unable to absorb them because of the soil's pH level. Most plants are somewhat tolerant of a soil with a higher pH—as opposed to a lower pH—than that preferred by the plant. A soil's pH is a product of its parent material, surrounding environment, and

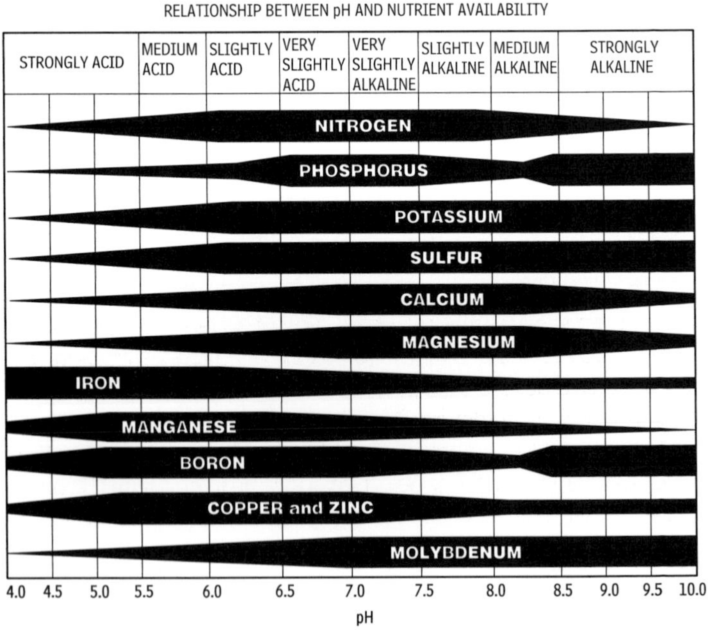

Figure 1.23   Specific nutrients' availability to a plant is dependent on the pH of the soil.
Source: Trowbridge and Bassuk, *Trees in the Urban Landscape.* Copyright John Wiley & Sons, Inc., 2004.

precipitation rate. It is difficult to effect long-term change in pH; therefore, it is always better to choose plants whose preferred pH range is a match to the soil's original pH level.

See the sections "Soil Amendments" and "Site Considerations and Tree Selection" in Chapter 4.

Organic Matter and Humus

Humus is produced by the decomposition of organic material that accumulates on the soil surface, such as leaves, branches, and lawn clippings. As this material decomposes, it is integrated into the top layer of soil by water, insects, and earthworms. The soil's humus content affects soil structure, porosity, moisture, and drainage.

Humus is often added to sandy soils to improve texture, water storage, and nutrient retention. Added to clayey soils, it can improve aeration and drainage. However, humus will need to be replenished as the existing material continues to decompose. If this is not likely as part of a maintenance plan, then selection of plants that are matched to the soil's existing organic content level should be considered.

In the field, digging a test pit about a foot or so deep to expose the "A" soil horizon can give a good indication of a soil's humus content. Soils with high organic content look rich and dark. In contrast, compacted soils or lighter sandy soils contain less organic material and are therefore considered less fertile.

Soil Salinity

High salt levels in soil dry out tree roots, making it difficult for a tree to grow or even survive. Trees may be subjected to high soil salt levels if planted in coastal areas (airborne salt spray) or adjacent to pavements likely to receive deicing salts (sidewalks, roadways, parking lots), or irrigated with well water that may have high salt levels. Soils in these areas should be tested for sodium levels and sodium absorption ratios. (See "Site Considerations and Tree Selection" for more information.) If conditions exist that represent potential salt problems, have the soil tested.

Electrical conductivity (EC) is used to measure salt content. The typical unit of measurement of how well electricity is conducted is micromhos per centimeter (mmhos/cm). This unit is derived from the typical unit of resistance, the ohm. Because conductivity is the opposite of resistance, the name of this unit is based on ohm spelled backward. A reading of zero indicates no electrical conductivity. There are many different kinds of salt, and the electrical conductivity test will provide the levels of salinity but not the type of salts present.

Soil salinity level test results per centimeter affect plant consideration as follows:

- *0–2 mmhos* — Low level, not a consideration in plant selection.
- *2–4 mmhos* — Plants sensitive to salt conditions will be affected.
- *4–8 mmhos* — Moderate salt levels that will affect many plants.
- *8–16 mmhos* — High salt levels; only salt tolerant plants should be considered.
- *Over 16 mmhos* — Indicates very high soil salinity that few plants will tolerate.

If well water is used for irrigation, have it tested. If the irrigation water conductivity is above 1 mmhos per cm, it may be contributing to poor plant growth and salt buildup in the soil.

▶ **Soil salinity levels can change significantly throughout the year. In areas where deicing salts have been used, salt levels can be extremely high in early spring. These levels can be significantly reduced if taken after a rainy spring when the soil has leached to lower levels. It would therefore be advisable to test for soil salinity in the early spring before salt levels are affected by spring rains.**

Moisture

Some plants tolerate a broad range of moisture levels in the soil, while others prefer very specific moisture conditions. Although irrigation can help plants that require more moisture than conditions can provide, it is advisable to select plants that match the existing soil moisture condition.

If possible, try to make field visits at different times of the year and during different weather conditions, to note where drainage appears poor or where soil seems to drain well. Take particular note of low-lying areas or areas that are at the base of a slope; they tend to be wetter than areas that are at higher elevations. Look for plant species that like wet conditions or those that prefer dry conditions; they can be a good indicator of soil moisture. Be guided accordingly in your planting location and species selection.

Soil Life

The presence of a broad spectrum of organisms in the soil indicates a healthy soil environment. Bacteria help decompose organic matter, earthworms integrate humus from the surface into the top layer of soil, and mycorrhizal fungi form symbiotic relationships with roots to help them absorb water and nutrients, to mention just a few of the beneficial qualities of soil life.

In the field, dig down and look for earthworms, insects, or white threadlike strands of fungi that would indicate a healthy soil. If none is found, investigate other possible causes of poor soil quality. In some soils, such as sandy soils, there may be beneficial microorganisms that cannot be seen.

Distance to Water Table

If a site has a shallow water table, trees that tolerate wet conditions should be considered. The distance to the water table often varies during the year. It might be several inches below the surface in the cooler season and drop several feet in the growing season because transpiration pulls it from the soil. If possible, test holes should be dug at different times of the year to avoid drawing incorrect conclusions.

Test pits or auger holes should be dug down to three feet. If any water appears in the hole over a three- to four-hour period, only trees that tolerate wet conditions should be considered. If water fills the hole to within 18 inches of the surface, moderate-sized trees should be considered, as larger trees will not be able to develop the deep anchoring roots to make them stable. See Figure 1.24.

In some cases, it may be possible to add a layer of stone beneath the root ball to keep it elevated above the water level (see Figures 1.25 and 1.26). This can keep water draining away from the root ball and allow root development in the soil above.

Depth to Bedrock

Minimum depth to bedrock, impervious horizon, or infrastructure surface such as an underground rooftop, should be at least 24 to 30 inches for most planting designs. A depth of 36 inches is nearly ideal for most situations.

Hazardous Materials

No known contaminants should be present anywhere within the profile or within the subbase below; otherwise, HAZMAT cleanup is required, unless the Environmental Protection Agency (EPA) and the appropriate state office have issued certificates of cleanup or isolation, and acceptance.

Figure 1.24 This tree pit fills with water as it is being dug, indicating a high water table and/or poorly drained soil.

Figure 1.25 After determining the water level, place a layer of stone on a geotextile fabric to elevate the root ball so that it is sitting above the water level.

Figure 1.26 The root ball is set on the stone with the tree flare slightly above the surrounding grade, keeping the root ball as high as possible.

Practices to Avoid

Avoid soils with coarse fragments (stones and/or building rubble). If present, they should be less than 2 inches in diameter and less than 25 percent by volume within 24 inches of the soil surface. Coarse fragments may increase with depth but should not exceed the limit. Remove excess coarse fragments by employing a rock rake after the stony soil has been loosened with a chisel plow or a spade tiller; adding sufficient stoneless, specified soil to the surface to provide an adequate depth of planting medium for the desired plants is another alternative, and is probably the least expensive. However, in extremely stony situations, the interface between the nonstony and stony material may create restricted rooting. For very stony areas, a planting design of simple scattered plants would require the removal of stones only in the planting pits. This technique is commonly employed in stony desert regions; usually, soil must be supplemented in the planting pits.

Designed Soil Mixes

Description

On sites that have very poor soil or damaged soil structure, or that have been disturbed by previous development, designed soil mixes can be used to restore the soil's ability to support healthy plants. Designed soil mixes can improve soil aeration, water storage, nutrient-holding capacity, and drainage.

Importing topsoil from undeveloped sites to be used on a project is discouraged and is not considered a sustainable approach. The Sustainable Sites Initiative's Guidelines and Performance Benchmarks further state:

- Imported topsoils or soil blends designed to serve as topsoil may not be mined from:
  - Soils defined by the Natural Resources Conservation Service as prime farmland, unique farmland or farmland of statewide importance
  - Other Greenfield sites, unless those soils are a byproduct of a construction process
- Soils must be reused for functions comparable to their original function (i.e. topsoil is used as topsoil, subsoil as subsoil, or subsoil is amended to become functional topsoil).

Proper design emulation of an appropriate local natural soil suitable for the desired plant palette ensures sustainability to the plant palette and the overall landscape design. Components of a designed soil may be recycled by-products such as composted organic materials, waste sand or ground glass as a sand substitute, tailings from stone quarry washers as silt and clay substitutes, and many others yet to be devised.

Designed soil mixes can be uniquely developed for very specific landscape uses such as high-use turf areas, steep slopes, wetlands, bio-retention, planting over structure or on roofs, and meeting the soil requirements for planting beds.

Assessing Site Conditions

Designed soil mixes can be considered on projects where the site's existing soil cannot perform the functions that are required for the proposed design. Some of the most common (and interrelated) existing soil conditions that can be modified with a designed soil mix are:

- *Compaction* — One of the most common and difficult existing soil conditions that require modification if vegetation is to thrive. Compacted soils usually have poor drainage characteristics, reduced aeration capacity, and densities that inhibit root growth.
- *Bulk density* — Inhibits root growth into the denser soils immediately outside the planting pit.
- *Damaged soil structure* — Damage to soil peds, macropores, and micropores results in poor drainage and aeration, and prevents root growth.
- *Poor drainage* — Excessively wet or saturated soils deprive plant roots of necessary oxygen.

The soil texture or particle size distribution is the physical property that has the greatest influence on many other soil properties, including density and susceptibility to compaction, structure formation, drainage and aeration, and relative fertility. Its overall effects are modified by the presence of organic matter. Therefore, it is the first property of concern in examining existing soils, or the first criterion considered for designing a soil.

See the sections "Soil Overview" and "Soil Assessment" in this chapter for additional information.

Acceptable Practices

When the existing soil material has been drastically altered or is totally unsuitable, then a designed soil mix should be considered for restoration. The overall goal is to return the soil to a condition that enables it to perform desired functions suitable for one or more land uses.

Design of a General Soil Profile

Designed soils are not necessarily natural soils, nor do they yet fit into the accepted USDA Soil Taxonomy; therefore, the following specifications are given to provide an arbitrary horizon designation system (Craul 1999):

- *S1: topsoil* — A medium loamy sand amended with mature composted organic matter to a content of 10 percent by weight.

Table 1.3 Range in Percent Passing Sieve Sizes for S2 Subsoil and Organic Amended S1

Sieve Size	Percent Finer
#10	100
#18	88–100
#35	70–80
#60	40–50
#140	29–39
#300	25–35
Silt range	10–30
Clay range	5–15

Source: Craul 1999.

- *S2: subsoil* — A medium loamy sand (USDA) conforming to the following specifications, which may contain 1 to 2 percent organic matter by weight (refer to Table 1.3). The range of silt should be within 10 to 30 percent, and the range of clay should be within 5 to 15 percent.
- *S3: drainage layer* — A gravelly sand (AASHTO #4) that provides a high rate of water flow from the bottom of the soil profile to the underdrainage system.

The table of percent passing for the stack of sieve sizes (Table 1.1) and the particle size envelope (see Figure 1.27) for each designed soil or for each separate horizon, where distinct horizons are required for a unique soil profile (for example, the S3 layer in the horizon designation system in Table 1.4), should always be provided in the specifications, for clarity and to ensure that the testing laboratory and landscape contractor receive the necessary information. It is also valuable and necessary data for such applications as rooftop projects and those involving slope stability and the like. Estimates of bulk density are also necessary, although not graphically represented.

Organic Matter

Organic matter is a very important component of soil, whether natural or designed. Design guidelines are as follows:

- The organic matter in natural soil is formed there as the result of soil formation and evolution, and the content may be determined by ASTM tests.
- Organic matter content and type must be specified as a component for designed soil.

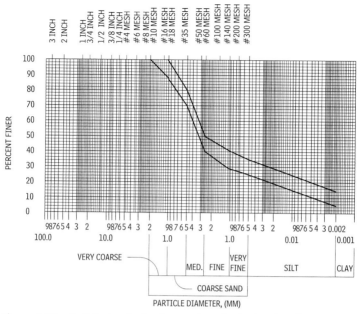

Figure 1.27 Particle size distribution envelope for the S2 subsoil loamy sand.
Source: Hopper, *Landscape Architecture Graphic Standards.* Copyright John Wiley & Sons, Inc., 2007.

- Peat moss is no longer recommended as a soil amendment, in light of LEED and Sustainable Site Initiative Guidelines and provisions.
- Composted biosolids have become a preferred source of organic matter amendment. Problems of uniformity in processing and

Table 1.4 Range in Percent Passing for AASHTO Aggregate #4 *Frequently Used as S3 Drainage Layer

Particle Size Class	Sieve Size	Percent Passing
Medium gravel	3/8″	100
Fine gravel	#4	95–100
Very fine gravel	#8	80–100
Very coarse sand	#16	50–85
Coarse sand	#30	25–60
Medium sand	#50	10–30
Fine sand	#100	2–10
Silt + clay**	—	1–2

Notes
*Sometimes called "highway sand."
**Determined by hydrometer method in ASTM F-1632.

meeting specifications have been overcome, and formulations are now more or less standardized. Availability is no longer a problem.

Experience has shown biosolids to be a very good source of organic matter, with reliable and acceptable field results when properly composted and installed. That said, problems have been encountered with excessively high pH values of alkaline-slaked biosolids, which should therefore be avoided.

Specifications for composted biosolids are as follows:

- *Carbon:nitrogen (C:N) ratio* — This should be in the range 10:1 to 25:1.
- *Stability* — The three tests for stability are:
  - Dewar self-heating test: Maximum heat rise <20°C above room temperature (of 20–25°C)
  - CO_2 evolution test: <1.5% carbon/day
  - O_2 respiration test: <0.8 mg/g VS/hr

Thus, per Table 1.5, only Classes IV and V are acceptable for mixing. The larger the number, the greater the degree of stability. Too often, contractors have delivered composted biosolids at a stability level of III or less.

- *Odor* — Compost has no unpleasant odor. Any odor of ammonia indicates that the compost is immature (Class III or less) and should not be applied until cured to mature (Class IV or V) stage.
- *Mineral/organic content and fineness* — Compost must contain more than 40 percent organic matter (dry weight), and 100 percent should pass a half-inch (13 mm) or smaller sieve. Debris (metal, glass,

Table 1.5 Four Levels of Stability/ Maturity by the Dewar Test

Stability Evolved Class	Stability Description	Temperature Rise	O_2 Evolved MG/G VS/HR	CO_2 Evolved Percent Carbon/Day
V	Very mature compost	0–10°C	< 0.5	< 0.8
IV	Maturing, curing compost	10–20°C	0.5–0.8	0.8–1.5
III	Material still decomposing	20–30°C	0.8–1.2	1.5–2.0
II	Immature, active compost	30–40°C	1.2–1.5	2.0–2.5
I	Fresh, very raw compost	40–50°C	> 1.5	2.5–3.0

Source: Switzenbaum, Craul, and Ryan 1996. Stability classes originally developed by Woods End Research Laboratory 1995.

plastic, wood other than residual chips) content should not exceed 1 percent dry weight.

- *Reaction (pH)* — This must be in the range of 5.5 to 8.0.
- *Salinity* — Soluble salts should not exceed 4.0 mmhos/cm (dS/m) or 2,560 ppm salt.
- *Nutrient content* — Nutrient content should be stated, giving: nitrogen, phosphorus, potassium, calcium, magnesium, sodium, and micro-nutrients, including iron, copper, boron, manganese, and molybdenum.
- *Heavy metals/pathogens/vector attraction reduction* — All these must meet the provisions of the 40 CFR Part 503 rule (EPA CFR, Part 503 Regulations, Table 3, page 9392, Vol. 58, No. 32, Friday, Feb. 19, 1993, *Federal Register*).

For a general topsoil specification, organic matter content may be 5 to 10 percent dry weight; for a subsoil, it should be from 1 to 3 percent dry weight. The values given here may appear to be low; however, these are weight basis. Approximate volume values are obtained by multiplying the dry weight by 2.2. It must be kept in mind that these values are to be used in mixes for landscape soils. Most people confuse the values with those for potting mixes, which always contain greater amounts of organic matter.

Blended Soils

Blended soils use natural topsoil as one component in the mix, which serves to limit the amount of topsoil used and conserve this valuable natural resource. Blended soils are composed of varying proportions of:

- *Natural topsoil* — Contributes silt, clay, and organic matter to the blended mix.
- *Uniform particle sand* — Contributes to the soil structure of the blended mix, including resistance to compaction.
- *Compost* — Provides organic matter to the blended mix.

Blended soil mixes for some typical uses include:

- *High-use lawn soils* — 3 parts sand; 1.5 parts topsoil; 1 part compost.
- *Passive lawn soils* — 2 parts sand; 1.5 parts topsoil; 1 part compost.
- *Planting beds* — Top layer of equal parts sand, topsoil, and compost; subsoil layer of equal parts sand and topsoil.

Overview of Mixing Procedures

At first, mixing the components in large quantities and ensuring a complete mix can be overwhelming (see Table 1.6). Fortunately, equipment and techniques are available on- or off-site to accomplish mixing

Table 1.6 Guide for Mixing Soil Components

Mixing Method	Comments and Cautions
Machine mixing	The most efficient method is by ball mill or tub mixer for large volumes. May be processed on- or off-site. Problem is variation among batches: Close inspection and frequent sampling is required. Usually not weather-dependent.
Windrowing	Appropriate for medium to small volumes. May be done on- or off-site but requires a large, dry, flat, solid surface; not on gravel or loose soil. Dry, compacted soil may suffice on approval by the landscape architect or the project soil scientist. Uniformity of mixing depends on the skill of the windrow equipment operator. Not recommended for large quantities, as it is very difficult to achieve thorough mixing as required in the specifications. Frequent inspection required. Weather-dependent and should be done when the materials are moist, not wet or dusty.
Spreading and mixing on-site	This method depends on the location (access), slope gradient, and general configuration of the site. Should not be used on slopes greater than 2:1. Cannot be used in very confined sites. Primary mixing machine is the tractor-mounted rototiller; the hand rototiller is too light for most applications. Weather-dependent and should be done when the materials are moist, not wet or dusty.

in an appropriate manner for any mixing volume (Switzenbaum, Craul, and Ryan 1996).

Testing

To ensure proper soil design function it is imperative that each soil component be clearly specified and tested before installation, and further tested as a system after installation for conformance and proper function. Close scrutiny throughout the entire project process is always required, as many contractors are not yet familiar with detailed soil specifications and the required testing for landscape projects.

ASTM standard tests and interpretation of results include the following:

- F-1632-03: Standard Method for Particle Size Analysis
- F-1815-97: Standard Method for Saturated Hydraulic Conductivity, Water Retention, Porosity, Particle Density, and Bulk Density
- F-1647-02a: Standard Method for Organic Matter Content of Putting Green and Sports Turf Root Zone Mixes
- D-3385-03: Standard Method for Infiltration of Soils in the Field Using Double Ring Infiltrometer

- D-4221-99: Standard Method for Dispersive Characteristics of Clay Soil by Double Hydrometer

▶ **Method F-1815-97 is the most appropriate general all-around test for the major physical characteristics of soil.**

For composted biosolids, if used as the organic matter source, the maturity test showing "mature" or "maturing" is absolutely necessary; "immature" is unacceptable (see the "Organic Matter" section earlier in this chapter for further details).

For the chemical properties of pH, nutrient content, soluble salts, and organic matter content, the tests and interpretations performed by the appropriate state agricultural experiment station are valid and should be used. If the existing or designed soil does not exhibit the appropriate chemical characteristics for the plant palette, then amendments are required to adjust them accordingly.

The landscape architect should always confirm that the soil materials delivered to the site are the same on which the tests were performed; thus, samples must be obtained from the bulk deliveries and tested again. Most laboratories can provide quick turnaround service (at extra charge) to facilitate installation.

Overview of Installation

Soil placement during installation requires following the appropriate soil mechanics procedures with respect to compaction of the soil. Close supervision of the soil installation process by the landscape architect or the soil scientist, if one is retained for the project, is absolutely necessary. See Chapter 3, "Earthworks," for more information.

Installation activities include:

- Proper inspection and sampling for tests of delivered soil materials.
- Supervision of soil placement in lifts to the proper degree of compaction.
- Prevention of excessive traffic over the placed soil.
- Proper sequencing of planting with soil placement, to greatly reduce disturbance to the placed soil.

▶ **The best practice is simultaneous placement of the topsoil and plants, if feasible. Contractors have stated that this practice has saved them time—hence, money. It also eliminates unwanted traffic over the topsoil final grade.**

Practices to Avoid

Some contractors attempt to bypass adhering to the specifications by inflating the estimated costs of the specified soils and then offering the client the contractor's own lower-cost materials. Be aware that substitutions of this type can lead to soil design mixes that do not meet the requirements of the project.

References

ALSO IN THIS BOOK

"Topsoil Preservation, Stripping, and Stockpiling"; "Construction Damage to Existing Trees"; and "Spreading and Grading Topsoil."

OTHER RESOURCES

American Society of Landscape Architects, the Lady Bird Johnson Wildflower Center and the United States Botanic Garden. *The Sustainable Sites Initiative-Guidelines and Performance Benchmarks 2009.* www.sustainablesites.org.

Craul, P. J. *Urban Soil in Landscape Design.* New York: John Wiley & Sons, Inc., 1992.

Craul, P. J. *Urban Soils: Applications and Practices.* New York: John Wiley & Sons, Inc., 1999.

Craul, T. A., and P. J. Craul. *Soil Design Protocols for Landscape Architects and Contractors.* Hoboken, NJ: John Wiley & Sons, Inc., 2006.

Hopper, Leonard. *Landscape Architectural Graphic Standards.* Hoboken, NJ: John Wiley & Sons, Inc., 2007.

Pine, Robert. *Specifying Soils for Complex Landscapes.* PowerPoint Presentation. ASLA, Chicago 2009.

Switzenbaum, M.S., P.J. Craul and T. Ryan. "Manufactured Loam Using Compost Material Phase 1: Feasibility." Final Report. Amherst, MA: University of Massachusetts Transportation Center, 1996.

Trowbridge and Bassuk. *Trees in the Urban Landscape.* Hoboken, NJ: John Wiley & Sons, Inc., 2004.

"Soil Science Education Home Page." Soil Structure and Images. 15 December 2010. NASA. 22 April 2011. http://soil.gsfc.nasa.gov/pvg/prop1.htm.

Urban, James. *Up By Roots.* International Society of Arboriculture, Champaign, IL, 2008.

Chapter 2

Earth Stripping and Stockpiling

Topsoil Preservation, Stripping, and Stockpiling

Topsoil Preservation, Stripping, and Stockpiling

Description

Topsoil is the top layer of undisturbed soil that contains organic material and nutrients essential to establishing and sustaining vegetative life. It is the living part of the soil that contains hundreds of trillions of beneficial organisms, bacteria, and fungi in just one cubic yard. It is the layer of soil where over three-fourths of all root growth takes place.

Ideally, existing topsoil should be identified and protected in place. If that is not possible, existing topsoil should be preserved by stripping it from areas that are to be disturbed, compacted, filled, or developed and stockpiling it for redistribution later in the construction process. The reuse of existing topsoil is a practical and economical approach to successful establishment of new vegetation on the site.

Assessing Site Conditions

An initial site assessment should map the locations and depth of healthy soils and soils that have been disturbed by previous development. Using that initial soil information as a guide during the preliminary design phase, a soils site plan should be developed that delineates which soils will:

- Remain in place and be protected.
- Be removed from the site.
- Be stripped and stockpiled for redistribution.
- Require restoration.

The areas designated for soil stockpiling should be chosen carefully, so as not to interfere with construction operations, disturb drainage patterns, or require relocating during the construction phase. Construction entrances, parking areas, material storage areas, and heavy equipment circulation routes should be clearly delineated on the plan to minimize compaction and damage to the soil structure. Encourage the use of size-appropriate construction equipment with tracks or large tires that distribute the equipment's weight over a large soil area, thus minimizing compaction.

▶ Compaction is the most common form of soil damage resulting from construction, and restoration measures can be costly. The contract documents should emphasize to the contractor that prevention of soil compaction during construction and efforts to minimize it have both ecological and economic benefits.

Prior to stripping the layer of topsoil, any large vegetative material and root masses should be removed. An inspection should be conducted to make sure the topsoil does not contain weeds or invasive vegetative species. If noxious weeds or invasive species are evident, treatment with a selective herbicide may be considered to prevent these seeds from being reestablished when the topsoil is redistributed.

All necessary erosion and sediment control measures should be called for on the plans and should be in place prior to the stripping of topsoil.

Although the topsoil layer is generally removed to a depth of approximately 6 inches, this depth can vary according to soil type and location. Core samples should be taken or test pits dug in several locations to determine the appropriate depth of topsoil to be stripped.

▶ The larger the site, the more critical the soil plan's impact and cost effectiveness. On some small urban sites with limited space and intense development, it may not be practical to preserve or reuse existing soil resources, and importing a soil mix and/or soil restoration may be the only feasible approach.

Acceptable Practices

Topsoil Preservation

It is best to preserve existing areas of healthy topsoil in place and protect them from negative impacts during construction. The initial site assessment of soils should help guide design development to take advantage of these opportunities. The Sustainable Site Initiative's Guidelines and Performance Benchmarks call for these areas to be designated as vegetation and soil protection zones (VSPZ) that must meet a set of specific requirements, including the following (partial summarized list):

- Construction impacts should not decrease the capacity of the VSPZ to support the desired vegetation, including construction activities outside the VSPZ, which should not change drainage patterns or microclimate effects within the VSPZ.

- The VSPZ should be protected with a fence or other physical barrier that protects this zone from equipment parking and traffic, storage of materials, and other construction activities.
- All construction and maintenance personnel should be educated about the locations and protective measures of the VSPZ, and the construction documents should include consequences to the contractor if the VSPZ provisions are not respected.

▶ See The Sustainable Site Initiative's Guidelines and Performance Benchmarks (www.sustainablesites.org) for a complete list of VSPZ requirements.

Topsoil Stripping and Stockpiling

In areas that have been designated for having topsoil stripped, the top 6 inches (or the depth determined by core samples or test pits) should be scraped and removed. This includes the stockpiling area itself, if it is not paved. The stripping process should be done when the soil is moist but not wet or overly dry, to protect soil structure when soil is being handled.

Where soil removal deeper than the level of topsoil is required, topsoil and subsoil should be stockpiled separately. Whenever multiple textures of topsoil are being stripped, an effort should be made to keep clay and silt soils separate from soils with a sandy texture. Ideally, the proposed design plans can call for reuse of the sandy soils in areas that may experience high use, such as lawns, while the clay and silt soils are reused in planting beds where compaction is less likely and plants will benefit from their nutrient- and water-holding capacities.

The removed topsoil should be stockpiled in areas located on the site plan. The area for stockpiling should not interfere with ongoing work on the site or disrupt drainage patterns or block drainage structures (see Figure 2.1). The slope of topsoil stockpiles should not exceed 2:1.

▶ Topsoil piles should be handled as little as possible, to minimize damage to soil structure.

Temporary measures should be used to contain sediment. Topsoil stockpiles can be covered to slow drying, prevent erosion, keep down dust, and prevent contamination by windblown seeds of weeds or invasive species. Stockpiles are best covered with a breathable material such as an unwoven geotextile (see Figure 2.2), which will allow air and water to penetrate. Nontoxic soil binders can be applied to

Figure 2.1 Stripped topsoil is stockpiled in a low continuous pile along the edge of the site, waiting for rough grading to be completed, and then redistributed over the site.
Photo by Mark K. Morrison, FASLA

Figure 2.2 This stripped topsoil is stockpiled on a paved surface and covered with a geotextile to protect it from erosion and contamination.

stockpiles for short-term stabilization. If topsoil stockpiles will not be redistributed within a year, they should be stabilized by planting a quick-growing erosion-preventing annual ryegrass or other vegetative cover.

The stockpiling of topsoil for periods of a month or more will likely result in the loss of beneficial soil microorganisms that are an integral component of healthy soils. In order to minimize the loss of microorganisms, create many small stockpiles rather than one large one, and keep them moistened. The Natural Resources Conservation Service recommends a maximum pile height of 4 feet for clay soils and 6 feet for sandy soils.

When stockpiled soil is properly maintained, there is likely to be a greater concentration and less loss of microorganisms in the upper layer of the topsoil stockpile. In order to distribute the microorganisms throughout the topsoil, the top foot or so of the stockpile should be mixed with the balance of the soil, prior to redistribution on the site. For topsoil stockpiled for a year or more, microorganism inoculants may need to be introduced into the soil mix prior to redistribution on the site.

Before topsoil can be redistributed, damage to subsoils, primarily due to compaction, will need restoration. This may include the area under the topsoil stockpile as well. Soil restoration and redistribution is generally one of the last phases of construction, after much of the hardscape and site amenities are in place. Therefore, concerns about damaging the new construction limit the equipment that can be used to perform these operations.

▶ On some sites, it may be necessary for contract documents to include phased restoration and topsoil redistribution that is coordinated with other construction completion, in order to ensure that these steps can be carried out effectively.

Practices to Avoid

- Topsoil is a valuable resource. Avoid the construction approach of cutting the topsoil layer away and using it in areas that require fill. In this way, the top organic layer, removed first, ends up at the bottom of the area to be filled, buried by the subsoil that is removed later and used to complete the filling operation. This puts valuable nutrients and organic material out of the reach of plant roots.

Figure 2.3   A large stockpile of mixed topsoil and subsoil makes it impossible to redistribute the topsoil, squandering a valuable natural resource.

- Where soil removal deeper than the level of topsoil is required, do not mix topsoil and subsoil together; they should be stockpiled separately. See Figure 2.3.
- Avoid stockpiling topsoil on steep slopes.
- Avoid leaving existing topsoil in areas designated for temporary staging or access, where compaction can destroy the topsoil structure. Strip and stockpile topsoil from these areas as well as those being directly disturbed or built on as part of the construction.
- Avoid covering stockpiles with plastic tarps; they prevent the flow of air and moisture, which can leave the soils too wet for redistribution and can contribute to higher temperatures that can kill beneficial soil organisms.
- Avoid spreading noxious weeds or invasives. If there is evidence of noxious weed or invasive plant growth, treat the soil with a selective herbicide before the soil is spread and before the stockpile is redistributed.

References

ALSO IN THIS BOOK

See sections "Grading," "Spreading and Grading Topsoil", and "Soil Erosion and Sediment Controls" found in Chapter 3.

OTHER RESOURCES

American Society of Landscape Architects, the Lady Bird Johnson Wildflower Center and the United States Botanic Garden. *The Sustainable Sites Initiative—Guidelines and Performance Benchmarks 2009.* www.sustainablesites.org.

Hopper, Leonard. *Landscape Architectural Graphic Standards.* Hoboken, NJ: John Wiley & Sons, Inc., 2007.

Hopper, Leonard. *Graphic Standards Field Guide to Hardscape.* Hoboken, NJ: John Wiley & Sons, Inc., 2010.

Thompson, J. William, and Kim Sorvig. *Sustainable Landscape Construction.* Washington, DC: Island Press, 2000.

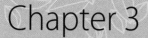

Chapter 3

Earthworks

Construction Damage to Existing Trees

Description

Wounding of the aboveground parts of a tree due to construction activities is more than unsightly; it can leave a tree vulnerable to infection by insect vectors or fungal diseases. Damage to the underground parts of a tree is typically less obvious but usually has a much greater impact on the health of a tree. A broken limb is relatively easy to repair, but soil compaction or root destruction is more difficult and takes much longer to repair (see Figures 3.1 and 3.2). Belowground damage to the root system may not be readily visible for two or three years

Figure 3.1 Several major roots have been torn by the backhoe excavating next to this large major tree. Note the lack of any tree protection. Care should be taken to bridge over any major roots instead of ripping them apart during the excavation.

Figure 3.2 Excavation along with a lowering of grade resulted in many of the large supporting roots of this tree being cut or damaged by the excavation for this concrete curb. Contract documents should have taken into consideration the critical root zone of this tree.

after construction damage, or when the tree is subject to unusual stress, such as drought. The initial obvious signs may be branch dieback and leaf drop, which can indicate a period of decline, leading to the ultimate death of the tree.

Trees are damaged during construction in four primary ways:

- The aboveground parts of a tree are subjected to physical damage, for example, broken limbs, scarring of trunks, and mechanical damage to roots protruding above grade.
- A tree's root system can be damaged during excavation.
- Chemical damage can be inflicted on the root system (cement, paint, acid, etc.) when the ground beneath the canopy is used as a washing/rinsing area for tools and other construction equipment.
- The soil is compacted within the critical root zone of a tree.

The root system of an established tree extends to, at minimum, a distance out from its trunk equal to the height of the tree (see Figure 3.3). Most tree roots are located in the top 6 to 18 inches of soil, and the majority of a tree's active root system exists in the top 8 inches of soil

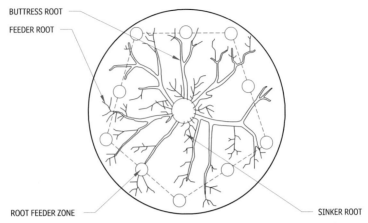

BUTTRESS ROOT

FEEDER ROOT

ROOT FEEDER ZONE

SINKER ROOT

Figure 3.3 Plan view of typical tree root system. The 10 gray dots indicate the general outline of the feeder root zone, which is located close to the drip line of the tree where the majority of absorption and other root/soil interface activities take place.

Source: Hopper, *Landscape Architecture Graphic Standards.* Copyright John Wiley & Sons, Inc., 2007.

in and around the drip line. A change in grade of as little as 4–6 inches either above or below this natural level can have devastating effects on the health of a tree.

▶ Although the area under the drip line of the tree is generally considered the minimum area to be protected, be aware that a healthy tree can have roots that extend out two to three times that distance.

In addition to supporting and anchoring the tree, the main functions roots serve are to extract oxygen, water, and nutrients from the soil and to transport them from the root hairs to the stem. All of these ingredients are essential for a tree to survive and are contained in the pore spaces within a soil. Tree roots exist and can survive only in the pore spaces between soil particles.

Understanding the critical function of roots, their relatively shallow soil habitat, and how extensive they are in relation to the aboveground parts of the trees (which they support), makes it obvious just how destructive it is to compact the soil in and around the drip line of any tree. The options for repairing damaged trees as a result of soil compaction are very limited. Therefore, prevention is far better than any attempt to cure (see Figure 3.4).

Figure 3.4 This tree has its trunk protected by vertical wooden slats wired together. The wood barrier protects the critical root zone from compaction by construction equipment and activities.

Assessing Site Conditions

The existing trees on the site should be evaluated using the following criteria:

- Tree value, including aesthetic, cultural, and ecological value.
- Tree health.
- Species tolerance to construction and other mechanical disturbance.
- Site suitability (postconstruction).

Certified arborists possess a unique body of knowledge and skills that make them the best choice for evaluating trees according to these criteria; they should be part of the site assessment team.

After all existing trees have been assessed, the certified arborist will advise whether a tree is suitable for retention. Existing trees that exhibit poor structure or poor health may not be designated for preservation. Occasionally, the certified arborist will recommend against retaining healthy trees that will inevitably be compromised by the impact of construction. If the tree is particularly valuable, the certified arborist may recommend an alternative construction technique and/or a design change. However, this information must be acted on *prior* to drawing the final design plans, in order to avoid costly and time-consuming changes during the actual construction phases.

Once a tree has been earmarked for retention, a tree protection zone (TPZ) must be identified. The TPZ comprises the area around the tree or groups of trees in which no grading or construction activities should occur. The tree and its protection zone should be clearly demarcated on all resulting plans and drawings that describe the installation of utilities and all demolition and construction activities, and the TPZ should be fenced off (see Figure 3.5).

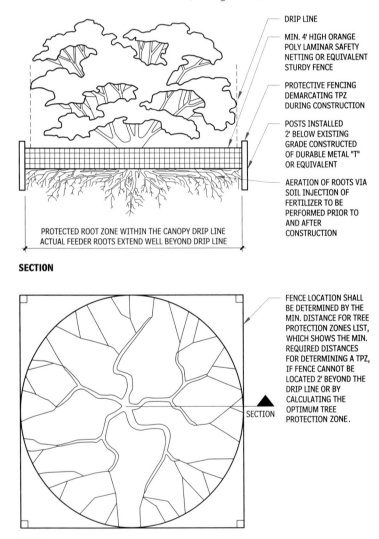

DRIP LINE

MIN. 4' HIGH ORANGE POLY LAMINAR SAFETY NETTING OR EQUIVALENT STURDY FENCE

PROTECTIVE FENCING DEMARCATING TPZ DURING CONSTRUCTION

POSTS INSTALLED 2' BELOW EXISTING GRADE CONSTRUCTED OF DURABLE METAL "T" OR EQUIVALENT

AERATION OF ROOTS VIA SOIL INJECTION OF FERTILIZER TO BE PERFORMED PRIOR TO AND AFTER CONSTRUCTION

PROTECTED ROOT ZONE WITHIN THE CANOPY DRIP LINE ACTUAL FEEDER ROOTS EXTEND WELL BEYOND DRIP LINE

SECTION

FENCE LOCATION SHALL BE DETERMINED BY THE MIN. DISTANCE FOR TREE PROTECTION ZONES LIST, WHICH SHOWS THE MIN. REQUIRED DISTANCES FOR DETERMINING A TPZ, IF FENCE CANNOT BE LOCATED 2' BEYOND THE DRIP LINE OR BY CALCULATING THE OPTIMUM TREE PROTECTION ZONE.

SECTION

PLAN

Figure 3.5 Typical tree protection zone.
Source: Hopper, *Landscape Architecture Graphic Standards.* Copyright John Wiley & Sons, Inc., 2007.

Acceptable Practices

Minimum Distances for Tree Protection Zones

To calculate the optimum tree protection zone, evaluate the species tolerance for construction damage (good, moderate, or poor), and identify tree age (young, mature, or overmature):

- Trees rated good, young need 2 inches of TPZ for every .5 inch of trunk diameter at breast height (DBH).
- Trees rated good, mature need 4 inches of TPZ for every .5 inch of trunk DBH.
- Trees rated good, overmature need 5 inches of TPZ for every .5 inch of trunk DBH.
- Trees rated moderate, young need 4 inches of TPZ for every .5 inch of trunk DBH.
- Trees rated moderate, mature need 5 inches of TPZ for every .5 inch of trunk DBH.
- Trees rated moderate, overmature need 6 inches of TPZ for every .5 inch of trunk DBH.
- Trees rated poor, young need 5 inches of TPZ for every .5 inch of trunk DBH.
- Trees rated poor, mature need 6 inches of TPZ for every .5 inch of trunk DBH.
- Trees rated poor, overmature need 7 inches of TPZ for every .5 inch of trunk DBH.

Multiply the TPZ needed by the trunk diameter to calculate the optimum diameter for the tree protection zone. Plot the resulting tree protection zone on the tree preservation plan (see Figure 3.6).

Tree Protection Zone Specifications

Tree protection zones should meet the following specifications:

- *Perimeter fencing* — Minimum 4-foot-high orange plastic safety fence, wood and wire snow fence, or chain-link fence.
- Mulch — Two inches of composted mulch spread evenly over a geo-textile fabric throughout the entire zone.
- Moisture — Maintain natural moisture levels.
- Drainage — Do not alter the existing natural drainage.
- Signage — Affix to fencing as close to eye level as possible, containing the following directions: No vehicle movement; No storage of materials; No washing of equipment; Contact [name and number] for inquiries.

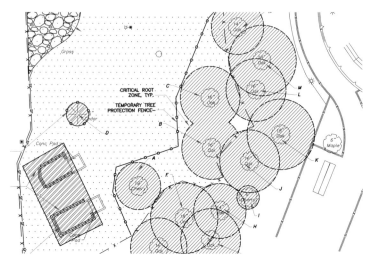

Figure 3.6 Construction drawing identifying the tree protection zones (referred to on this plan as critical root zones) of the trees that are to be protected (single cross hatching) and the location of the temporary tree protection fence. These trees were also photographed to document their condition prior to the start of any construction activities.

- Fertilizers — Healthy trees generally don't need to be fertilized; however, fertilizer is beneficial to compensate for root loss and to stimulate the growth of new feeder roots closer to the trunk. An efficient method of applying nutrients to large trees is to inject the soil with a water-based solution.

▶ Prior to establishing a tree protection zone, prune the trees to be protected, focusing on removal of dead or broken branches. The purpose of this maintenance is primarily safety, but it also serves as a monitor for any new damage that may occur during construction.

Construction Activities within the Tree Protection Zone

If, during the course of construction, it does become necessary for activities to take place inside the tree protection zone, then a certified arborist should be consulted. The consulting certified arborist will recommend the most appropriate way to undertake such activities, or will suggest possible alternatives.

Vehicle and pedestrian movement can be particularly damaging to trees, causing soil compaction. A 6-inch layer of mulch over a geotextile

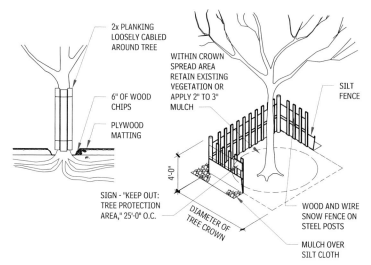

2x PLANKING
LOOSELY CABLED
AROUND TREE

WITHIN CROWN
SPREAD AREA
RETAIN EXISTING
VEGETATION OR
APPLY 2" TO 3"
MULCH

SILT
FENCE

6" OF WOOD
CHIPS

PLYWOOD
MATTING

4'-0"

SIGN - "KEEP OUT:
TREE PROTECTION
AREA," 25'-0" O.C.

DIAMETER OF
TREE CROWN

WOOD AND WIRE
SNOW FENCE ON
STEEL POSTS

MULCH OVER
SILT CLOTH

Figure 3.7 Tree trunk and root protection within the tree protection zone.
Source: Hopper, *Landscape Architectural Graphic Standards.* Copyright John Wiley & Sons, Inc., 2007.

fabric with an overlay of ¾-inch-thick plywood sheets, along with 2 x wood planking loosely cabled around the tree trunk, is the recommended approach to reduce the effects of construction activity within the tree protection zone. See Figure 3.7.

When trenching or excavation is to be undertaken in areas where tree roots are likely to exist, the use of an air tool that forces high-speed air through a tube can move soil without damaging the roots. These types of tools can also be used to loosen compacted soils around roots, which can then be amended with organic matter and backfilled around the roots to create a more suitable environment for root growth. See Figure 3.8.

▶ **Wherever possible, consider installing utilities by tunneling under the tree (see Figure 3.9). Tunneling causes less damage to the root structure than trenching.**

When trenching or excavation is to be undertaken and roots need to be cut, it is important that the roots be severed cleanly rather than torn with a backhoe or other excavation equipment. The best way to achieve this is to expose the roots first and then cut them cleanly with a sharp saw or loppers. Roots with a diameter larger than 2 inches should be tunneled under, where practical.

▶ **Before severing any major roots, consider whether bridging over the roots is a feasible alternative.**

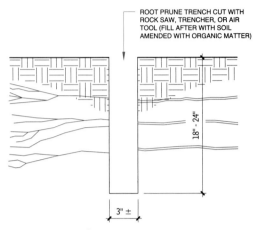

ROOT PRUNE TRENCH CUT WITH
ROCK SAW, TRENCHER, OR AIR
TOOL (FILL AFTER WITH SOIL
AMENDED WITH ORGANIC MATTER)

18" – 24"

3" ±

Figure 3.8   Root prune trench.
Source: Hopper, *Landscape Architectural Graphic Standards.* Copyright John Wiley & Sons, Inc., 2007.

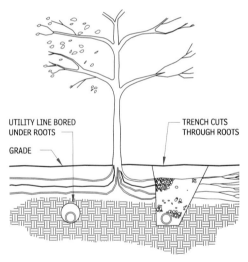

UTILITY LINE BORED
UNDER ROOTS

GRADE

TRENCH CUTS
THROUGH ROOTS

Figure 3.9   Underground utility line installation near existing trees.
Source: Hopper, *Landscape Architectural Graphic Standards.* Copyright John Wiley & Sons, Inc., 2007.

▶ The tree protection zone must be monitored during construction to ensure compliance by the contractor. If any tree is accidentally damaged, appropriate actions to mitigate the damage should be implemented.

Grade Changes within the Drip Line of Existing Trees

A change in grade either above (Figure 3.10) or below (Figure 3.11) the tree's natural level due to construction activity or design changes should be avoided. However, if a grade change is absolutely necessary, proper procedures for filling or cutting around an existing tree (Figure 3.12) should be employed to protect the tree.

Tree Damage Treatments

If, despite efforts to prevent construction damage to existing trees, damage does occur, measures to mitigate the damage should be implemented as soon as possible. Measures to mitigate construction damage include the following:

- Pruning may be required to remove branches that have been broken or torn during construction. In some cases, low-hanging branches may need to be removed in order to provide necessary clearance below. Any dead, diseased, or otherwise hazardous branches should be removed. Proper pruning techniques should be employed.

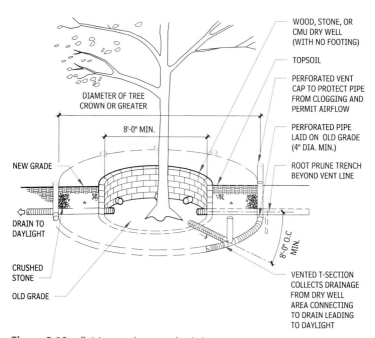

Figure 3.10   Raising grade around existing tree.
Source: Hopper, *Landscape Architectural Graphic Standards.* Copyright John Wiley & Sons, Inc., 2007.

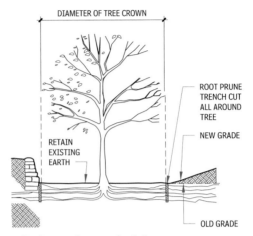

Figure 3.11   Cutting grade around existing tree.
Source: Hopper, *Landscape Architectural Graphic Standards.* Copyright John Wiley & Sons, Inc., 2007.

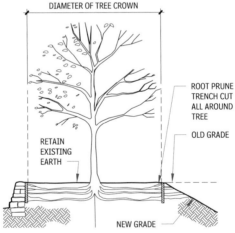

Figure 3.12   Filling around an existing mature tree utilizing a retaining wall to reduce the amount of fill within close proximity to the tree.
Source: Hopper, *Landscape Architectural Graphic Standards.* Copyright John Wiley & Sons, Inc., 2007.

▶ Although compensatory pruning of the crown to offset root loss during construction was once considered a standard practice, research indicates that this practice may reduce the tree's food-making capacity and stress the tree further.

▪ If any trunk bark is damaged by construction vehicles, loose bark should be removed and any jagged edges cut cleanly with a sharp knife.

▶ **Unless aesthetically desirable, use of a wound dressing over cut branches or damaged bark is not considered necessary and does not speed the healing process or prevent insect infestation or disease.**

▪ Keep the root zone adequately irrigated by applying a thorough, deep penetrating supply of water. Frequent shallow applications of water are not beneficial to roots below the top surface of soil.

▪ Apply a 3- to 4-inch layer of organic mulch over the root zone to retain soil moisture, reduce competition from weeds, and moderate temperature fluctuations.

▪ If soil compaction has occurred, consider vertical mulching or radial aeration (see Figure 3.13). Vertical mulching involves drilling 3- to 4-inch-diameter holes, 12 inches deep, on a 3-foot-on-center grid within the root zone and filling the holes with organic matter. Radial aeration involves creating a spoke-and-wheel trenching pattern; utilizing an air tool or hydrovac, a 6-inch by 6-inch trench can be excavated radially, starting 5 feet from the base of a tree and extending to the edge of the critical root zone (CRZ). See Figure 3.14. Each trench should be connected by a 6-inch by 6-inch trench that will demarcate the outer edge of the CRZ. The minimum amount of the CRZ trenched must be 40 percent of the total area of the CRZ. The

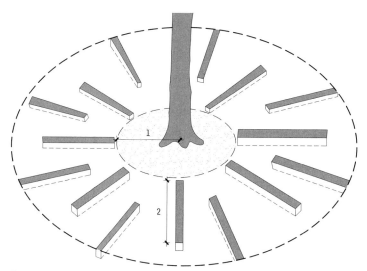

Figure 3.13 Typical radial aeration trenching diagram.
Photo courtesy of James Urban/ISA

Figure 3.14 Aeration trenching by having soil removed by a hydrovac. Water is being applied to aid in the soil removal. Trench will be backfilled with amended planting soil mix.
Photo courtesy of James Urban/ISA

trenches should then be backfilled with soil amended with either organic material or dehydrated manure.

Monitor trees carefully after construction, keeping an eye out for visible indicators of decline such as:

- Branch dieback in the crown.
- Smaller and fewer leaves produced during the spring.
- Premature fall color and/or leaf drop.
- Cracks, splits, or cavities in the trunk.
- Evidence of insects, disease, or decay.

Immediate action can often save a tree from spiraling rapid decline and prevent loss of the tree.

Transplanting Existing Trees

There may be times where fairly young trees can be transplanted to another location if they are in conflict with the proposed design, or if they are likely to be damaged by construction. Although there is no guarantee that a tree will survive the stress of transplanting, the following steps will provide the best opportunity for success (see Figures 3.15 through 3.17):

- If possible, root prune a year before the tree is to be transplanted.
- Dig as large a root ball as possible.
- Transport the tree carefully to its new location. See Figure 3.18.

Figure 3.15　Before digging the tree to be transplanted, a hole is dug in the new location using a skid steer digger attachment. After the hole is dug, the smoothly scraped sides should be scarified to create a better interface between the backfill and surrounding soil.
Photo by Kenneth Petrocca

Figure 3.16　Before digging the tree to be transplanted, the lower branches are tied to minimize any damage.
Photo by Kenneth Petrocca

Figure 3.17 A skid steer tree spade is carefully lined up with the tree centered between the tree spade blades.
Photo by Kenneth Petrocca

Figure 3.18 The tree is carefully lifted from its existing location and transported to the new location where it is to be planted.
Photo by Kenneth Petrocca

- Backfill carefully with a planting mix that includes a mycorrhizal fungus or biostimulant to promote new root development. See Figures 3.19 and 3.20.
- Provide adequate and deep-penetrating irrigation to keep the root area moist.

Figure 3.19　The tree is carefully lowered into the new planting hole.
Photo by Kenneth Petrocca

Figure 3.20　The tree hole is backfilled in gently but firmly tamped multiple layers. The tree in the background has a ringed berm around the planting hole, ready to be watered and then covered with a layer of mulch.
Photo by Kenneth Petrocca

- Provide a 3- to 4-inch layer of organic mulch over the root zone to help retain moisture, reduce competition from weeds, and moderate temperature fluctuations.

Practices to Avoid

- Avoid construction activities that result in soil compaction within the drip lines of trees. If soil compaction remediation is required, consider remediation with either vertical mulching or radial aeration.
- Avoid tearing roots with construction equipment. If roots are torn rather than cut cleanly, the resulting wound will have a much larger surface area that will take longer to heal and be vulnerable to infection.
- Avoid changing the existing drainage patterns around trees to be protected. Any increase or decrease in water can have devastating effects on tree health and stability. Changes in drainage patterns should not undermine roots or inundate trees with excessive water. If the natural runoff toward a tree has been cut off, or if a site is being artificially drained after construction, then irrigation will be required to maintain tree health, particularly if substantial root loss has occurred.
- Construction contractors should never undertake any pruning during the course of construction, unless directed to do so.
- Do not allow trees to be damaged in the final stages of construction by the landscape installation. Rototilling under the drip line, adding planting soil over the root zone, or trenching for an irrigation system can negate any earlier tree preservation efforts.
- Avoid fertilizing damaged trees after construction unless soil tests indicate a specific deficiency. Nitrogen can push green leaf growth at a time when roots are just beginning to recover. Excess salts can draw critical water away from the roots and into the soil. Any deficiencies should be compensated with low application rates, using a slow-release fertilizer.

Grading

Description

Grading is the reshaping of the ground surface by moving earth on a site to desired finished elevations or subgrade elevations as shown on a proposed grading plan.

Grading can involve lowering the elevation in some areas (cutting) or raising the elevation in some areas (filling). Grading operations on a site can involve moving the existing earth already on the site to attain the desired elevations (balancing cut and fill). It may also require that additional material be brought to the site or that excess material be removed from the site.

▶ Most grading plans strive to balance cut and fill. If site constraints prevent that approach, it is usually more desirable (and less costly) to remove material from a site than to import additional material.

Assessing Site Conditions

During the preliminary design phase, the existing grades, slopes, and drainage patterns of the site should be evaluated. Because almost every site improvement involves some grading, understanding the existing conditions is a critical first step before considering grading changes. Thinking of grading as a strategy that should be integrated with other strategies to arrive at the final design—rather than just a function that needs to be worked out later—maximizes the design impact of a creative grading plan as part of a comprehensive site improvement.

Existing site elements, trees, and vegetation that could be negatively impacted by grading operations should be noted and addressed in the grading plan. There are several approaches to saving trees when the design requires that the grade around them change:

- Any changes in grade should be made as far away from the drip line as possible.

- If the grade around the tree needs to be raised significantly, a well can be created around the tree—ideally, out to the drip line—to retain the existing soil and grade in the area of the feeder roots. A dry well or perforated pipe system should be installed to provide drainage within the well.
- If the grade around the tree needs to be raised only a few inches, the existing root zone can be carefully scarified before adding a sandy loam mixed with organic matter. If the root zone area is compacted, compaction reduction techniques should be employed before adding any material over the root zone.
- If the grade around the tree needs to be raised a foot or more, a layer of large open graded stone and geotextile mat should be included in the profile, to provide a positive drainage layer and allow air to penetrate through to the original soil layer. A well will need to be constructed around the trunk, allowing room for growth, to keep the raised soil level away from the tree trunk itself.
- If the grade around the tree needs to be lowered, a tree wall should be constructed just outside the drip line to accommodate the change in grade. Drainage provisions should be made in the wall.

▶ **There are many variables involved when changing the grade around trees that are to be saved. Although general approaches provide a guide to techniques that can be used, the unique circumstances of each situation need to be studied in detail, in order to tailor the approach to the specific situation.**

Erosion and sediment control measures should be implemented prior to the grading operations. Vegetated buffer strips outside of the area to be graded, as well as other areas, should be incorporated into the plan to help provide temporary or permanent storm water control. Areas for stockpiling earth during the grading process should be identified, and the stockpiles protected from erosion.

Prior to any grading operations, potential damage to adjacent properties or installations should be evaluated. Where the potential for damage is high, a geotechnical engineer should be consulted to thoroughly evaluate the situation and propose mitigating.

Utility installation should be performed after rough grading operations have been completed and the surface drainage patterns are established. Storm sewers for site drainage are generally the first to be installed, as they usually require the deepest and widest trench excavation. Depending on the project, the remaining utilities (sanitary, water, electric, gas, etc.) are installed immediately afterward, or at the same time, if there are no conflicts with location of the required trenches and utility routes.

Backfilling and compacting over installed utilities (or existing utilities where fill needs to be added) should be performed with lighter equipment compacting the layers in smaller lifts, before heavier grading equipment is brought in to grade and compact the earth, in order not to crush or damage the utility.

Acceptable Practices

General

Based on the grading plan, the contractor (with the help of a surveyor, if necessary) positions stakes on the site that represent a layout of the work that is to be done, with the specified elevations required for each stake point. Often a ribbon or painted line on the stake indicates the required grade for the contractor to meet. See Figure 3.21.

Figure 3.21 Stake with painted line and string indicating grade to be met.

The grading plan should be studied to develop an efficient plan to cut and fill without having to haul earth long distances. Ideally, the soil would be scraped from high areas directly to low areas (basically cutting and filling in one operation). If possible, grading should be sequenced in a way that does not require moving equipment over areas that have already been cut or filled.

Large areas can be graded using a scraper to cut areas to the required grades and move thin layers of soil to areas that require fill. Some scrapers are equipped with laser units to help set the equipment to grade more precisely. Graders, bulldozers, and compactors are also used in the grading operation to complete grading done by the scraper and to get into areas that are not accessible to the scraper.

Areas of fill should be compacted in 6- to 12-inch lifts (layers), depending on the type of soil, the equipment being used, and the desired level of compaction. Fill depths greater than 12 inches generally cannot be compacted effectively.

Rough Grading

Rough grading is the initial operation of shaping the earth on the site to within a few inches of the desired elevation. It involves moving, removing, or importing the quantities of earth into or from the locations where the rough grading will take place. Rough grading will establish elevations that will parallel the elevations and slopes of the final grades. The rough grading operation includes any required compaction of areas that are filled. Proper compaction will require the addition of some water, to provide the right moisture content that will allow the soil to be compacted to the required density.

Slopes that are created as part of the rough grading operation should be stabilized. This is particularly important with fill slopes that are difficult to compact without any restraint along the edge.

Fine Grading

After rough grading has been completed, fine grading establishes the elevations of the site at precisely the desired elevations to receive the proposed pavements or topsoil, which will bring the areas up to the finished grades shown on the grading plan. Fine grading is usually accomplished by using a grader and steel drum vibratory or rubber tire roller.

Grading Slopes

The maximum slope for lawn areas that will require mowing is 3:1 (three horizontal feet for one foot of vertical change in height). The maximum for other vegetated slopes is generally considered to be 2:1. These slopes will need to be stabilized until final grading is complete or vegetation is established. Slope roughening can provide easy, inexpensive, and immediate erosion control immediately after grading operations have been completed.

Slopes should be roughened using machine tracks or other attachments prior to seeding or planting, in order to:

- Help vegetation get established from seed.
- Minimize erosion and trap sediment.
- Maximize storm water infiltration by slowing runoff velocity and increasing the surface area of the soil.

Some techniques to stabilize slopes after fine grading are:

- Stairstep grading with the horizontal step sloped back toward the uphill slope (see Figure 3.22). The ratio of vertical cut distance to horizontal distance should be less than 1:1, with vertical cuts not to exceed 2 feet in soft soils or 3 feet in rocky material. Each step catches material from above and provides a fairly level surface for vegetation to become established.
- Grooving the slope with a tiller, harrow, or teeth of a front-end loader, forming grooves perpendicular to the slope (see Figure 3.22). Grooves should be at least 3 inches deep and no more than 15 inches apart, with each series of grooves cut in the direction opposite to that of the preceding set of grooves, to avoid buildup of loose material at one end.
- Tracking by running a tracked machine up and down the face of the slope, with the tracks leaving their horizontal impression perpendicular to the slope (see Figure 3.23). Excessive compaction should be avoided by making as few passes as possible with the tracked equipment.

Finish Grading

Finish grading establishes the elevations that are indicated on the grading plans. For landscaped areas, this would include the elevations shown on the grading plan after the spreading of new soil mix or stockpiled topsoil.

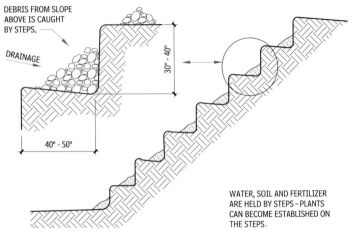

DEBRIS FROM SLOPE
ABOVE IS CAUGHT
BY STEPS.

DRAINAGE

30" – 40"

40" – 50"

WATER, SOIL AND FERTILIZER
ARE HELD BY STEPS – PLANTS
CAN BECOME ESTABLISHED ON
THE STEPS.

STAIRSTEPPING CUT SLOPES

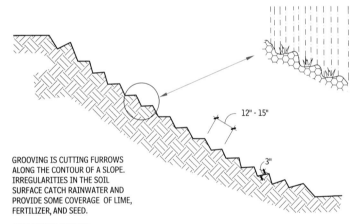

12" – 15"

3"

GROOVING IS CUTTING FURROWS
ALONG THE CONTOUR OF A SLOPE.
IRREGULARITIES IN THE SOIL
SURFACE CATCH RAINWATER AND
PROVIDE SOME COVERAGE OF LIME,
FERTILIZER, AND SEED.

GROOVING SLOPES

Figure 3.22   Stairstep grading and grooving slope diagram.
Source: Hopper, *Graphic Standards Field Guide to Hardscape.* Copyright John Wiley & Sons, Inc., 2010.

EACH LIFT OF THE FILL IS COMPACTED, BUT THE OUTER FACE OF THE SLOPE IS ALLOWED TO REMAIN LOOSE SO THAT THE ROCKS, CLODS, ETC. REACH THE NATURAL ANGLE OF REPOSE.

FILL SLOPE TREATMENT

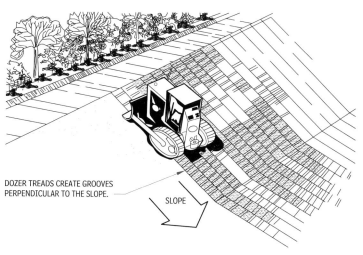

DOZER TREADS CREATE GROOVES PERPENDICULAR TO THE SLOPE.

SLOPE

TRACKING

Figure 3.23 Tracking creates impressions perpendicular to the slope.
Source: Hopper, *Graphic Standards Field Guide to Hardscape.* Copyright John Wiley & Sons, Inc., 2010.

Practices to Avoid

- Do not place fill on saturated or frozen ground.
- Do not cut or fill very close to adjacent properties without providing protection against erosion, sedimentation, slippage, or any other slope-related problem.
- Avoid placing fill adjacent to a water channel bank where it may cause bank failure with deposition of sediment downstream.
- Avoid grading adjacent to water bodies without leaving a vegetated buffer strip, berm, or filter fabric fence to prevent erosion and sedimentation.
- Avoid excessive compaction in areas that will be vegetated. It inhibits germination and growth, and also increases runoff quantity and velocity.

Spreading and Grading Topsoil

Description

Topsoil is usually spread during finished grading to provide a suitable level of positive characteristics, nutrients, and organic matter to encourage the growth of vegetation. It is the layer of soil where root development and biological activity occur. The coarser texture of topsoil increases its infiltration capacity and makes it less susceptible to erosion.

Topsoil to be spread can be from stockpiles of existing topsoil that has been stripped and stockpiled early in the construction phase, or it can be an imported soil blend.

Assessing Site Conditions

Existing topsoil stockpiled for spreading during final site preparation should be used to provide a positive growing medium for vegetation. Before importing soil from another site, the restoration of existing soils on site should be considered. The addition of soil amendments can improve the quality of the existing soil characteristics to match the qualities of healthy local soils.

Existing or imported topsoil should be evaluated for quality, foreign matter, weed seeds, and the feasibility of distributing and grading topsoil on the site. In some cases, it may be more practical to enhance the quality of the soil or subsoil on site than to transport and spread topsoil. If the existing soil or subsoil cannot be amended, or if the depth is not adequate to provide sufficient area for roots to develop, or if the soil contains materials that may be toxic to vegetation, addition and spreading of topsoil may be the only alternative.

Because topsoil generally has a high level of infiltration, the soil beneath needs to be tested to determine if it is well-draining. The different infiltration rates between the base soil and the topsoil overlay can create a situation where water will drain horizontally along the interface of the two different soil types. Low pockets created during the finished grading process can trap water beneath the surface. A percolation test should be performed to determine the rate of infiltration and the need for any modification to the existing soil, to improve its drainage characteristics to make it compatible with the topsoil overlay.

▶ Before spreading topsoil, be sure that erosion and sediment control devices have been put into place.

Acceptable Practices

Overview of Installation

Topsoil spreading and grading include the following steps:

- Proper inspection and sampling for tests of delivered soil materials.
- Supervision of soil placement in lifts to ensure the proper degree of compaction.
- Prevention of excessive traffic over the placed soil.
- Proper sequencing of planting with soil placement, to greatly reduce disturbance to the placed soil.

▶ Close supervision of the soil installation process by the landscape architect or the soil scientist, if one is retained for the project, is absolutely necessary.

Topsoil Spreading and Grading

- Prior to topsoil spreading, be sure fine grading has established even and proper elevations as indicated on the plans, without low spots or other irregularities.
- The surface of the existing soil should be loosened and roughened to a depth of approximately 6 inches, to create a bond between the existing soil and topsoil layers. This can be accomplished by running a disk over the area or using the teeth of a backhoe or loader to scarify the surface.
- It should be anticipated that some storm water will flow under the topsoil layer and along the surface of the subsoil; therefore, drainage may be required at low points.
- Topsoil should be spread uniformly over the area and compacted enough to bond the topsoil to the layer below and provide even storm water infiltration.

- Use low-impact equipment to minimize overcompaction and soil structure damage.
- On slopes that will not be mowed, the surface can be left rough to minimize erosion.

Topsoil Spreading and Grading on Slopes

Installation of topsoil on slopes carries the potential risk that it can slip down along the interface with the subsoil. In order to minimize this possibility, consider:

- Stepping the subgrade to provide a rougher surface.
- Providing an intercepting swale at the top of the slope to minimize the storm water runoff down the face of the slope.
- Installing soil stabilizers, such as a geoweb.

▶ Surface matting is not effective in preventing topsoil from slipping down a steep slope.

Installation of Soil in Lifts

The soil should always be placed in lifts, preferably not to exceed 6 inches in thickness. This ensures the elimination of air pockets and soft spots of inadequate filling, as well as providing adequate compaction to prevent settlement or subsidence. See Figure 3.24.

If a loamy sand to sandy loam designed soil is installed with less than 10 percent volume basis organic matter, the density as placed will normally be at 85 to 90 percent, using the Proctor test. If compactive force is required, it should be applied with a lightweight roller of not more than 75 to 100 pounds per foot-width of the roller.

In many cases, traffic from soil-spreading equipment—such as a "speeder-skidder" or a light, wide-track bulldozer—can apply sufficient

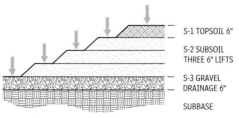

S-1 TOPSOIL 6"

S-2 SUBSOIL THREE 6" LIFTS

S-3 GRAVEL DRAINAGE 6"

SUBBASE

Figure 3.24   Installation of soil in lifts. The arrows indicate compaction of each lift as installed.
Source: Hopper, *Landscape Architecture Graphic Standards.* Copyright John Wiley & Sons, Inc., 2007.

force for compacting soil to a Proctor of 85 to 90 percent for landscape purposes, without exceeding plant root penetration density of 1.65 Mg/m^3 for fine-textured cohesive soil and 1.70 Mg/m^3 for sandy noncohesive soil.

Overview of Placement of Soil on Slopes

The placement of soil on a slope must be done with somewhat more care than on level areas. The existing slope surface should be prepared to receive the designed soil as cover, especially if the slope is greater than 3:1; however, it is always wise to prepare the subbase even on a gentler slope, to ensure slope stability.

Soil should not be placed on a slope with compacted soil or a very stony smooth surface acting like a pavement. Both conditions act as an interface between the initial surface and the placed soil, and will become a potential failure plane, especially if water is contributed to the site from upslope drainage.

The surface should be deeply scarified (6 inches or more, using a chisel plow), with removal of some of the stone in the case of the stony surface. On steeper slopes, the existing soil material (subgrade) should be stepped or terraced (see Figure 3.25).

▶ The best practice is simultaneous placement of the topsoil and plants, if feasible. Contractors have stated that this practice has saved them time—hence, money. It also eliminates unwanted traffic over the topsoil final grade.

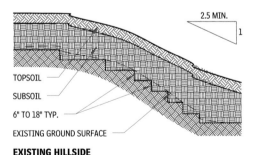

2.5 MIN.

1

TOPSOIL

SUBSOIL

6" TO 18" TYP.

EXISTING GROUND SURFACE

EXISTING HILLSIDE

Figure 3.25 "Stepping" preparation of a sloping subgrade. The designed soil is backfilled into the benches. Upslope drainage should be cut off by curtain drains if excess downslope drainage is a problem. Underdrainage may be required at the foot of the benched slope. Width of each bench depends on existing slope angle.
Source: Hopper, *Landscape Architecture Graphic Standards.* Copyright John Wiley & Sons, Inc., 2007.

Practices to Avoid

- Do not spread topsoil while it is frozen or muddy, or when the sub-grade is wet or frozen.
- Do not apply topsoil to slopes steeper than 2:1, as it will likely slip down to the toe of the slope.
- Do not apply topsoil over a subsoil of a significantly different texture and infiltration rate.
- Avoid spreading topsoil on subsoils with high clay content, particularly on slopes.
- Avoid low spots in the grading of subsoils prior to topsoil spreading, because they will hold water.
- Avoid having equipment repeatedly run over the area where topsoil has been previously placed, to avoid compaction; loosen the soil if necessary.

Soil Erosion and Sediment Controls

Description

The control of erosion and subsequent transport of sediment from project sites is a critical part of the design and development process. Modification of land and land use can have severe impacts on-site, as well as upon adjacent lands and downstream areas. Most of the impacts can be mitigated by proper planning, implementation, and active maintenance of soil erosion and sediment control measures.

This has become a critical issue in recent years, and many local jurisdictions now require an erosion control plan as a part of the construction document package. The goal of erosion control measures is to protect areas outside of the project boundary, particularly bodies of water such as streams and lakes, from the harmful effects of increased silt load. Several types of methods can be used, including erosion control fencing (see Figure 3.26), bales of straw placed in drainage channels, or "bio-bags," or filtration fabrics placed over the openings of catch basins or other drainage structures that are downhill from the site (see Figure 3.27). Once construction is completed, these can be removed, but not until all work is completed.

Assessing Site Conditions

Land-Disturbing Activity Plan

Successful control of erosion and sedimentation from construction activities involves a system of Best Management Practices that target each stage of the erosion process. The most efficient approach involves minimizing the potential sources of sediment from the outset. This means limiting the extent and duration of land disturbance to the minimum needed, and protecting surfaces once they are exposed.

A Land-Disturbing Activity Plan is a document set specifying the types of erosion and sediment control measures, their locations, and the

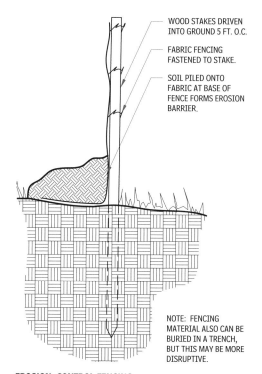

WOOD STAKES DRIVEN
INTO GROUND 5 FT. O.C.

FABRIC FENCING
FASTENED TO STAKE.

SOIL PILED ONTO
FABRIC AT BASE OF
FENCE FORMS EROSION
BARRIER.

NOTE: FENCING
MATERIAL ALSO CAN BE
BURIED IN A TRENCH,
BUT THIS MAY BE MORE
DISRUPTIVE.

EROSION–CONTROL FENCING

Figure 3.26   Erosion control fence detail.
Source: Hopper, *Landscape Architecture Graphic Standards.* Copyright John Wiley & Sons, Inc., 2007.

Figure 3.27   Protective snow fencing with silt fence and hay bales to control erosion and prevent sediment from entering the river at the bottom of the embankment.

specific installation and maintenance practices to be followed for a given project. The plan typically includes soil erosion and sediment control plans superimposed on site grading, drainage, utility, or other building construction plans, indicating the locations of measures to be taken. The most effective Land-Disturbing Activity Plan is one that has been integrated throughout the entire design process, resulting in a site plan that minimizes land disturbance by fitting the proposed use to the existing topography and soils. For the plan to be effective, it must minimize the size of the disturbed area, stabilize disturbed areas immediately, retain or safely accommodate runoff, retain sediment on the site, and protect existing watercourses from disturbance.

The Land-Disturbing Activity Plan includes a narrative component that describes the existing site conditions (land use, soil, topography, drainage, and vegetation), the proposed project and development phases, the proposed construction period and schedule of activities, and a detailed description of four major programs: the erosion control program, the sediment control program, the storm water management program, and the maintenance program. All standards, details, and specifications are included in the document set and are typically required to be housed at the construction site on a 24-hour basis.

The permitting process for land disturbance may vary from site to site, based on local, state, and federal jurisdictional authorities. Any land disturbance proposed within or adjacent to watercourses, wetlands, other water bodies, or shorelines will require permitting through state and federal authorities. Make significant time allowances in planning for the permitting process.

Construction Sequencing

Construction sequencing is a specified work schedule that coordinates the timing of land-disturbing activities and the installation of erosion and sediment control measures. The goal of a construction sequence schedule is to reduce on-site erosion and off-site sedimentation by performing land-disturbing activities and installing erosion and sediment control practices in accordance with a planned schedule. See Table 3.1.

Construction site phasing involves disturbing only part of a site at a time, to prevent erosion from dormant parts. Grading activities and construction are completed and soils are effectively stabilized on one part of the site before grading and construction commence at another part.

Table 3.1 Scheduling Considerations for Construction Activities

Construction Activity	Schedule Consideration
Construction access, entrance to site, construction routes, areas designated for equipment parking	This is the first land-disturbing activity. As soon as construction begins, stabilize any bare areas with gravel and temporary vegetation.
Sediment traps and barriers, basin traps, sediment fences, outlet protection	After the construction site is accessed, install principal basins. Add more traps and barriers as needed during grading.
Runoff control diversions, perimeter dikes, water bars, outlet protection	Install key practices after installing principal sediment traps and before land grading. Install additional runoff control measures during grading.
Runoff conveyance system, stream bank stabilization, storm drains, channels, inlet and outlet protection, slope drains	If necessary, stabilize stream banks as soon as possible, and install a principal runoff conveyance system with runoff control measures. Install the remainder of the systems after grading.
Land clearing and grading, site preparation (cutting, filling, and grading, sediment traps, barriers, diversions, drains, surface roughening)	Implement major clearing and grading after installing principal sediment and key runoff control measures, and install additional control measures as grading continues. Clear borrow and disposal areas as needed, and mark trees and buffer areas for preservation.
Surface stabilization, temporary and permanent seeding, mulching, sodding, riprap	Apply temporary or permanent stabilizing measures immediately to any disturbed areas where work has been either completed or delayed.
Building construction, buildings, utilities, paving	During construction, install any erosion and sedimentation control measures that are needed.
Landscaping and final stabilization, topsoiling, trees and shrubs, permanent seeding, mulching, sodding, riprap	This is the last construction phase. Stabilize all open areas, including borrow and spoil areas, and remove and stabilize all temporary control measures.

Source: U.S. Environmental Protection Agency

Acceptable Practices

A wide variety of vegetative and structural measures may be used to limit erosion and prevent the transport of sediment off a disturbed site. The following measures are commonly referred to as soil erosion and sediment control measures:

- *Buffer zone* — A vegetated strip surrounding disturbed areas or along water body margins that filters solids and sediment from sheet flow used as a buffer on construction sites. Sometimes used with a level spreader to distribute runoff evenly.
- *Level spreader* — Converts concentrated runoff to sheet flow and disperses it uniformly across a slope without causing erosion. This structure is particularly well suited for returning natural sheet flows to exiting drainage that has been altered by development, especially for returning sheet flows to receiving ecosystems such as wetlands, where dispersed flow may be important for maintaining preexisting hydrologic regimes. Particular care must be taken to construct the outlet lip completely level in a stable, undisturbed soil to avoid formation of an outlet channel and subsequent erosion.
- *Streambank stabilization* — Vegetative and structural practices to prevent or reduce bank erosion. See Figure 3.28.

Figure 3.28   Streambank stabilization with rock and vegetation.
Photo by Russell Adsit, FASLA

Figure 3.29   Check dam.
Source: U.S. Environmental Protection Agency

- *Check dam* — A temporary structure to control concentrated storm water flows in channels, slowing velocity and catching sediment. See Figure 3.29.
- *Vegetated swale* — Used to help infiltrate runoff and convey storm water. Vegetation should be established before water flows are introduced. See Figures 3.30 and 3.31.
- *Channel stabilization* — The creation, improvement, or stabilization of channels for safe conveyance. See Figure 3.32.
- *Temporary slope drain* — A flexible conduit, serving as a temporary outlet to conduct flows safely down slopes. It reduces soil erosion and creation of gullies until permanent drainage measures can be employed. The ends of the flexible pipe can have flared metal collars attached, and the pipe itself needs to be anchored along the slope. The outlet should empty to a location that is erosion-resistant and should be checked regularly for blockages or conditions that would render it ineffective. For flatter slopes, a half-pipe or channel can be used. See Figures 3.33 and 3.34.

Figure 3.30 Vegetated swale, usually dry except in rainfall events, channels storm water runoff.

Figure 3.31 A series of culverts allows water of vegetated swales to flow uninterrupted under pedestrian and vehicular circulation routes.

Figure 3.32 Grass-lined channel with offset wattles to control velocity and stabilize channel banks during heavy storm water runoff.
Photo by Russell Adsit, FASLA

Figure 3.33 Temporary slope drain.
Photo by Russell Adsit, FASLA

Figure 3.34 A series of hay bales and slope drains used in conjunction with stone apron employed to prevent erosion.
Photo by Russell Adsit, FASLA

- *Grade stabilization structure* — A temporary or permanent structure designed to accommodate vertical grade change in natural or man-made channels, dropping water to a lower elevation without causing erosion or gullies.
- *Chemical stabilization* — In areas where other measures to stabilize exposed soils are not effective, the spraying of vinyl, asphalt, or rubber onto the soil surface can effectively bind and stabilize. The obvious environmental concerns of using these chemical stabilizers must be weighed against their erosion control value.
- *Rock filter dam* — A temporary or permanent dam used in streams or drainage channels to filter sediment and slow flow velocity. It forms a pool from which water flows downstream through a riser pipe or through the gravel of the rock dam.
- *Retaining wall* — A structural method to reduce slope face exposure to erosive forces. The use of a soil retaining structure during the construction phase can reduce steep slopes during construction. If the structure is to be permanent, careful sequencing of the construction can facilitate grading operations and keep workers safe, without hindering the construction activities. The effect of changes to the site's drainage pattern needs to be considered.

Figure 3.35   A stone or riprap apron is the most common measure for temporary storm water outlet protection.
Photo by Russell Adsit, FASLA

- *Storm drain outlet protection* — Typically, a rock or concrete device to reduce storm water velocity, dissipate flow energy, and prevent channel erosion at pipe outlets. See Figure 3.35.
- *Surface roughening* — Creating horizontal grooves running across a slope can decrease runoff velocity and erosion, improve water infiltration, and help establish vegetation. They can be created by using grooving disks, tillers, or heavy tracked machinery.
- *Temporary seeding* — Planting rapid germinating and growing annual grasses or other vegetation can be an effective measure to stabilize a slope. Surface roughening, fertilizer, and raking in of seed are helpful to germination and growth. Hydroseeding mixes seed with mulch and fertilizer in one application.

These measures, plus those described in the following construction details, provide a palette of possible solutions to specific site conditions (see Figure 3.36). Numerous trade products have been introduced that can simplify the installation and/or maintenance of many soil erosion and sediment control measures. Application of some measures varies by region; refer to local and state standards for specific requirements, limitations, or regional adaptations. Most states have a manual of soil erosion and sediment control standards specifically tailored to regional conditions.

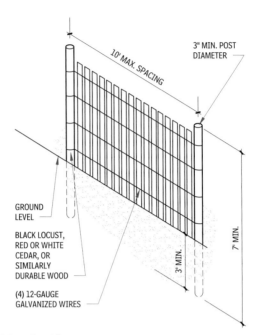

Figure 3.36a   Sand fence.

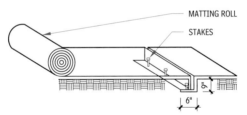

Figure 3.36b   Erosion control mats.

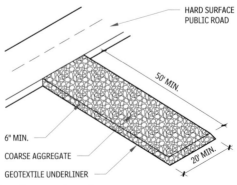

Figure 3.36c   Construction exit.

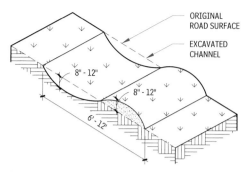

Figure 3.36d Diversion channel.

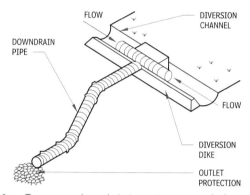

Figure 3.36e Temporary slope drain in conjunction with diversion channel.

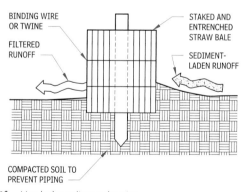

Figure 3.36f Hay bale sediment barrier.

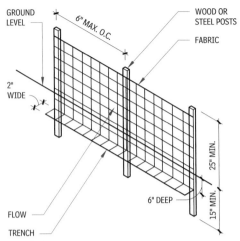

Figure 3.36g Silt fence.

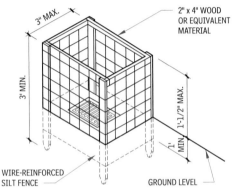

Figure 3.36h Fabric and frame sediment trap.

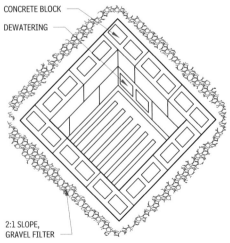

Figure 3.36i Block and gravel sediment trap.

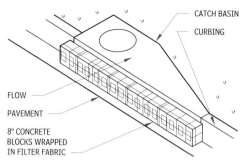

CATCH BASIN

CURBING

FLOW

PAVEMENT

8" CONCRETE
BLOCKS WRAPPED
IN FILTER FABRIC

Figure 3.36j "Pigs in a blanket" sediment trap.

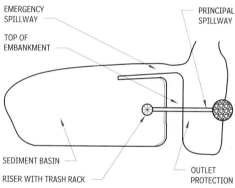

EMERGENCY
SPILLWAY

TOP OF
EMBANKMENT

PRINCIPAL
SPILLWAY

SEDIMENT BASIN

RISER WITH TRASH RACK

OUTLET
PROTECTION

Figure 3.36k Sediment basin plan.

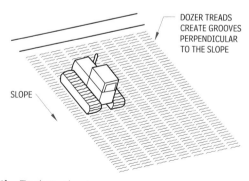

DOZER TREADS
CREATE GROOVES
PERPENDICULAR
TO THE SLOPE

SLOPE

Figure 3.36l Track roughening.
Source: Hopper, *Landscape Architectural Graphic Standards.* Copyright John Wiley & Sons, Inc., 2007.

Practices to Avoid

- Unless areas are designated for clearing, there should be no removal, cutting, or destruction of existing trees or other vegetation without explicit approval of the owner or owner's representative.
- Avoid problems during the design approval process and construction phase. Check the permitting process for land disturbance, as it may vary from site to site, according to local, state, and federal jurisdictional authorities.
- Limit any land disturbance proposed within or adjacent to watercourses, wetlands, other water bodies, or shorelines, which will require permitting through state and federal authorities.

▶ If required, include adequate time allowances in planning for the permitting process.

Storm Water Pollution Controls

Description

Storm water pollution control is required to prevent sources of pollution from affecting the quality of storm water discharge from the site. The identification of potential sources of pollution that might affect storm water discharge quality and the measures that will be taken to address those concerns are very often outlined in a Storm Water Pollution Prevention Plan (SWPPP). The SWPPP should be part of the contract documents and monitored throughout construction to ensure compliance. A copy of the SWPPP should be kept on-site at all times.

Assessing Site Conditions

The following steps are part of the initial site condition assessment:

- Identify the location of all storm drainage structures, drainage swales, and streams (or other water bodies) on or near the site.
- Identify all vegetation that is to be preserved before clearing at a height that will be visible to equipment operators.
- Identify potential sources of pollution that may be expected to affect the quality of storm water discharge from the site.
- Develop a set of measures that will be used to prevent sources of pollution from affecting the storm water discharge (the EPA has a description of Best Management Practices that can be used as a reference).
- Check that practices and measures that will be taken are in compliance with federal EPA as well as state and local requirements.
- Outline required filings, notifications, required permits, and any other administrative tasks related to the temporary storm water pollution controls necessary during the construction.

Acceptable Practices

Storm water pollution controls are often described as a series of Best Management Practices (BMPs), a list from which applicable choices for a specific project or set of conditions can be chosen and implemented. Some temporary storm water pollution control BMPs that can be considered during construction are:

- Vegetation provides erosion control, storm water detention, biofiltration, and postconstruction aesthetic value. Existing vegetation outperforms new vegetation in every category and is valuable to preserve. Preservation and protection of existing vegetation usually include some type of temporary fencing.
- Construction entrances should be stabilized with rock aggregate or other nonerodible material placed over a geotextile fabric (see Figure 3.37). Where choices are available, it is most desirable to locate the construction entrance at a high point where storm water runoff from the construction site will not be directed toward the entrance. The construction entrance should not extend into the street, nor should it block or disrupt the flow of storm water in the gutter.

Figure 3.37 A stone construction exit lined with filter fabric, to agitate the vehicle in order to reduce the amount of soil being transported off-site. If mud needs to be removed from the tires, the tires should be washed, with the wastewater drained to an area where the sediment can be trapped.
Photo by Russell Adsit, FASLA

- Construction exits should be stabilized with coarse rock aggregate over a geotextile fabric. A steel grid, strong and wide enough to accommodate the heaviest and widest construction vehicles anticipated, should be firmly installed, to agitate the tires in order to loosen and remove soil build-up. This grid is typically constructed of a series of 3"-diameter or greater pipes or tubes, a minimum of 8' long, elevated 8" above the ground, and spaced $4\frac{1}{4}$" apart or greater.

- A tire wash-down area shall be provided at the construction exit so that on rainy days, or when there is mud on the site, all vehicle tires can be washed with pressurized water to remove any mud or debris, in order to prevent material from leaving the site or being dropped on streets. The tire wash-down area shall be sloped to divert any debris or soil back onto the site.

- Erosion control can be provided by using vegetated buffer strips (existing or newly planted vegetation). They slow storm water runoff, preventing soil erosion; filter sediment; and allow storm water to percolate through the soil, recharging groundwater supplies. The width and slope of the vegetated buffer strips should be determined by the size and slope of the drainage area they need to accommodate.

▶ Vegetated buffer strips at the construction site perimeter trap sediments and remove pollutants in runoff from exposed areas.

- Erosion control of sheet flow on the down-slope side of a construction site can be provided by the use of hay bales placed with their ends perpendicular to the slope (contours) to trap sediment.

- Erosion control on slopes can be provided by the use of soil retention blankets anchored to the slope with wire staples 6" long and 1" wide (see Figures 3.38 and 3.39). All rocks or other debris that would prevent the soil retention blankets from lying flat in direct contact with the soil need to be removed. The edges of the mat should be buried into a 6"-wide by 6"-deep trench, backfilled and tamped. Joints should be overlapped a minimum of 12" to provide a continuous blanket. Soil retention blankets can be made from jute mat (jute yarn woven very loosely together), a wood fiber mat (constructed of wood fibers enclosed in nylon, cotton, or other type of netting), or a synthetic matting, creating a three-dimensional web to control erosion or facilitate vegetation establishment. See Figure 3.40.

▶ Soil retention blankets can help new vegetation by holding seeds, fertilizer, and topsoil in place.

- Erosion control can be provided by the use of silt fence composed of a nonwoven geotextile fabric (permeable to water but retaining sediment) supported by galvanized or painted metal posts (driven a

Figure 3.38 A soil retention blanket controls erosion on a newly seeded slope.

Figure 3.39 The soil retention blanket is held in place by wire staples.

Figure 3.40 Three-dimensional web for erosion control.
Photo courtesy of Presto Geosystems

minimum of 12" into the ground and spaced a maximum of 6' on center) on the down slope from the construction site. A wire backing or other temporary fencing should be used to help support the geotextile. Lengths of geotextile should be overlapped a minimum of 12" at stakes to provide a continuous barrier. A 6"-deep and 6"-wide trench should be dug on the side of the fence disturbed by construction, and a 6" toe of the silt fence left at the bottom should be buried in the trench, backfilled, and tamped firm. The ends of the silt fence should be turned up perpendicular to the slope (contours) to create a sediment trap. Accumulated silt should be removed and redistributed on the site. If a chain-link fence is used along the same lines as the silt fence, it may be possible to attach the silt fence to the chain-link fence. See Figure 3.41.

▶ Tilt the posts of the silt fence slightly, in an "uphill" direction, for additional strength.

- On larger sites, the excavation of a temporary detention structure may be a viable approach to containing storm water discharge and controlling erosion. If a common low point can be identified, the area can be excavated to serve as a temporary storm water detention area.

- A temporary sediment trap can be formed by creating an embankment or excavating to capture sediment and debris on drainage areas less than three acres. Sediment traps are often constructed with a

Figure 3.41 Double silt fence with hay bales sandwiched between. The silt fence on the gravel construction entrance side is supported by chain-link mesh attached to galvanized posts.

pipe and stone outlet. They are usually created by excavating an area at the outlet of a channel, slope drain, swale, construction site entrance/exit, or any storm water conveyance or discharge, to capture any sediment or debris that it might be carrying.

- Rock check dams can be used to control erosion and sediment loss in areas of concentrated storm water flow. They slow velocity and catch sediment as the water runs through them, and are an effective measure used in drainage swales and ditches. When check dams are constructed in series, the top elevation of the downstream check dam should be set at the toe elevation of the adjacent upstream check dam, and the top elevation of the last upstream check dam set to the invert elevation of the last stabilized portion of the drainage swale or ditch. The center of the check dam should be lower than the sides, in order to channel water overflows away from the sides, preventing erosion.

- Rock berms of well-graded riprap or open graded stone, secured with wire sheathing, can be installed at the base of slopes to control erosion and trap sediment while allowing water to pass through.

- Stabilized earth berms are an effective perimeter control, keeping storm water runoff from leaving the site, as well as preventing storm water runoff from entering the site from the adjacent properties.

- Diversion dikes are constructed by forming a ridge of compacted soil, often accompanied by a ditch or swale with a vegetated lining, at the top or base of a sloping disturbed area. When on the up-slope side of a site, they help to prevent surface runoff from entering a disturbed construction site. When located on the down-slope side of a site, they divert sediment-laden runoff created on-site to sediment-trapping devices, preventing soil loss from the disturbed area.

- An interceptor swale channels storm water runoff to a stabilized outlet or sediment trap, in order to prevent off-site runoff from entering the construction site or prevent storm water from carrying sediment off the site.

- A thick layer of fibrous natural mulch (minimum 3″) can be used to control erosion and limit storm water runoff from the site. Mulch material can be straw, wood chips, shredded wood, post-consumer paper content, and yard-trimming compost. Mulch can be used on slopes where establishing vegetation can be difficult, or can help on slopes until seeded or planted areas can become established. When used on steeper slopes or in areas of concentrated runoff, the mulch should be held in place by netting anchored to the ground below. See Figure 3.42.

Figure 3.42 Natural mulch material held in place to stabilize slope and control erosion.
Photo by Russell Adsit, FASLA

- Hydromulch with seed can be used in place of regular seeding, wherever seeding is being considered as an erosion control measure.

▶ **Hydromulch stabilizes the slope and applies seed and fertilizer all in one application.**

- Storm drain inlet protection prevents soil and debris from entering into the structure. There are several protection measures: (1) excavating around the inlet and letting water slowly pass through a filtering device, (2) placing a fabric barrier around the inlet, and (3) forming a gravel barrier around the inlet. See Figures 3.43 and 3.44.

An initial inspection and review of all measures taken to control erosion and storm water pollution should be conducted prior to the start of any site-disturbing construction activities. After initial implementation of the temporary storm water pollution protection measures, unusual or unforeseen conditions may still need to be addressed, and additional measures may need to be taken.

The contractor should be responsible for maintaining all installations, equipment, and services required for the temporary storm water pollution controls to remain effective until completion of construction. Any damage to storm water controls should be repaired immediately. Modifications or additional measures should be made to address

Figure 3.43 Storm drain inlet protection during construction.
Photo by Russell Adsit, FASLA

Figure 3.44   Storm drain inlet protection along street curb.
Photo by Russell Adsit, FASLA

changing site conditions or circumstances during the course of construction. All temporary storm water pollution control measures shall be removed after the completion of construction, and the contractor should provide any necessary restoration to return those areas to their previous condition (or to improve them).

Practices to Avoid

- No construction dewatering should be discharged into sewers, storm drains, or water bodies.
- Do not allow sediment to accumulate in storm water pollution control measures. Inspect them regularly and remove sediment when necessary.

References

ALSO IN THIS BOOK

See section "Topsoil Preservation, Stripping, and Stockpiling" in Chapter 2.

OTHER RESOURCES

Dillaha, T. A., J. H. Sherrard, and D. Lee. "Long-Term Effectiveness of Vegetative Filter Strips." *Water Environment and Technology* 1:418–421, 1989.

Hopper, Leonard J. *Graphic Standards Field Guide Hardscapes*. Hoboken, NJ: John Wiley & Sons, Inc., 2010.

Hopper, Leonard J. *Landscape Architectural Graphic Standards*. Hoboken, NJ: John Wiley & Sons, Inc., 2007.

Smolen, M. D., D. W. Miller, L. C. Wyatt, J. Lichthardt, A. L. Lanier, W. W. Woodhouse, and S. W. Broome. *Erosion and Sediment Control Planning and Design Manual*. Raleigh, NC: North Carolina Sedimentation Control Commission, NC Dept. of Natural Resources and Community Development, 1988.

Urban, James. *Up by Roots*. Champaign, IL. International Society of Arboriculture, 2008.

USEPA (U.S. Environmental Protection Agency). *Storm Water Management for Industrial Activities: Developing Pollution Prevention Plans and Best Management Practices*, EPA 832-R-92-006. Washington, DC: U.S. Environmental Protection Agency, Office of Water, 1992.

USEPA. *Guidance Specifying Management Measures for Sources of Nonpoint Pollution in Coastal Waters*, EPA-840-B-92-002. Washington, DC: U.S. Environmental Protection Agency, Office of Water, 1993.

USEPA. *Storm Water Management for Construction Activities: Developing Pollution Prevention Plans and Best Management Practices*. EPA 832-R-92-005. Washington, DC: U.S. Environmental Protection Agency, Office of Water, 1992.

PART II
PLANTING

Chapter 4

Trees

Nursery Stock Standards

Description

The green industry has attempted to develop regulations and is urging compliance. But compliance is voluntary and only enforced to the degree that the public or consumer demands that it be enforced. That said, as the green industry evolves into a formidable economic industry, and as plant materials are commonly shipped across the country and internationally, the demand for universally accepted standards is growing.

For many years, the American Nursery and Landscape Association (ANLA) has been publishing the *American Standard for Nursery Stock*, ANSI Z60.1, and has encouraged its adoption throughout the industry. It is the intent of ANLA to provide "buyers and sellers of nursery stock with a common terminology in order to facilitate transactions involving nursery stock." Further, the document states, "The standards establish common techniques for (a) measuring plants, (b) specifying and stating the size of plants, (c) determining the proper relationship between height and caliper, or height and width, and (d) determining whether a root ball container is large enough for a particular size plant" (ANLA 2004).

▶ The most recent publication, ANSI Z60.1-2004, can be downloaded from a number of different websites and is a valuable resource.

Assessing Site Conditions

Overview of Plant Nomenclature Standards

When specifying plants, it is important to use standard nomenclature. All plants have a Latin binomial name—the "scientific name"—and pertinent botanical variety, form, or cultivar names. Only the scientific name is standardized across regions, states, and countries. Because the scientific name is standardized, it has legal standing and helps to ensure that the species and cultivars are delivered to the job site as specified.

Plants also have a "common name," which consists of the pertinent variety, form, and/or cultivar identifications, in addition to the name commonly used in the region in which they are grown or sold. The common names of plants vary throughout the country and the world; therefore, they have not been standardized. For example:

- *Scientific name* — *Acer* (genus, italicized and capitalized); *rubrum* (species, italicized and lowercase); 'October Glory' (cultivar, capitalized and with single quotation marks).
- *Common name* — October Glory (cultivar, without quotation marks); red maple (commonly used but may vary).

As another example, *Acer saccharinum* (scientific name) is commonly called a silver maple, but in Ohio many call it a water maple. In Kentucky, an *Acer negundo* is commonly called a water maple, but in other parts of the country it is called a common box elder or an ash-leaf maple.

Certain species may not be grown in the hardiness zone where they are going to be relocated; therefore, it is best to specify cultivars if hardiness may be an issue. The hardiness of named cultivars is ensured by USDA regulations.

▶ A request for a substitution for a species or cultivar by a contractor should be allowed only if it is certain that the substitution is not substantially different from the species or cultivar specified.

Two sources for more information are available online. The International Plant Name Index (2004), published on the Web at www.ipni.org, contains all known plants by genus and species. It does not include cultivars, however. The USDA Natural Resources Conservation Service (NRCS) Plant List of Accepted Nomenclature, Taxonomy and Symbols (PLANTS), at http://plants.usda.gov, is a dynamic database that provides online accessibility to standardized plant information. It contains information on plant names, symbols, growth habit, plant growth, vegetative specifications, distribution, wetland indicator status, and threatened and endangered status. This nomenclature is used by most U.S. federal agencies and is the required reference on federal projects.

Acceptable Practices

Overview of Plant Quality Standards

Plant quality tends to be somewhat subjective, since we are dealing with living material that varies in growth habit within species, and with the conditions under which it was grown. For this reason, it is necessary to write specifications that are detailed enough to ensure receipt of the quality desired. One of the major factors in obtaining high-quality plant material is the reputation of the nursery in which the plants are grown. A good, but not certain, indicator is whether the nursery belongs to one or several of the state or national organizations. In addition, nearly all wholesale producers publish catalogs that provide descriptive information relative to the plant in question—for example, cultivar, size, hardiness zone, form and height of expected growth, rate of growth, bloom time and color, and other pertinent characteristics.

Quality standards fall into two categories for all plants: aboveground standards and belowground standards. If this information is followed, the odds are very good that plant material of a high quality will be received.

Quality Standards: Aboveground Considerations

- Ensure that plants are nursery grown under favorable conditions. Nursery-grown plants have a better survival rate and do not disturb the natural ecosystem by their removal. It is not recommended that trees collected from the wild be specified or accepted, both from a quality and an ecological perspective.
- Verify that the ratio of height to caliper is proportional and typical of the species.
- Select trees that have well-spaced structural branches that are oriented uniformly around the trunk.
- If a tree is a type that has a strong central leader, ascertain whether the trees in question manifest that characteristic.
- Ascertain the general health of the plant. Check for mechanical damage, frost cracks, and herbicide damage to the bark. Check for any signs of serious insect or disease problems. Also examine foliage color, density, and length of shoot extension as signs of general health.

Quality Standards: Belowground Considerations

Soil ball wrapping:

- Natural, untreated burlap is best. Treated, or rot-resistant, burlap, which retards decomposition for up to three months and binds well with the soil after decomposition, is also acceptable.
- Plastic or poly tree ball wrap is not acceptable, and should be specified as such. If plants are shipped with a nonorganic wrapping, it must be removed prior to planting.

- Ball-supporting devices, such as wire baskets or rope and twine, should hold the ball firmly and in rigid condition. Rope or twine, if it is organic, should be loosened from the top of the tree ball. Synthetic twine or rope must be removed completely.

Soil ball:

- The size of the soil ball should meet minimum standards, as indicated in ANSI Z60.1-2004 standards.
- The burlap and other materials used to wrap the ball must be very tight, to reduce risk of ball damage from shipping and handling.
- The trunk of the tree should be in the center of the soil ball.

Overview of Plant Material Standards

Plant materials are classified by ANSI Z60.1-2004 into the following categories:

- Shade and Flowering Trees
- Deciduous Shrubs
- Coniferous Evergreens
- Broadleaf Evergreens
- Roses
- Bulbs, Corms, and Tubers
- Herbaceous Perennials
- Ornamental Grasses
- Ground Covers
- Vines

Because anomalies can and do occur, not all plants will conveniently fit into a selected category. This document establishes standards for measuring plants; specifying and stating the size of plants; determining the proper relationship between height and caliper, or height and width; and determining what size root ball or container size is appropriate for a specified size of plant. It should be referenced whenever specifying plant material for a project, to ensure that you are requesting plants that adhere to a national standard with which the nursery trade that is supplying the material is familiar. Other characteristics or desirable attributes can be listed as part of the plant list in addition to the minimum standards set forth in the ANSI Z60.1-2004 standards.

Overview of Plant Hardiness Standards

Hardiness is the capability of a plant to survive and grow in the landscape of a given region. The United States Plant Hardiness Zone Map (USHZ) presently consists of 11 zones, with Zone 1 being the coldest and Zone 11 being the warmest. The zones are based on the average climatic conditions of each area. A Zone 6 plant, for example, generally will endure winters in that zone and will withstand the warmer zones below. Since local climates and conditions, such as soil, rainfall, length of growing season, and the like, can dramatically differ within regions, the hardiness zone map should be used only as guide for plant selection. This is especially the case when a region is on the cusp of two zones.

In 2004, the American Horticultural Society (AHS) produced a Heat-Zone Map that is similar in form to the USHZ Map and based on the "number of days per year above 86°F (30°C) and establishes the point at which plants experience damage to cellular patterns." When used in conjunction with the USHZ Map, both cold-hardiness and heat-tolerance ranges can be used to select plants that are appropriate to the climatic condition under consideration. Plants are now being coded for both conditions.

More information on plant hardiness can be found at the following sources:

- The 2003 U.S. National Arboretum Web version of the USDA Plant Hardiness Zone Map (USDA Miscellaneous Publication No. 1475, issued January 1990) is located at www.usna.usda.gov.
- The American Horticultural Society Heat-Zone Map is located at www.ahs.org/publications.
- Canada has a Plant Hardiness Zones Map (2000) similar to the USHZ map, which "outlines the different zones in Canada where various types of trees, shrubs and flowers will most likely survive." It is located at http://sis.agr.gc.ca/cansis/nsdb/climate/hardiness/intro.html.

Overview of Plant Guarantees

Plants shipped from a nursery, which are purchased wholesale, should be guaranteed to be true to name, of the appropriate size and quality, and in good viable condition. Claims regarding disease or viability are to be reported to the supplier. Seldom do guarantees for survivability emanate from a wholesale nursery or supplier. The installation contractor, in addition to these requirements, is responsible for plant survival.

Under normal conditions, plants are to be guaranteed for one year from the date of planting. Sometimes, however, specifications are written as "one growing season" in lieu of one year, for guarantee purposes. And for large trees, it is common to require a two-year guarantee.

It is the responsibility of the owner to maintain the plant material in the specified manner during the guarantee period. Specifications can be written to require the installation contractor to include maintenance as part of the cost of the plant during the guarantee period—which will add to the cost of the plant.

Overview of Plant Quarantines and Inspection

"The USDA, Animal and Plant Health Inspection Service, Plant Protection and Quarantine Program (USDA APHIS PPQ) and the plant health agencies in each of the 50 states, regulate the shipment of nursery stock in an effort to minimize the spread of harmful insects, diseases, and other pests" (www.nationalplantboard.org). The National Plant Board (NPB) is the USDA agency responsible for bringing "out greater uniformity and efficiency in promulgation and enforcement of plant quarantines and plant inspection practices in the various states" (National Plant Board 1999). This is an organization of state plant health regulatory officials who are responsible for nursery licensing, certi-fication, quarantines, and other pest prevention efforts. "They inspect plants and commodities for export so that required phytosanitary certification can be provided" (National Plant Board 1999).

Phytosanitary and Plant Inspection Certificate

The plant inspection certificate certifies that the plants in question meet the requirements of the destination states or countries. Each state and territory in the United States regulates the growing and sale of nursery stock for its state or territory. It is their responsibility to examine or inspect plants, plant material, or nursery stock located or grown on the business location or any other applicable location, to affirm that all plants or other regulated articles meet phytosanitary (quarantine), nursery inspection, pest freedom, plant registration or certification, or other legal requirements. All plant material shipped interstate and to other countries must be accompanied by a Nursery Stock Certificate, verifying compliance with registration or certification requirements. While specific regulations vary by state and territory, all plants shipped interstate must meet the NPB health criteria.

Overview of Freight and Shipping

Freight and shipping parameters are as follows:

- Not all plants can be shipped during all months, due to weather, digging, or order restrictions.
- All costs of shipping, including inspections, duty, and brokerage, are the responsibility of the customer.

- Shipments, for the most part, are FOB the nursery.
- All stock travels at the risk of the buyer; claims for damage during transit must be filed with the forwarding company.
- Most wholesale nurseries arrange for bulk shipment of stock by independent truckers and brokers who specialize in hauling nursery stock.
- All interstate and international shipping must be accompanied by the appropriate federal and/or state phytosanitary certificates.

Overview of Invasive Plant Species

Plants that have been moved from their native habitat to a new location are typically referred to as "nonnative," "nonindigenous," "exotic," or "alien" to the new environment. Only those nonnative plants that cause serious problems in their new environment are collectively known as "invasive species." By Executive Order 13112 (February 3, 1999), a National Invasive Species Council was formed and charged with developing a National Invasive Species Management Plan. The council noted that the number of invasive species and their cumulative impact are accelerating at an alarming rate. In response, the council developed a comprehensive plan for federal action, in coordination with other nations, states, and local and private programs. The objective of the plan is "to prevent the introduction of invasive species, provide for their control, and minimize their economic, environmental, and human health impacts" (www.invasivespecies.gov).

Actions that can be taken by site designers to control the spread of invasive species include:

- Recognize and understand the severity of the problem.
- Attempt to minimize the impact of invasive species.
- Become informed as to which plant species are considered invasive.
- Refuse to use invasive species on site plans.
- Encourage clients to eradicate existing invasive species from sites as development is ongoing.
- Encourage the restoration of areas impacted by invasive species.

There are numerous sources whereby one can become knowledgeable about which species of plants are considered invasive. The federal government, all states, and nearly all communities have ordinances prohibiting the use of invasive species on public works projects. Lists of invasive species are published by these organizations and are on numerous web sites, including www.invasivespecies.gov, the gateway to federal efforts concerning invasive species. This site provides a very good overview with regard to the use or nonuse of invasive species in the landscape.

The Plant Conservation Alliance (PCA) has also published an excellent, comprehensive inventory of invasive plants called "Alien Plant Invaders of Natural Areas," which is available at www.nps.gov/plants/. The PCA, an organization under the auspices of the National Park Service, is dedicated to promoting "the conservation and restoration of native plants and native ecosystems."

Overview of Poisonous Plant Species

In the interest of public health, safety, and welfare, it is advised that consideration for the potential toxicity of plants be given appropriate attention. The two web sites referenced here present data on plants that cause poisoning in livestock, pets, and human beings. These caveats must, however, be noted in regard to the data on poisonous plants:

- Much literature on poisonous plants is anecdotal and may be of limited reliability.
- Many plants are only mildly poisonous or are dangerous only when prodigious quantities of material have been consumed.
- Nonetheless, poisonous plants can be, and are, deadly; for example, *Taxus* (Japanese yew) will kill domestic farm animals.

These databases give the name of the plant, the species affected, and the primary poison:

- Cornell University Poisonous Plants Database: www.ansci.cornell.edu/plants/
- USDA Agricultural Research Service: www.ars.usda.gov

Practices to Avoid

- Do not specify plant material without consulting and referencing the sources in this section.
- Do not select or tag plant material at the nursery without a copy of ANSIZ60-1 as a reference.
- Do not inspect or accept plant material delivered to the planting site without a copy of ANSIZ60-1 as a reference.

Site Considerations and Tree Selection

Description

The selection of the right tree is based on matching its characteristics with those of the site where it is to be planted. Tree selection has long-term implications, and making a decision involves several factors including:

- Purpose
- Characteristics
- Location

▶ The large tree circles drawn on the planting plan that are so integral to the design will only be realized if site characteristics are identified and evaluated before tree selection is decided.

Assessing Site Conditions

Assessing existing site conditions to identify any characteristics or constraints that will affect tree selection is an important initial step prior to tree selection (see Figure 4.1). Trees will have a greater potential to survive and develop a mature size and shape characteristic of their species if they are compatible with the existing site conditions. Fundamental environmental and physical constraints as well as unique, sometimes less obvious factors, their combination and interaction, need to be considered.

Trees have specific requirements and conditions that need to be met if they are to grow to their full potential over the long term. Some important site conditions to assess before making a tree selection are:

- Determine the site's hardiness zone, and identify any microclimate conditions that need to be taken into account.
- Identify soil type and characteristics, including drainage.
- Evaluate exposure to sun or shade.
- Evaluate exposure to various wind conditions.
- Determine water requirements.

Climate

USDA Hardiness Zone

__ 7a __ 6a __ 5a __ 4a __ 3a
__ 7b __ 6b __ 5b __ 4b __ 3b

Microclimate Factors

__ Frost pocket __ Wind __ Accumulated heat

Surface Soil

Texture

__ Clayey
__ Loamy
__ Sandy

pH

__ Above 7.0
__ 6.0 to 7.0
__ 5.0 to 6.0
__ Below 5.0

Subsoil

Texture

__ Clayey
__ Loamy
__ Sandy

pH

__ Above 7.0
__ 6.0 to 7.0
__ 5.0 to 6.0
__ Below 5.0

Drainage Characteristics

__ Mottled, clayey soil
__ Low-lying area

Indicator plants suggest site drainage is:

__ wet __ well-drained __ dry

Percolation test results (in./hr.)

__ poorly drained (<4 in./hr.)
__ moderately drained (4–8 in./hr.)
__ excessively drained (>8 in./hr.)

Compaction Levels

__ Severe __ Moderate __ Uncompacted

Past/Recent Treatment

__ Wooded/native state
__ Existing landscape
__ Excessive machinery resulting in compacted soil
__ Presence of construction debris
__ Undisturbed meadow/field
__ Eroded hillside/slope
__ Evidence of recent construction
__ Evidence of excessive road salt

Depth Favorable to Roots

	Soil overlies	
---	Pan*	Bedrock
Variable, shallow to deep within short distances	—	—
Very shallow (0–10 in.)	—	—
Shallow (10–20 in.)	—	—
Moderate (20–30 in.)	—	—
Deep (30–48 in.)	—	—
Very deep (>48 in.)	—	—
Upper bedrock more or less solid		
Upper bedrock scattered		

Access Limitations

__ None to slight __ Moderate __ Severe

Sunlight and Irrigation Levels

__ Full sun (6+ hours) __ No supplemental irrigation
__ Part sun or filtered light __ Automatic irrigation system
__ Shade __ Frequency and amount _____

Structural Factors

Limitations to aboveground space

__ Overhead wires __ Nearby buildings and structures __ Other

Limitations to belowground space

__ Underground utilities
__ Approximate rooting volume for site
__ Length __ Width __ Depth

Marked Hazards to Survival and Early Growth

__ None __ Surface flooding
__ Wetness (poor aeration) __ Drought
__ Frosts __ Heavy grass/brush competition
__ Invasive weeds/plants __ Active erosion
__ Other

*Pan refers to a hardened clay layer caused by cementation of soil particles.

Figure 4.1 Site assessment checklist.

Source: Trowbridge and Bassuk, *Trees in the Urban Landscape.* Hoboken, NJ: John Wiley & Sons, Inc., 2004.

- Evaluate site space constraints such as buildings, pavements, walls, fences, underground and overhead utilities.
- Consider what proposed site modifications will impact the trees that will be planted on the site.
- Inventory the diversity of the tree population in and around the site.
- Determine the level of care, maintenance, and abuse the tree is likely to receive.

Once these factors have been identified, considered, and evaluated, the list of compatible trees can be narrowed by overlaying it with the functional and aesthetic characteristics desired, such as tree form, leaf texture, fall color, flower, attractive bark, and the like.

Acceptable Practices

Hardiness Zone and Microclimate

The hardiness of a tree is a measure of its ability to survive in the extreme temperature spectrums of a specific geographic area. Specific trees are tolerant of certain extremes of cold, heat, and sometimes both. To help with the selection of trees for particular geographic areas, the United States Department of Agriculture (USDA) has developed the Plant Hardiness Zone Map (see Figure 4.2).

The Plant Hardiness Zone Map divides Canada, Mexico, and the United States into 11 different zones based on the lowest temperatures that

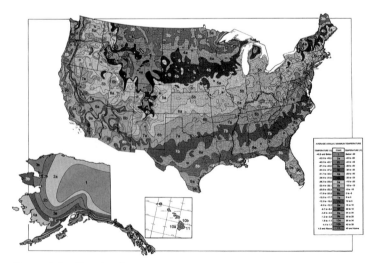

Figure 4.2 Plant hardiness zones.

can be expected each year. Zones 2–10 are further broken down into sections a and b, which represent 5 degrees F differences within the 10 degrees F difference represented by each zone (the lighter color representing the colder section, and the darker color the warmer section). The recent addition of Zone 11 represents areas where the average annual minimum temperature is above 40 degrees F, and is generally considered frost free. The map contains "island zones" that are created by higher elevations that may be colder than the immediately surrounding areas, or by urban environments that may be warmer than the immediately surrounding area.

Identifying the hardiness zone for the proposed tree planting allows trees that are identified as hardy for that zone to be considered for selection. This first step in the tree selection process is followed by the other physical and environmental factors that may need to be considered, which will further narrow the number of appropriate choices.

Microclimates—small areas that have different climate characteristics than the zone that they are within—can expand the zone-appropriate tree selection list. Areas that are sheltered from winter winds and have a southerly solar orientation provide the opportunity to plant trees that may be marginally zone appropriate. In the same way, where microclimate conditions may leave a tree exposed to harsher conditions, plant selection would best be limited to either the appropriate hardiness zone or perhaps even a zone lower.

Soil Conditions

Tree-planting success requires that soil characteristics be properly identified and evaluated. A soil test should be performed to test for nutrients, pH, organic matter and soil type (proportions of sand, silt, or clay), drainage, salinity, and depth to water table.

For previously undeveloped areas, the Natural Resources Conservation Service may be able to provide soil surveys containing a broad spectrum of information, including percolation rates, hardpan characteristics, soil type, and other research that can provide valuable insight into soil conditions. In urban or suburban areas or where new construction has left debris or possible soil contamination exists, soil tests will identify these conditions. If soil tests indicate the presence of hazardous materials or contamination, specific remediation strategies may be required.

The disruption and tendency for construction to mix debris, subsoil, and good topsoil all together in an unplanned, haphazard way will often result in widely varied soil conditions on the same site. More soil tests may be necessary in critical tree-planting locations throughout the site, as conditions can vary.

The results of these soil tests will help identify compatible species of trees for selection. If tests reveal more serious concerns with the soil quality, then fertilizers or other soil amendments may be necessary. In some cases, removal of the existing soil and replacement with a good-quality planting mix may need to be considered.

▶ Good soil on a site is a valuable resource. Every effort should be made to strip and stockpile good soil properly prior to the start of construction, for later distribution and use for tree planting and other vegetated areas of the site.

Soil Drainage

All tree roots require oxygen in addition to nutrients and water, in order for the tree to survive. Tree pits that do not drain well deprive the roots of oxygen by having the voids within the soil fill with water. Trees prefer well-drained loamy soil, as opposed to heavy clay soils that drain very poorly. Although there are some species that tolerate wet conditions, water that fills a tree pit without draining can become stagnant and result in root rot that will eventually kill the tree.

▶ Soils that drain poorly often have a foul smell and gray color that can be very noticeable while digging the hole for the percolation test.

See the section "Soil Assessment" in Chapter 1 for more information on how to conduct an informal percolation test.

Soil Compaction

Soil that is very compacted contributes to poor drainage, lacks oxygen, and discourages root growth. If soil is compacted for the entire depth of the tree pit and beyond, drainage will be poor, and trees tolerant of wet conditions should be considered. Loose soil spread over a compacted subsurface soil layer will encourage root growth only in this top layer. Without roots growing deeper into the compacted soil layer, these shallow-rooted trees can become unstable as they grow larger, making more moderate-sized trees a better choice. Shallow roots can also create a conflict with turf areas and damage curbs, sidewalks, and other pavements.

▶ If only the top layer of soil is compacted, this layer should be broken and loosened as far from the tree pit as practically possible, to improve tree growth by encouraging better drainage and root development in the top 12–18 inches of soil.

▶ If possible, as part of a preconstruction soil compaction protocol that can be written into the contract documents, areas where trees will be planted should be declared "off limits" to heavy machinery, minimizing soil compaction in these protected areas during construction.

See the section on "Soil Assessment" in Chapter 1 for information on bulk density testing.

Soil pH Testing

The soil pH determines whether nutrients in the soil will be available to the tree, as well as the level of microorganism activity. Some trees have trouble growing in alkaline soils, while others prefer this higher pH level. Most trees will grow well in soils that are moderately acidic (pH 4.8) to slightly alkaline (pH 7.2), with a pH of 7.0 considered neutral. Few trees grow in soils with pH levels higher than 9.0.

See section on "Soil Assessment" in Chapter 1 for information on pH testing.

Soil Texture

Soil texture has both short-term and long-term impact on the selection and maintenance of newly planted trees.

▪ Soils that are higher in clay content generally drain poorly, and trees that are wet-tolerant should be considered. If irrigation will be provided, levels will need to be monitored so that the soil does not remain saturated, depriving the tree roots of oxygen and killing the tree.
▪ Sandy soils tend to drain faster, which may require that newly planted trees be irrigated more often in hot, dry weather. If irrigation is not likely to occur, more drought-tolerant tree species should be considered.
▪ Nutrients tend to leach down below the root zone faster in sandy soils than in clay. If maintenance is not likely to include regular fertilization, trees that are better suited to growing in sandy soils would best be considered.

Soil Salinity

High salt levels in soil dry out tree roots, making it difficult for a tree to grow or even survive. Trees may be subjected to high soil salt levels if planted in coastal areas (airborne salt spray) or adjacent to pavements likely to receive deicing salts (sidewalks, roadways, parking lots), or if irrigated with well water that may have high salt levels. Soils in these areas should be tested for sodium levels and sodium absorption ratios. Well water, if it will be used for irrigation, should be tested, especially in coastal areas.

If any of these conditions exist, or are likely to occur, trees with good salt tolerance should be considered. Trees within several hundred feet of major roadways that receive deicing salt regularly should be tolerant of aerosol salt spray. Those planted adjacent to salted roadways or parking lots should be tolerant of soil salt because salty water splashes or runs off from pavement into the root zone.

For tree planting in paved parking areas or roadways, raised planters or berms to keep the salt water away from the tree roots can minimize the negative impact of the deicing salts. It may be possible to grade the paved area in such a way that the salt-laden snow runoff and snow removal storage areas can be directed away from the tree plantings. However, any of these approaches need to be balanced with storm water management strategies that would be beneficial to the trees at most times of the year.

See the section "Soil Assessment" in Chapter 1 for testing information.

Soil Depth

Limited amounts of available soil for roots to develop can affect tree growth and stability. If conditions such as bedrock or other impenetrable layers are close to the surface, providing only minimal depth for soil above, more moderate-sized trees should be considered. Larger trees that aren't able to develop deeper anchoring roots can be blown over in storms more easily as they grow to maturity.

For more information, see "Soil Assessment," in Chapter 1, which includes the sections "Distance to Water Table" and "Depth to Bedrock."

Sun or Shade Conditions

The amount of full sun, partial shade (3–6 hours of direct sun), or dense shade (fewer than 3 hours direct sun or filtered sun or shade) will affect tree selection. Most trees prefer full sun and will do moderately well in partial shade. The list of trees that do well in dense shade or as understory plantings is much shorter. The tree selection should be matched to the sun exposure if good long-term growth, development of the tree species characteristics, and flowering (if applicable) are to be expected.

A sun diagram can be helpful in projecting shadows of other trees and buildings. Sun diagrams are available for different times of the year and can help the landscape architect anticipate shadows at different times of the year when the angle of the sun changes. If trees that have higher sun requirements are planted in the shadow of other trees or buildings, they will bend toward the sun and may develop a one-sided canopy. While this may provide an interesting special effect, more often than not, this result is completely unanticipated and does not fulfill the designer's intent or vision.

Trees that are planted near buildings, particularly on southern and western exposures, can be subjected to additional heat gain from reflective surfaces of buildings. Glass buildings and white or light-colored surfaces have the highest reflectivity. The added heat stress can cause trees to have an increased need for water, to compensate for water lost through their leaves. Drought-tolerant trees should be considered for these locations.

Increasing the distance between the tree and the building surface can significantly reduce the amount of heat gain. In addition, providing a large area of soil for roots to explore often helps trees withstand reflected light, by providing more soil from which to absorb water. Irrigation would also be helpful. Leaves on trees receiving reflected light in a restricted-soil area often turn brown along the edges in summer (called marginal leaf scorch) unless provided with ample water.

Slope Exposure

Take note of a site's slope solar orientation. Some trees have weaker barks that are sensitive to direct sun and drying that can be a factor on slopes that have a southern or western exposure. This can cause the bark to dry and split. Tree trunks of these sensitive species can be protected by painting the trunks with white latex paint or special tree wraps. This isn't always an acceptable approach in designed landscapes, and it might be best to consider trees that are less sensitive to these more intense solar exposures.

Slopes that face north are protected from direct solar radiation, and slopes that are oriented east are less affected by the morning sun, as temperatures are generally relatively cooler. The southern and western slopes, angled for more direct solar radiation, tend to dry out more quickly. This increases the evaporation of water from the soil and increases the transpiration rate of the tree leaves. Trees that do well in dry conditions should be considered for these locations, or adequate irrigation should be provided to compensate for the sun's effect.

Wind

Trees planted in sites that experience extensive periods of windy conditions, or increased velocity of wind, can experience adverse effects. Excessive winds can dry out soils and increase transpiration from the leaves, leaving the tree with less than its required amount of water. Higher velocities of wind can damage branches and uproot newly planted trees before their root system can develop sufficient anchoring capabilities.

In addition to tree species that tolerate windy conditions, additional watering or irrigation may be required, especially in urban areas or areas where the roots are confined by pavements and buildings. As irrigation in urban areas and other environments isn't always practical, proper species selection is the best approach to addressing wind concerns. Drought-tolerant trees can be considered; however, the soil should drain fairly well. Poorly drained soil will require that trees tolerate both wet and windy conditions.

It is especially important to take note of soil conditions and provide a soil environment that will encourage good root development, to enhance the tree's ability to absorb water and grow strong anchoring roots for stability.

▶ In windy conditions, special staking to provide support until a well-developed root system can be established should be specified.

Water Requirements

Different species of trees have different water requirements. While some trees may require a great deal of water, others may be more tolerant of drought conditions. In addition to matching a tree to basic climate conditions and annual rainfall, it is important to take into consideration any existing drainage patterns or proposed design features that may have an impact on the amount of water a tree will receive.

The proposed design may modify the existing drainage patterns so that newly planted trees are located in an area with the grades directing the water away from the tree. Conversely, the new design may modify the grades in a way that directs storm water runoff toward the newly planted trees. How the proposed plan will affect drainage patterns and direct storm water runoff will affect how much water a tree will receive.

Changing the drainage pattern can also affect the health of existing trees. Trees that have grown under certain drainage conditions can be negatively impacted if paving or grading modification substantially increases or decreases the amount of water that is made available to the tree.

Site Space Constraints

There are many different types of space constraints that need to be considered as part of the tree selection process. Some are visible aboveground, and some that are underground are not visible at all. Some may only exist intermittently, such as potential damage from a passing vehicle. The key factor in evaluating space constraints is to use the tree's mature height and spread as a basis for determining whether the grown tree will be in conflict with any of the existing (or proposed) site elements.

Buildings

The classic example is the all too common planting of a large tree too close to a building or other structure (see Figure 4.3). Although the temptation is to plant the small, young tree in a location where it will look good for the first few years, as it grows it will quickly look out of proportion with the adjacent structure, and the spreading branches

Figure 4.3   Large trees planted too close to the house have to be cut back along one side and still totally obscure the front of the house.
Photo by Shastine Vugt.

will often need to be severely pruned, leaving half a tree with none of the characteristics that might have contributed to its initial selection. Trees with more narrow canopies or columnar species are more suitable choices to consider when planting close to a building.

Trees ideally strive to develop a root system that is relatively evenly spaced around the tree. When tree roots encounter a building wall or other barrier, they will tend to spread laterally along the barrier or, in well-drained soil, may be deflected downward. The result is an unbalanced root system that leaves a tree susceptible to blowing over in storm. This can be compounded if the soil is poorly drained or compacted, preventing the tree from developing deeper anchoring roots for stability. Moderate-sized trees should be considered for planting close to a building.

▶ **Mature height and spread should be considered when selecting a tree and planting location in close proximity to a building or other structure.**

Street Trees

The space constraint evaluation for street trees needs to take into account the type of traffic that is expected on the street. Particularly on a commercial street, trucks making curbside deliveries and buses using the curb lane for travel can cause a great deal of damage to trees that have low, horizontal branching habits. On any street, the branching habit needs to be considered so that it does not interfere with visibility by blocking traffic control signs or signals at intersections. If the space for street trees is adjacent to the curb, as it often is, trees with narrow branching and growth habits are more compatible with these conditions.

The selection of location and tree species and the relationship of these elements to street or site lighting are important space constraints. Trees that are too close to a light pole or species with low branching habits or dense foliage can interfere with the intended light distribution. Because this can be a safety and security issue, the response is often the severe pruning and limbing up of a tree, destroying its natural characteristics. The location, branching habit, and foliage density of the tree species selected should be compatible with the height of the fixture, the type of luminaire, and the photometrics of its light distribution pattern, to avoid possible conflicts as the tree grows to maturity. See more under "Lighting" in the "Utility Conflicts" section of this chapter.

Root Space Constraints

The mature growth of a tree needs to be considered aboveground and belowground. The root system for a healthy tree will spread to the drip line and beyond. Water, air, and nutrients are necessary for proper root system development, tree growth, and health. Does the site allow space for the root system to develop, or will pavements, curbs, or walls (see Figure 4.4) interfere with root growth?

During tree selection, it is important to consider the volume of soil that roots will have available for growth and development. There is a direct relationship between volume of soil and tree growth (height and canopy). Matching the mature size of the tree selected to the soil volume available is critical to its successful growth, health, and longevity. See Figure 4.5.

In urban areas, the soil volume is limited to the size of the tree pit. The soil under the surrounding pavements is either unsuitable or too compacted to allow root development. This should limit the choice and sizes of trees to be considered. However, the tendency is to select large canopy trees, with the vision of having streets lined with mature

Figure 4.4 Uprooting caused by constraints to the tree's root system (concrete curb on one side, sidewalk and retaining wall on the other side) that inhibited sufficient root system development to stabilize the tree. Notice how few roots extend out from the tree on the curb side. Roots on the other side appear to have grown under the sidewalk and then been cut to allow installation of the relatively new retaining wall.

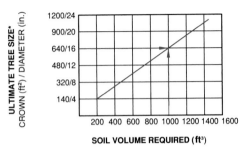

* THE ULTIMATE TREE SIZE IS DEFINED BY THE
PROJECTED SIZE OF THE CROWN AND THE DIAMETER OF
THE TREE AT BREAST HEIGHT.

Figure 4.5 Graph showing relationship of soil volume to tree growth. In this example, a 16-inch tree would require 1,000 cubic feet of soil.
Source: Hopper, *Landscape Architecture Graphic Standards.* Copyright John Wiley & Sons, Inc., 2007.

trees growing together to provide shady sidewalks and a pleasant streetscape (just like those large circles drawn on the planting plan). Any tree planted in a small opening in the pavement, surrounded by curbs or walls, will not survive very long. The reality is that trees in these locations only survive for approximately 10 years, with the last few years characterized by stunted growth and progressive branch dieback.

Therefore, tree selection in areas where root development is constrained requires the design discipline to work with a much narrower list of possible tree choices, accepting the reality that they will be more limited in their size and impact. If large street trees are critical enough to the design, then alternative approaches for providing additional soil volume for root development under the surrounding pavements can be considered. The space constraints presented by these site elements will need to be mitigated and countered with special planting techniques and procedures, if the tree planting is to be successful over the long term. These different strategies are detailed in Chapter 7, "Planting in Difficult or Special Situations."

Utility Conflicts

The location of above- and belowground utility lines should be an important consideration in the tree selection process. Aboveground lines that can include telephone, electric, and cable services are the most visible. These same services, along with water, sewer, natural gas, and steam lines, may be located belowground.

It is always best to obtain a site utility plan that will provide the location of belowground utilities. Many municipalities have "one-call centers" that will mark underground utilities so that they will not be damaged during construction. However, even before obtaining this belowground documentation, preliminary site visits should note the locations of manholes, valve boxes, utility vaults, and the like that are visible on the surface. Their locations can often provide a good idea of where belowground utility lines may be running, at a very preliminary stage.

Aboveground Utility Lines

As a basic rule, tall-growing trees should not be planted directly under aboveground utility lines. Tall trees have the potential to damage utility lines, and falling branches can interrupt service. Utility companies prune large trees to keep them away from the lines, usually resulting in large portions of the middle of the tree being cut away (see Figure 4.6), ruining the aesthetic value of the tree.

Generally, trees planted under utility lines should have a mature maximum height of approximately 30 feet. This restriction would apply

Figure 4.6 Tree pruned for aboveground utility. In this case, the entire center of the tree has been cut away.

Figure 4.7 Newly planted medium-sized trees under aboveground utility, chosen to avoid conflict. In this case, the tree was an *Acer campestre* that was recommended by both the county and the utility company.

directly under the utility lines and 15 or 20 feet to each side of the utility lines, depending on the species of tree selected (see Figure 4.7). Columnar trees or trees with a narrow or tapering head could be planted closer to the minimum distance, and broad-crown trees or those species with horizontal branching should be more toward the maximum distance.

▶ Check with the utility company for any specific requirements and ask if they have a list of recommended trees for planting in close proximity to aboveground utility lines.

Belowground Utility Lines

The primary conflict with belowground utilities occurs when excavating for the tree pit. Prior to any excavation, the utility companies or "one-call center" should be contacted to mark out the location of any belowground utilities.

Although a tree should not be planted directly on or immediately adjacent to a utility line, most utility lines and tree roots can peacefully coexist in close proximity. However, as the tree matures and the roots spread, there can be a conflict if the utility needs to be repaired, and necessary excavation damages the root structure. Therefore, when considering a tree location and species, and the potential conflicts with belowground utilities, it is important to consider the root structure of the mature tree, and not just the area around the root ball at the time of planting.

Lighting

Tree locations that are too close to a light pole, or species with low branching habits or dense foliage, can interfere with the intended light distribution. This can result in the need for regular pruning and can mean that the natural shape of the tree will be sacrificed to provide better light distribution. The best approach is to select the right tree to be planted at an appropriate distance from any existing or proposed light. Many municipalities have regulations that guide how close a tree can be planted to a streetlight.

As a general guideline for most types of site lighting:

- Major trees should be planted a minimum of 30 feet from street lighting.
- If trees are planted closer than 30 feet from a light, consider selecting a tree with a narrow growth habit or an open, less dense canopy that will not impede light distribution.
- If a light is less than 20 feet tall, it is possible to plant a large major tree less than 30 feet away, if proper pruning protocols can be established and the tree trained to have its canopy spread above the light fixture. If proper pruning cannot be specified or practically implemented, there is a risk that the tree will be pruned to stay below the light, which would completely ruin its mature form. Smaller-scaled trees would not be a good choice, as their canopies would most likely be in direct conflict with the intended light distribution pattern.
- For lights that are between 20 and 40 feet tall, neither large nor moderate-sized trees are good choices to plant in close proximity. These lights are too tall to have a large tree canopy spread over the top of the light, and the canopy branches of more moderate-sized trees will be in direct conflict with the light. Trees with a very narrow growth habit or small minor trees might be considered.
- If lights are taller than 40 feet, smaller minor trees, medium-sized trees, and smaller major trees will not block their light. In situations where lighting may be a security concern, trees with narrow growth patterns, open canopies, or less-dense leaf structure will allow light to filter through below.

Signage

The location of existing or proposed signage needs to be considered as part of the tree selection process. Smaller trees are generally compatible with taller signs. Large, major trees will grow above lower signs, but may need some selective pruning of lower limbs in the early years to keep the sign visible. Trees with narrow growth habits or open, less-dense canopies allow signs to be seen through their branching.

Particular attention should be directed toward stop signs, yield signs, stop signals, or other traffic control devices that could create a serious safety hazard if covered or made less visible from a distance.

Municipalities often have regulations that govern how close a tree can be planted to an intersection, traffic light, or other structures in the public right of way. Be sure to check before developing your street tree planting plan, and take accurate notes as to the location of any of these existing features.

Level of Care and Maintenance

An important factor in tree selection is the anticipated level of care and maintenance the tree will receive. Also a consideration is the level of intentional or unanticipated adverse conditions that the tree will have to endure.

Ideally, the tree selected will receive proper care and maintenance, which broadens the palette of trees that can be planted. However, too often, trees are subject to adverse conditions and neglect, which limits the selection of trees to a smaller list of the hardiest species.

Some factors for consideration are:

- Will the area in and around the tree be subject to soil compaction, limiting the amount of air and water that will be available for proper root growth and development?
- Is the tree planted in a paved area likely to receive additional care that will compensate for its difficult location?
- Is the tree likely to be vandalized, suffering snapped limbs, cuts into the trunk or other inflicted damage?

The selection of tree species, including any necessary protection and initial planting size, needs to respond to anticipated conditions that will be less than favorable. As much effort as possible needs to be focused on the initial tree selection and related planting measures to counter the adverse conditions anticipated later (see Figure 4.8). There

Figure 4.8 Street tree plantings with guards and flowers receive additional care and water.

are lists of trees that do well under adverse conditions such as urban environments and dusty conditions (trees that are drought tolerant, pollution resistant, salt tolerant, etc.). Conversely, trees that will not do well under these conditions will be less likely to survive and thrive over the long term.

Insects and disease can have an effect on most trees. Some trees require a higher level of maintenance to keep them free of insects and disease. If this level of maintenance is not likely to occur, the tree selection process should be directed toward trees that are insect and disease resistant.

Tree Selection

After consideration of the existing conditions and site factors affecting tree selection, and the development of a list of potential tree species, considerations of function, design, and aesthetics can be applied, to narrow the list and ultimately select a specific tree. Trees can be used to address the design needs of a project by directing pedestrian or vehicle movement, framing vistas, screening objectionable views, and defining and shaping exterior space. Trees can also be used to modify the microclimate of a site and to help conserve building energy use by heating, cooling, and lighting systems.

Environmental Function

The physical environment of the site, the design needs of the project, and the design character of the trees are all factors that must be considered in selecting trees and preparing a landscape plan. Trees can have an impact on the following environmental and microclimate factors:

- *Glare protection* — The vertical angle of the sun changes seasonally; therefore, the area of a building subject to the glare of reflected sunlight varies. Trees of various heights can screen sun (and artificial light) glare from adjacent surfaces.
- *Air filtration* — Large masses of trees physically and chemically filter and deodorize the air, reducing air pollution. Particulate matter trapped on the leaves is washed to the ground during rainfall. Gaseous pollutants are assimilated by the leaves. Fragrant plants can mechanically mask fumes and odors. As well, these pollutants are chemically metabolized in the photosynthesis process.
- *Runoff reduction* — Mature trees absorb or delay runoff from storm water at a rate of four to five times that of bare ground.
- *Shade provision* — In summer, trees obstruct or filter the strong radiation from the sun, cooling and protecting the area beneath them. In winter, evergreen trees still have this effect, while deciduous trees, having lost their leaves, do not.
- *Sound attenuation* — A combination of deciduous and evergreen trees and shrubs reduces sound more effectively than deciduous plants alone. Planting trees and shrubs on earth mounds increases the attenuating effect of a buffer belt.
- *Wind protection* — Shelter belt wind protection reduces evaporation at ground level, increases relative humidity, lowers the temperature in summer, and reduces heat loss in winter, and reduces blowing dust and drifting snow. The amount of protection afforded is directly related to the height and density of the shelter belt.
- *Climate control* — The amount of solar radiation received by people or objects in the landscape can be increased or decreased through strategic site design. During cool seasons, people will receive high levels of solar radiation in areas that are also sheltered from prevailing winter winds. During warm seasons, people will be able to sit or stand in dense shade, a more thermally comfortable microclimate. See Figure 4.9.
- *Modifying winds* — Wind speed will be low behind trees with approximately 50 percent porosity and branches that extend to the ground, and the wind reduction zone will be relatively large; behind lightly leafed and leafless deciduous trees and coniferous trees whose

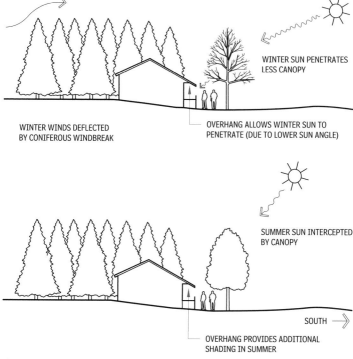

WINTER SUN PENETRATES
LESS CANOPY

WINTER WINDS DEFLECTED
BY CONIFEROUS WINDBREAK

OVERHANG ALLOWS WINTER SUN TO
PENETRATE (DUE TO LOWER SUN ANGLE)

SUMMER SUN INTERCEPTED
BY CANOPY

SOUTH

OVERHANG PROVIDES ADDITIONAL
SHADING IN SUMMER

Figure 4.9 Seasonal modifications of solar radiation.
Source: Hopper, *Landscape Architecture Graphic Standards.* Copyright John Wiley & Sons, Inc., 2007.

branches don't extend to the ground, wind speed will be nearly the same as in the open.

- *Modifying microclimate* — Tree selection and planting designs should consider modification of both wind and solar radiation to provide the most beneficial microclimates.

- *Thermal comfort* — Movement through the landscape from one microclimate to the next is experienced by a person as a change in his or her thermal comfort. For example, on a hot day, a person moving from a sunny microclimate into the shade of a densely leafed deciduous tree would experience this as a move to a "cooler" microclimate. However, it is a common misconception that the air temperature is lower in the shade of the tree. The temperature of the ground and other surfaces in the sun would likely be considerably higher than that of shaded surfaces, but because the air is a very efficient mixer, temperature differences are lost by the time the air is measured at a standard height of 5 feet, a height that is more representative of the air that affects people's thermal comfort level. In this case, it is the reduction in solar radiation received by the person that is being interpreted as a cooler microclimate. Similarly, moving from a windy sidewalk on a cold day into the shelter of a row of coniferous trees would be experienced as moving to a "warmer" microclimate. Again, the air temperature would be essentially the same in the two microclimates, and it would be the reduction in convective cooling of the wind that gives the impression of a warmer microclimate.

- *Wind and shadow patterns* — Figure 4.10 shows prevailing micro-climatic conditions in a typical urban landscape during the winter and spring seasons. Area 1 would be inherently comfortable (sometime known as a *sun-catch*), while Area 2 would be inherently too cool or cold to use in spring. In Figure 4.11, Area 1, which was inherently comfortable in springtime, might be inherently too hot in summer, as it

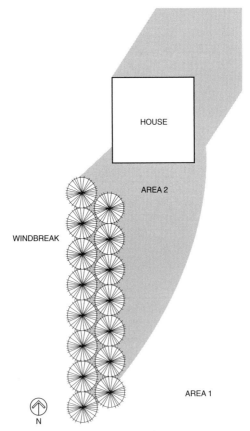

Figure 4.10   Winter/spring wind and shadow patterns.
Source: Hopper, *Landscape Architecture Graphic Standards.* Copyright John Wiley & Sons, Inc., 2007.

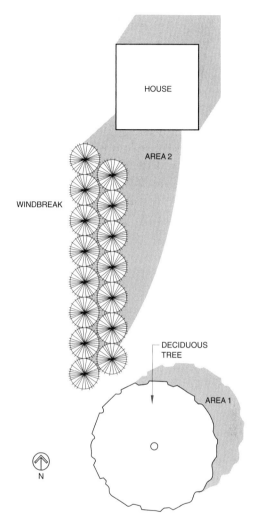

Figure 4.11   Summer wind and shadow patterns.
Source: Hopper, *Landscape Architecture Graphic Standards.* Copyright John Wiley & Sons,
Inc., 2007.

would be open to full sun, and would not experience any cooling
breezes. To make it more comfortable for summer use, a deciduous
tree could be located so as to cast a shade on Area 1 in midsummer.
The lack of leaves in the spring would allow much of the solar radiation to pass through at this time, warming the people. Dominant
summer winds in this location are typically from the south and south-
east, while winter/spring winds are dominantly from the west. This
provides an opportunity to use a windbreak to slow the winter/spring

winds, but leave the site open to the desirable summer southerly and southeasterly winds.

Design Characteristics

The design character of the trees themselves plays a part in the choice of species best suited for a particular application. The shape of a tree can be columnar, conical, spherical, or spreading, and the resulting height and mass will change over time as the tree matures. Some trees grow quickly and others more slowly, and their color and texture vary from coarse to medium to fine, affecting their character. The appearance of deciduous trees changes with the seasons, while the effect of an evergreen remains relatively constant.

Trees can be selected for their foliage, bark, flowering, and fruit characteristics in an effort to provide year-round interest. Fruit can be an issue for consideration in areas heavily traveled by pedestrians or vehicles, as the fallen fruit can be messy or slippery. Cleaning up after these tree fruits is considered an added maintenance burden. Trees without fruits, or with less-messy fruits, are often considered a more desirable choice for these areas.

Species Selection

There is a historical design tendency to plant groups of the same tree species in order to meet design principles and objectives. This monoculture approach to tree species selection can cause serious problems when insects or diseases attack that specific tree species. This has led to the decline of overplanted and popular species and the devastation of tree-planting designs that relied on one species. Municipalities that have relied heavily on one species for their street tree planting have been particularly hard hit when that species develops insect or disease problems. Whenever possible, a diverse selection of tree species will help avoid these problems in the future.

Because many design principles are based on the uniformity of the trees, planting a more diverse grouping of tree species with different design characteristics is not always an acceptable aesthetic alternative. Where uniformity is a design priority, it is advisable to select several different tree species that share the same size, form, branching, and leaf characteristics. This may include some cultivars of the same species that have been developed to be more disease or pest resistant or to adapt better to certain growing conditions. By carefully grouping the different species, uniformity can be achieved without risking the disadvantages of a monoculture planting.

▶ Be sure to check if there is a prevalent species already planted in the area. Avoid adding more of the same species. Ideally, no single species should make up more than 10 percent of an area's tree population.

Practices to Avoid

- Do not select a tree species to be planted without having a soil test performed to test for nutrients, pH, organic matter and soil type (proportions of sand, silt, or clay), drainage, salinity, and depth to water table.
- Space constraints need to be considered as part of the tree selection process. Do not forget to consider those belowground, those that may be imposed by the proposed design, and those that may occur intermittently (such as passing trucks that could cause damage).
- Avoid the common mistake of planting a large tree too close to a building or other structure.
- Do not limit your space constraint evaluation to the size of the tree at planting, but consider its mature height, canopy spread, and root system.
- Avoid selecting trees that will block distribution from site lighting or streetlights.
- Avoid selecting trees that require more soil volume for growth and health than can be provided, as these trees will not achieve their full potential.
- Avoid potential conflicts with any utilities by selecting trees that will not need to be pruned for aboveground utilities. Avoid planting in locations where their mature root system may be damaged by underground utility repairs or upgrades.
- Municipalities that have relied heavily on one species for their street tree planting have been particularly hard hit when that species develops insect or disease problems. Avoid monoculture tree selections, and contribute to a diverse selection of tree species, which will help avoid these problems in the future.

Tree Selection at the Nursery

Description

Initial inspection and selection of good-quality trees at the nursery is a critical step in maximizing a tree's potential to survive and thrive through maturity. Trees should be selected from a reputable nursery that has a reputation for proper care and development of their nursery stock.

▶ Proper planting and care may not be enough to overcome the problems associated with poor-quality trees.

Assessing Site Conditions

Nursery Conditions

Reputable nurseries attach a good deal of importance and pride to the measures they have taken to ensure that the trees they are offering are of good quality. When selecting trees at the nursery for a project, look for visible signs of good nursery practices, which differentiate reputable nurseries from those that exhibit less attention to how their tree stock is cared for.

Be observant, as the tree selection and tagging process takes place, by noting the following:

- How are the trees lined out in the field? Tree spacing affects tree form, canopy, growth rate, and trunk quality.
- What is the condition of the nursery's facilities and equipment?
- Are the growing areas free from unwanted vegetation? Weeds and turf compete with the trees for water and nutrients.
- How are the trees cared for as they grow to a sellable size?
- How are they dug?
- How are they transported?
- How are they cared for after digging?

These visual clues can provide valuable information about the nursery's horticultural practices that can directly affect the quality of the plant material (see Figures 4.12 and 4.13).

Figure 4.12 This nursery exhibits poor weed control, lower branch management, and pruning practices necessary to produce good branch structure and canopy development.
Courtesy Dr. Ed Gilman, University of Florida.

Figure 4.13 This nursery is representative of good horticultural practices, with good weed control, strong trunk development, and good branch structure and canopy development.
Courtesy Dr. Ed Gilman, University of Florida.

Tree Size and Planting Site Conditions

Matching the right size tree to be selected from the nursery with the anticipated conditions at the planting site can increase the potential for a tree to survive and thrive after planting. The following factors should be considered to determine the size of tree that will be best suited to the planting conditions and anticipated care at the site (see Table 4.1):

- *Watering* — Evaluate the likelihood that the newly planted tree will be provided with adequate water to become established. If the climate or microclimate of the planting site contributes to dry conditions, this will put further stress on the newly planted tree. If adequate watering is not likely to be provided, smaller trees will have a better chance of survival than larger tree stock.
- *Drainage* — Smaller trees may do better when destined for planting sites that tend to be wet or have poor drainage characteristics. Large trees with bigger root balls may have their lower roots sitting in water that will eventually kill the roots. Smaller trees or trees grown with shallow, wider root balls have a better chance to sit above any standing water.
- *Tree pit maintenance* — If weeds are not controlled either chemically or by a layer of mulch, this unwanted vegetation will compete with the tree for water and nutrients. Smaller trees establish more quickly and are better able to compete with any other vegetation.

Table 4.1 Comparing Small-Sized with Large-Sized Nursery Stock

Criterion	Small-Sized Nursery Stock	Large-Sized Nursery Stock
Establishment period	Quick	Slow
Irrigation period after planting	Brief	Extended
Susceptible to drought or flood	Briefly after planting	For an extended period
Number of trees planted per dollar	Large	Small
Pruning needs	High	Moderate
Cost of nursery stock	Inexpensive	More expensive
Suitability for compacted or poorly drained soils	Well-suited	Could be poorly suited

Sources: The University of Florida and Dr. Ed Gilman.

- *Wind* — Smaller trees, because they establish faster, are better able to resist damage by windy conditions or storms than larger tree stock.

▶ Small trees generally transplant more successfully than large trees. Newly planted trees do not produce new shoot growth until the original ratio of branch to root has been reestablished. Because larger trees likely have had more of their roots removed when dug and inherently have more roots to reestablish, smaller trees produce new growth sooner and after several years will have "caught up" in size to a larger tree planted at the same time.

Standards

The American Standard for Nursery Stock (ANSI Z60.1) is a set of standards that nurseries and buyers use to facilitate a common set of criteria and expectations for growing, specifying, and inspecting plant material. Some key criteria included in the standards are:

- How trees are to be measured, and how their size is specified.
- The relationship between caliper, height, and spread.
- The size of the root ball, container, or box for a given size tree.

▶ It is important to be familiar with these standards when selecting trees at the nursery.

Acceptable Practices

Trees at the nursery will be available in three different root conditions (see Table 4.2):

- *Bare root* — These trees are field-grown; they are dug and sold without soil around the roots. They must be dug, transported, and planted within their dormant season.
- *Balled and burlapped* (B&B) — These trees are field-grown; they are dug with a ball surrounding the roots that is held intact by tightly wrapped and tied burlap. Larger trees often include wire baskets around the burlap for additional support. They are dug during their dormant season but can be held aboveground, with proper care, for planting later in the season.
- *Container-grown* — These trees are grown in containers aboveground. They are transferred to larger containers as they grow. All roots are intact within the container. Container-grown plants can be planted throughout the year if required.

Table 4.2 Choosing Among Tree Production Methods Based on Weight, Staking, and Irrigation Capabilities at the Planting Site

Production Method	Root Ball Weight	Need for Staking	If Irrigation after Planting Is:	Then Tree Growth Will Be:	And Survival Will Be:
Containers, aboveground or pot-in-pot	light	frequently	frequent	very good to excellent	very good to excellent
			infrequent	fair to good	fair
Fabric containers, in ground	light to moderate	usually	frequent	excellent	very good to excellent
			infrequent	good	poor to fair
B&B, not root pruned	heavy	sometimes	frequent	good	fair to good
			infrequent	fair to good	poor to fair
B&B, root pruned	heavy	sometimes	frequent	excellent	excellent
			infrequent	good	good
Bare root	very light	usually	frequent	excellent	excellent
			infrequent	good	good

Sources: The University of Florida and Dr. Ed Gilman.

Aboveground Characteristics of High-Quality Trees

Good nursery stock should have a uniform height, trunk thickness, crown, branching, and leaf size and quantity from tree to tree. Some visible characteristics that distinguish good quality trees from those that are not include the following.

Tree Size

Trees are measured by their height for smaller sizes and by caliper (diameter of the trunk) for larger sizes. Trees less than 4 inches in diameter have their caliper measured 6 inches above the ground. Trees that are 4 inches and larger in diameter have their caliper measured 12 inches aboveground.

Trees are classified by the average of the largest caliper measured and the caliper perpendicular to the largest caliper measured (the trunk is rarely perfectly round). Caliper is typically measured with a diameter measuring tape or a special tool that is called a "caliper." The measuring tape, usually used for larger trees, will convert the circumference to a diameter. The caliper is a tong-like instrument with forks that can be closed down on each side of the trunk. A scale along one of the forks indicates the tree's caliper. See Figures 4.14 through 4.16.

Figure 4.14   Tree caliper measured 6 inches above grade.

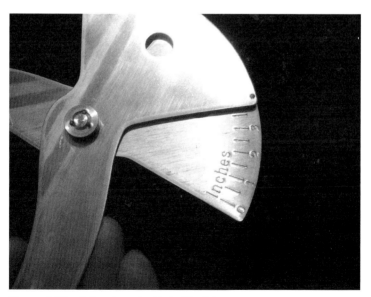

Figure 4.15   Caliper is marked in half-inch increments.

Figure 4.16   A mature tree trunk diameter being measured with a caliper tape that converts the circumference to a diameter. The tree trunk diameter is measured at breast height (4-1/2 feet above the ground) and referenced as DBH. On sloping sites, the 4-1/2 feet is measured on the uphill side. If the tree forks below breast height, each trunk is considered separately.

Trees are generally classified in half-inch caliper increments. For example, a 2½– 3"-caliper tree could be a tree with a caliper from 2½" up to, but not including, 3".

Tree Form

Trees should have well-spaced branches uniformly around the trunk. A good-quality tree will have a strong central leader (if typical for the species) without co-dominant stems or competing acute-angled branching at the top. Trees that are grown for street tree planting should have been limbed up over several years and require minimal pruning of lower branches at the time of planting. The crown form should be full, uniform, and typical for the species of tree being selected. There should be no branch dieback.

Look for previous pruning cuts, and evaluate whether they were performed properly. There should be no indication of flush pruning cuts. See Figures 4.17 through 4.23.

▶ Mark the north side of the tree so that the tree orientation at the site can be matched to the orientation in which it was grown.

Figure 4.17 This recently tagged and planted tree has a strong structure with well-spaced branches along the trunk and a uniformly tapering central leader.

Figure 4.18 This tree selected at the nursery has clustered branches that are not well spaced along the trunk, which weakens the tree. The reduction in diameter of the central leader above the cluster of large branches toward the top of the photo indicates that the branches are growing more aggressively than the leader.

Figure 4.19 This newly planted tree exhibits a desirable strong central leader.

Figure 4.20 This tree has developed co-dominant competing leaders, which is not desirable.

Figure 4.21   This row of recently planted street trees represents poor selection at the nursery. They have bent trunks, multiple leaders, and poor branch structure.

Figure 4.22   This recently planted street tree has poor branch structure and competing multiple leaders.

Figure 4.23 This tree exhibits a series of flush pruning cuts performed at the nursery and should not have been selected for planting.

Tree Trunk

The trunk should be fairly straight with a consistent taper and a visible root flare at the base. Taper is the increase in trunk diameter close to the ground. The trunk should be sufficiently developed to be able to support the tree without the need for staking. The trunk should be free of mechanical wounds and evidence of incorrect pruning techniques (see Figures 4.24 through 4.28). Torn or split bark caused by contact with herbicides impacts movement of nutrients and water up into the canopy. Openings in the bark make the tree susceptible to disease and pests. There should be no indication of borers, cankers, scale, pests, or disease.

Several factors affect strength of the trunk and trunk taper. Stronger trunks often translate to quicker growth and better-quality trees. Some influencing factors that encourage good trunk strength are:

- Adequate spacing between trees.
- Good lower branch management.
- No staking.

Figure 4.24 A proper pruning cut being made by sawing beyond the root collar straight and perpendicular to the branch.
Courtesy Dr. Ed Gilman, University of Florida.

Figure 4.25 A good pruning cut with branch collar clearly visible.

Figure 4.26 Evidence of an improper flush cut freshly made on a young tree. Avoid selecting trees that exhibit flush pruning cuts.
Courtesy Dr. Ed Gilman, University of Florida.

Figure 4.27 Callus is having difficultly forming with no sign of the branch collar, which is indicative of a flush pruning cut.

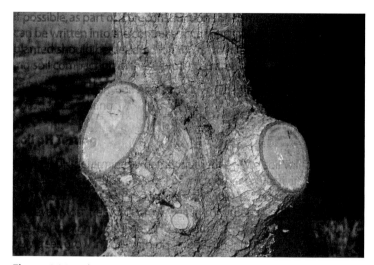

Figure 4.28　These are examples of good pruning cuts, with branch collar clearly visible.
Courtesy Dr. Ed Gilman, University of Florida.

If selecting a tree with a multi-stem, look for trunks that are well separated at the ground line. As the trunks expand, they may squeeze together, which can cause vertical cracks that can result in complete fracture during a storm (see Figure 4.29).

▶ Look for any indication of trunk injury or broken branches. Look under any trunk wrap, as it may be covering an injury.

Branches

The tree should have evenly spaced branches growing both radially and vertically around the trunk at an angle of 45 degrees or greater with no included bark. Branch diameter should be no greater than ⅔ the diameter of the trunk, measured 1 inch above the branch. (See Figures 4.30 through 4.34.) There may be some small-diameter temporary lower branching on smaller trees, which is acceptable nursery practice.

Evaluate the annual shoot growth length. It should increase in length each year, unless there is some extenuating circumstance affecting growth. Stunted growth can be caused by drought conditions, lack of nutrients, or recent transplanting. Stunted growth during the season before the tree is dug will result in a tree having fewer reserves to help with establishment after planting.

Branches should be firmly attached, and none should be dead, damaged, or distorted. Weak branch attachment can occur if a branch and

Figure 4.29 Multiple branches with bark inclusion squeezed together with vertical crack developing. The tree will be susceptible to splitting as it grows older.

Figure 4.30 Branch diameter almost equal to trunk diameter, growing at an angle of less than 45 degrees, is unacceptable.

Figure 4.31 These branch diameters are acceptable, and the angle of branching is 45 degrees or greater.

Figure 4.32 Branches with bark ridges visible on the top of the union indicate firm branching.

Figure 4.33   Branches with bark inclusions are weak and can split from the trunk.

Figure 4.34   Trees with co-dominant stems, bark inclusion, and V-shaped unions should not be selected.

trunk are squeezed together. As the diameters of both increase, dead spots or cracks develop below the point of attachment of the branch to the trunk, which can cause breaking or further cracking during storms. The same condition can result from several branches that are attached at the same position on the trunk.

Leaves

The size, shape, and color of leaves should be typical of the species being selected. Light green or yellowish leaves can indicate a nutrient deficiency that can have an effect on how long the tree will take to get established after planting.

Leaves should not have any indication of being eaten by pests or discolored by fungi. There should be no signs of wilted, shriveled, or dead leaves. There should be no branch dieback.

Belowground Characteristics of High-Quality Trees

Although the aboveground characteristics are the most visible and are the first to get attention, it is the belowground characteristics that are responsible for a tree's survival after being planted. Inspection of belowground factors should be a critical component of the tree selection process at the nursery. Too often, this aspect of the tree selection process is not given the attention required or is overlooked completely. A poorly developed root system has a direct impact on tree survival and future growth.

General Tree Root Condition

Good root management at the nursery is essential to the development of a good root system, whether the tree selected will be bare root, container-grown, or balled and burlapped. A good root system helps the tree get established quickly after planting and thrive in the years after. Root problems, particularly those close to the trunk, can be difficult to correct and may not affect a tree's growth until many years later, when they can lead to premature death of the tree.

Some root conditions can be visibly checked at time of selection; others may not be able to be seen until time of planting. How a nursery cares for its tree stock can be an indicator of root conditions that are not readily seen.

Some root conditions that should be noted at time of selection are:

- There should be no circling, girdling, or kinked roots at the top of the root ball around the trunk (some soil removal may be necessary to

Figure 4.35 An example of a circling root. This should be corrected before planting by cutting this root back to where the root is oriented radially from the trunk.
Photo Courtesy of James Urban/ISA.

check this). Trees with circling roots near the trunk should not be selected or planted. See Figures 4.35–4.46.

- Trees should not be planted too deep. The root flare should be visible at the soil line of the container or root ball. See Figures 4.47 and 4.51.
- The top roots from the trunk (the root collar), if not visible at the soil surface, should be within an inch or so of the top of the root ball. See Figure 4.48.
- There should not be too few roots in the root ball or too many roots matted against the outside edge. See Figures 4.49 and 4.50.
- Weeds or unwanted vegetation should not be growing within the root ball.
- The tree should be rooted firmly into the root ball. If the tree trunk is gently pushed, it should bend slightly, not move loosely at the top of the root ball. For container-grown trees, the root ball should remain intact when removed from its container.

Figure 4.36 Visible indication of roots stopping at limit of old container diameter. A surveyor's pin is being used to detect the root locations along the dashed line (diameter of old container).
Courtesy of James Urban/ISA.

- The size of the container or root ball should be appropriate for the size of the tree (ANSI Z60.1).

Bare-Root Conditions

Trees available as bare root are a very economical approach to buying trees that will be planted in relatively protected areas. They are seldom specified for urban areas because their inherently smaller sizes are more susceptible to vandalism.

Bare-root trees are dug while they are dormant; the roots must be kept moist and stored at temperatures below 40 degrees F prior to shipping and planting. Their delivery and planting should be coordinated at the site so that they can be set into the ground as soon as possible after arrival. The longer the gap between delivery and planting, the less likely that the trees will survive.

Figure 4.37 Container root package cut in half to reveal many circling roots along the limits of the old container diameter (inner dashed line). Courtesy of James Urban/ISA.

Figure 4.38 A low-quality root ball from a #15 container showing deflected roots developed before the tree was moved from a #3 container. Courtesy of Dr. Ed Gilman, University of Florida.

Figure 4.39 A high-quality root ball from a #15 container showing no evidence of deflected roots developed before the tree was moved from a #3 container.
Courtesy of Dr. Ed Gilman, University of Florida.

Figure 4.40 A good example of the root structure of a tree that was moved evenly from a #3 container to a #15 container.
Courtesy of Dr. Ed Gilman, University of Florida.

Figure 4.41 These roots from a tree in a #15 container show good, straight, radial root growth right to the edge of the root ball.
Courtesy of Dr. Ed Gilman, University of Florida.

Figure 4.42 Examples of girdling roots at the surface. If a tree does not have a developing trunk flare visible, a girdling root below grade may be the cause.
Courtesy of James Urban/ISA.

Figure 4.43 Girdling roots have grown around the trunk and few roots grow into the surrounding soil, contributing to tree instability.
Courtesy of James Urban/ISA.

Figure 4.44 Girdling root, seen from above to the right of the trunk, can be removed.
Courtesy of James Urban/ISA.

Figure 4.45 Girdling root after removal.
Courtesy of James Urban/ISA.

Figure 4.46 Kinked roots can be deflected back by the container side and grow back toward the trunk.
Courtesy of Dr. Ed Gilman, University of Florida.

Figure 4.47 Trunk flare and root collar are visible, with top roots within an inch of the top of the root ball growing radially from the trunk.
Courtesy of Dr. Ed Gilman, University of Florida.

Figure 4.48 A root collar inspection is performed at the nursery using an air knife to remove the soil and expose the root flare. Any circling or girdling roots should be removed. The elevation of the root flare or main roots should be marked to aid planting at the proper depth at the site.
Courtesy of James Urban/ISA.

Figure 4.49 Roots tightly matted to inside of container. These roots must be loosened and directed outward at time of planting.
Courtesy of James Urban/ISA.

Figure 4.50 This tree has poor root distribution and no trunk flare.
Courtesy of Dr. Ed Gilman, University of Florida.

Figure 4.51 This tree has good root distribution and a clearly visible root collar and trunk flare.
Courtesy of Dr. Ed Gilman, University of Florida.

Container-Grown Root Conditions

Although container-grown trees have the advantage of having 100 percent of their root structure intact at time of planting, container-grown trees can be susceptible to several root problems. Proper care and root management as the tree grows and is planted into larger containers, as well as the type of container itself, will contribute to a healthy root system free of major problems that can affect survival.

Tree roots have a tendency to grow to the container wall, where they are deflected downward or begin to circle around the container edge. These conditions can cause serious root defects, particularly if the tree is left in the same size of container too long. Descending and circling roots should be cut by the nursery every time the tree is planted into a larger size container, to keep roots growing straight in a balanced radial pattern from the trunk.

Containers come in different shapes, sizes, and designs to accommodate specific conditions and encourage better root growth. Some special examples are:

- Trees grown in tall containers may be better suited to planting sites that are well drained without irrigation. Although the roots in the upper portion of the root ball may dry out and die, those deeper down have a better chance of surviving and growing out into the surrounding soil.

- Trees grown in short, wide containers may be better suited to planting sites with poorly drained or compacted soils. The roots closer to the surface will benefit from the air in the soil, whereas if the roots were deeper down, where the soil is wet or saturated, they would die from the lack of air.
- Air-pruned containers are manufactured with holes along their sides and bottoms. The concept is that root tips growing into the holes die from contact with the air, and the root branches farther back in response. This reduces the number of circling and descending roots.

Balled and Burlapped Root Conditions

Trees that are dug, balled, and burlapped should have the trunk flare visible at the top of the root ball. The diameter and depth of the root ball should be compliant with ANSI Z60.1.

Nurseries will use both natural burlap and treated burlap to wrap the root balls. Natural burlap will begin to decay after four to six weeks if stored in a mulch bed and may require a new layer of burlap to be wrapped around the root ball before the tree is transported, to prevent the root ball from breaking apart. Treated burlap, which will resist decay caused by soil fungi, will last three months or more when stored in a mulch bed. Either burlap will bind with the soil and allow water and air to move through easily.

▶ Plastic-wrapped tree balls should be avoided.

The burlap should be wrapped tight around the ball to prevent damage during transport. Wire baskets, if provided for additional support, should be tightly crimped. It is best if the burlap is secured with twine rather than plastic or nylon. The tree trunk should be centered in the root ball.

▶ It is a good idea to untie the top of the burlap and check for major support roots in the top inch or two of the root ball. If there are no major roots close to the surface, the tree may have an undersized root system. It would be best to pass over this tree, rather than have problems with survival after planting.

Root balls that are deeper than the minimum standards may be better suited to planting in areas of well-drained soil that will receive no additional irrigation. Their deeper roots will have access to the moist soil farther from the surface where the soil will tend to dry out sooner. Shallow root balls may be better suited to wet conditions where the roots will be located closer to the surface, instead of deeper down in the soil where compaction or poorly drained soil types keep the soil saturated and there is poor aeration.

Fertilization and Root System Development

Ask how the trees are fertilized at the nursery. Where fertilizer is applied to the soil that will be dug with the tree, trees exhibit a higher number of fine roots within the root ball, as opposed to trees that are fertilized over a larger area. These finer roots increase the tree's survival rate and help it get established more quickly after planting.

Irrigation and Root System Development

Observe or ask how the trees are irrigated at the nursery. Trees that receive water concentrated around the trunk, in the soil that will be dug with the tree, develop a denser root system within the ball than trees receiving the same amount of irrigation over a larger area or trees that are not irrigated at all.

Root Pruning

Good nursery practice will root prune trees on a regular basis and one or two growing seasons before they are dug for transplanting. This results in the development of a more compact, dense root structure containing a larger percentage of smaller-diameter and fine roots that are necessary to absorb water and nutrients. See Figures 4.52 through 4.54.

Figure 4.52   Example of the root structure of a tree that has not been root pruned.
Courtesy of Dr. Ed Gilman, University of Florida.

Figure 4.53   Example of the root structure of a tree that has been root pruned.
Courtesy of Dr. Ed Gilman, University of Florida.

Figure 4.54   A root ball that has been root pruned exhibits a much denser root system of different-diameter roots. In this example, you can see new finer roots growing from where the original roots were pruned.
Courtesy of Dr. Ed Gilman, University of Florida.

Root pruning is accomplished by cutting the roots with a spade just inside the line of where the tree ball diameter would likely be at time of digging. Some nurseries will add fabric to the bottom of the planting hole that, in conjunction with root pruning, will further increase root density.

▶ **The inability for a tree to absorb water, and the related stress, are the largest cause of dying in newly planted trees. Proper irrigation and the presence of smaller, fibrous root systems will ensure a greater potential for newly planted tree survival.**

Low Branch Management

Good nursery practice involves leaving low branches on the tree as it grows, to encourage strong trunk development and quicker trunk diameter growth. This involves pruning back lower branch growth in a balanced approach that keeps the tree canopy growth in better proportion to the size of the tree. These lower branches are considered temporary and are usually removed at time of transplanting. Keeping these temporary low branches relatively small in diameter minimizes large pruning cuts when these branches are eventually removed. See Figures 4.55 through 4.60.

Good low branch management is particularly important for trees that will be planted along streets, where they are typically required to be limbed up 7 feet or more.

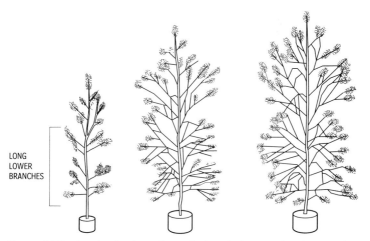

LONG LOWER BRANCHES

Figure 4.55   Leaving low branches quite long before pruning them, and then pruning them back just the right amount, allows the trunk to increase in diameter rapidly. Leaving low branches long also modulates top growth and helps prevent the tree from stretching too tall.
Courtesy of Dr. Ed Gilman, University of Florida.

Figure 4.56 Low temporary branches help the root system and lower trunk grow. They protect the trunk by forming a barrier to mechanical injury. As the trunk and canopy develop to the desired marketable size, lower branches will be removed in their final year of production in the nursery. Courtesy of Dr. Ed Gilman, University of Florida.

Figure 4.57 Long low branches encourage root growth. Trees with short low branches, or those with low branches removed too soon, can develop weak root systems unable to hold the tree erect. Courtesy of Dr. Ed Gilman, University of Florida.

Figure 4.58 Weak trunks can result from removing too many low branches. These trees will often require a stake to keep them from falling over.
Courtesy of Dr. Ed Gilman, University of Florida.

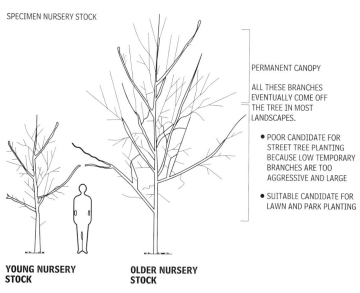

SPECIMEN NURSERY STOCK

PERMANENT CANOPY

ALL THESE BRANCHES
EVENTUALLY COME OFF
THE TREE IN MOST
LANDSCAPES.

- POOR CANDIDATE FOR
  STREET TREE PLANTING
  BECAUSE LOW TEMPORARY
  BRANCHES ARE TOO
  AGGRESSIVE AND LARGE

- SUITABLE CANDIDATE FOR
  LAWN AND PARK PLANTING

**YOUNG NURSERY
STOCK**

**OLDER NURSERY
STOCK**

TRAINING TREES FOR SPECIMEN AND STREET TREE USE

Figure 4.59 Example of specimen stock with low branching most suitable for lawn or park setting.
Courtesy of Dr. Ed Gilman, University of Florida.

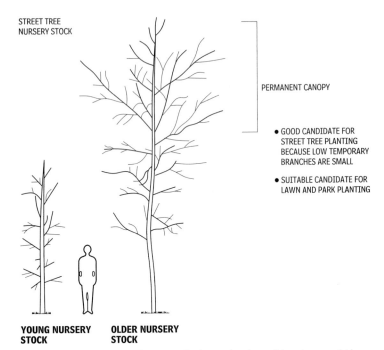

STREET TREE
NURSERY STOCK

PERMANENT CANOPY

- GOOD CANDIDATE FOR
  STREET TREE PLANTING
  BECAUSE LOW TEMPORARY
  BRANCHES ARE SMALL

- SUITABLE CANDIDATE FOR
  LAWN AND PARK PLANTING

**YOUNG NURSERY
STOCK**

**OLDER NURSERY
STOCK**

Figure 4.60 Example of a tree with shorter low branching that would be suitable for a street tree planting.
Courtesy of Dr. Ed Gilman, University of Florida.

Staking

Staking is done in the nursery to keep trees upright and to help develop a straight trunk. Staking does not necessarily inhibit trunk growth or strength if accompanied by good low branch management. Trees that are being selected for planting in the landscape should be able to support themselves without staking.

Proper Tree Harvesting at the Nursery

After the trees that will be planted at the site have been evaluated, selected, and tagged in the field, they are dug, balled and burlapped, and readied to be transported. This is a critical phase of the tree selection process that will play a large role in the survival and success of the trees once they are planted on the site. See Figures 4.61 through 4.63.

▶ Freshly dug trees that are transported and planted directly in the landscape can be subject to greater transplant shock than trees that have been dug and benefited from extra care and attention to irrigation in the nursery.

Figure 4.61   Trees should always be carefully lifted by the root ball. This tree is being lifted by a system of ropes attached to the galvanized wire basket.
Courtesy of Dr. Ed Gilman, University of Florida.

Figure 4.62   Sometimes balled and burlapped trees will be stored aboveground in sawdust, wood chips, or mulch. Roots will typically grow through the burlap and out into the mulch in the holding area.
Courtesy of Dr. Ed Gilman, University of Florida.

Figure 4.63 This recently dug tree developed new roots growing through the burlap while being stored and will likely transplant well into the landscape. Courtesy of Dr. Ed Gilman, University of Florida.

Transporting Trees to the Planting Site

On certain species, branches normally are tied together close to the trunk to prevent breakage during shipping. They can be secured with string, plastic straps, fabric, and other material. The root ball should be firm and securely tied. See Figures 4.64 through 4.66.

Some nurseries will ship trees with plastic wrapped around the root ball to reduce water stress by keeping the root ball moist. See Figure 4.67. The plastic should be removed if the tree is to be left in the sun for any length of time, and, of course, should be removed before planting.

Trees should be tied securely in the truck to prevent movement and excessive vibration that can loosen or damage the root ball. Trees in open trucks should always be covered so that air moves over the trees, not under the cover and through the trees. See Figure 4.68.

When trees are delivered to the site, they should be inspected for any damage as well as any signs of moisture loss. There should be no signs of trunk damage, broken branches, or broken root balls. If there are leaves present, there should be no wilting, shriveling, dead leaves, or evidence of branch dieback. The root ball should be tightly wrapped

Figure 4.64   Root ball tied securely and ready for transport.
Courtesy of Dr. Ed Gilman, University of Florida.

Figure 4.65   Trees should always be handled by the root ball or basket, never the trunk.
Courtesy of Dr. Ed Gilman, University of Florida.

Figure 4.66 Trees are delivered to the site on a flatbed trunk. Branches are tied together to prevent damage.

Figure 4.67 Root ball wrapped in plastic to reduce desiccation during transport. The plastic must be removed prior to planting.
Courtesy of Dr. Ed Gilman, University of Florida.

Figure 4.68   The flatbed truck has a special attachment that pulls burlap over the trees as they are being transported.

and moist, with no signs of damage or excessive moisture as indicated by discoloration or bad odor.

▶ Holding the trunk and gently rotating it in a circular motion can determine whether the root ball has been properly prepared and the roots sufficiently developed. The trunk and root ball should move as one; if the trunk moves around loosely and the tree ball remains stationary, the tree should be rejected.

Trees in closed trucks should be unloaded as soon as possible and not allowed to sit in the sun, which can effectively bake the tree, killing it before it even gets planted in the ground. If the trees cannot be unloaded when the truck arrives, it should be directed to a shady location until unloading can begin.

Trees need to be unloaded just as carefully as they've been loaded, to prevent damage to the root ball. Proper equipment for lifting and handling the trees by the root ball and gently lowering them onto the ground should be ready on the site on delivery day. See Figures 4.69 and 4.70.

▶ Trees should never be dropped off the truck onto the ground or dragged by the trunk or branches.

Figure 4.69 Trees are lifted off the truck with straps attached to the root ball.

Figure 4.70 The tree is carefully placed between forks and strapped in place, in order to transport it sideways through the fence opening with limited vertical clearance. Skid steer moves slowly so that bumps or vibration will not loosen soil in the root ball.

It is best to coordinate the planting on the same day as the trees are delivered. If the trees are to sit out for any length of time, they should be kept moist, particularly the root ball.

If the trees cannot be planted the same day, a holding area should be created that will safely store the trees for a few days until they can all be planted. They should be placed in an upright position and clustered together to provide their own shade from any sun conditions and protect each other from drying out by wind. A proper holding area should have the following characteristics:

- A shady location that is sheltered from the wind.
- Availability of water for irrigation.
- Soil, compost, mulch, or other organic material that can cover the sides of the root ball and keep it moist.

The holding area should be maintained to keep the trees moist at all times. Special attention should be paid to trees in black or dark plastic containers that can heat up quickly in direct sun and kill the root system. Bare-root trees must be covered immediately with sphagnum moss or other moisture-holding material, although bare-root trees should always be planted immediately upon delivery. Although plastic sheets can be used to control moisture loss, care should be taken, as any direct sun on the plastic will raise the temperature and bake the tree roots.

Practices to Avoid

- Avoid costly remedial techniques or replacement by examining trees carefully at the nursery.
- Trees that are disproportionately tall for their caliper may have been collected from forests or grown too close together. Either way, these trees should not be selected, as they may have diminished potential for survival after planting.
- Trees with crossing, parallel, or closely spaced branches should be avoided, as these will grow into each other as the tree matures.
- Avoid selecting trees with circling roots.
- Avoid selecting trees with trunk wounds from insects or impacts, or large wounds from pruning. Be sure to check under trunk wraps for damage. Any of these can lead to serious problems after planting.

Soil Amendments

Description

Traditionally, specifications called for the removal of the soil dug from the planting hole and a topsoil mixture backfilled in its place. However, recent research suggests that the soil removed from the planting hole generally makes the best backfill.

There may be some situations where amending or replacing the soil is recommended. However, the wholesale replacement of removed soil should not be the accepted standard. Indiscriminate replacement of existing soil with topsoil can even be detrimental.

Assessing Site Conditions

Removing good topsoil from one site and delivering it to another site is environmentally unsound on many levels. The protection and reuse of existing soil resources is the most sustainable approach.

A soil assessment is needed to determine what the existing soil characteristics are and what amendments may be beneficial, if any at all. One of the primary desirable characteristics of backfill is the increased aeration. This can often be accomplished with the existing soil. The action of removing the soil, loosening it, and breaking up any large clods will, in itself, improve the aeration of the soil when it is backfilled.

Where soil is determined to be of extremely poor quality and soil replacement is necessary, the most effective approach is to replace the soil in the area surrounding the planting hole, not just in the hole itself. As part of the site assessment, note how large an area is available for soil replacement (see "Acceptable Practices").

Acceptable Practices

The preservation of existing soil during construction should protect it from compaction and contamination. It is best protected in place, with stripping, stockpiling, and redistribution after construction an acceptable alternative.

The most common objectives in amending soils are:

- Reducing bulk density to encourage root growth into the backfill.
- Increasing aeration.
- Improving drainage.
- Improving soil structure.

It is difficult to reach these objectives with inorganic soil amendments, such as sand, as the amounts needed to make a significant improvement are great and, if improperly specified, can actually reduce aeration and have a negative effect on drainage.

The addition of organic soil amendments can have desirable effects. It is most effective when spread over a larger area around the planting hole and tilled to a depth of 18 inches, the depth at which most roots grow. To make a meaningful difference, enough organic material must be added. A compacted sandy loam would require a minimum of 25 percent by volume. For a heavy clayey soil, a minimum of 50 percent by volume would need to be added.

Organic amendments include:

- Peat moss
- Peat humus
- Composted organic waste

▶ Peat products are harvested from wetlands and usually transported great distances to where they are sold and used. For these reasons, their use is not considered a sustainable approach, and the use of local composted organic material is much preferred.

▶ Composted amendments must be completely composted and should be tested for pH, soluble salts, nutrient availability, and organic content. Well-composted organic waste is usually dark brown to black in color, with few if any of the original materials' parts visible.

Improving the drainage of only the backfill can create a bathtub of standing water that cannot penetrate the surrounding soil at the same rate as the backfill. If the soil under the backfill is poorly drained, a subsurface drainage system may be needed to carry the excess water away from the plant roots.

Adjusting pH

It is difficult to make a significant change in pH prior to planting. If the soil where the tree is to be planted is not suitable for the desired pH of the plant, it is best to choose another tree or another location.

Some modification of the soil pH is possible. Tables 4.3 and 4.4 provide recommendations to raise and lower pH.

Table 4.3 Changing Soil pH: Adding Limestone to Raise Soil pH
Liming Materials

Source	Calcium Carbonate* Equivalent %	Rate of pH Change
Burned lime	180	Very fast
Hydrated lime	140	Fast
Ground or pulverized limestone	75–94	Slow
Dolomitic limestone+	75–95	Slow
Pelletized limestone	75–95	Fast

*Liming power of a material.
+Contains magnesium (recommended only if the pH is low and magnesium is low).

Preplant Application to Raise Soil pH to 6.5: Pounds of Ground Limestone/100 Square Feet, Incorporated into Upper 6 Inches of Soil

Existing pH	Sandy Loam	Loam	Clay
4.5	12.6	25.3	34.8
4.6	12.4	24.8	34.1
4.7	12.0	24.1	33.1
4.8	11.7	23.4	32.2
4.9	11.2	22.2	30.7
5.0	10.6	21.1	29.0
5.1	9.9	19.8	27.2
5.2	8.9	17.7	24.3
5.3	7.2	14.3	19.7
5.4	5.3	10.7	14.6
5.5	4.2	8.4	11.6
5.6	3.6	7.2	9.8
5.7	3.1	6.2	8.6
5.8	2.6	5.1	7.1
5.9	2.0	4.0	5.6
6.0	1.7	3.3	4.5

Source: Trowbridge and Bassuk, *Trees in the Urban Landscape*, John Wiley & Sons, Inc. © 2004, p. 58.

Table 4.4 Changing Soil pH: To Lower Soil pH.
Pounds of Elemental Sulfur/100 SF   Incorporate into the Upper 6 Inches of Soil

Existing pH	Desired pH	Sandy Loam	Loam	Clay
8.0	7.0	1.2	2.4	3.3
	6.5	1.7	3.4	4.7
	6.0	2.2	4.5	6.1
	5.5	3.1	6.1	8.4
	5.0	5.1	10.2	14.0
7.5	7.0	0.5	1.0	1.4
	6.5	1.0	2.0	2.7
	6.0	1.5	3.1	4.2
	5.5	2.4	4.7	6.5
	5.0	4.4	8.8	12.0
7.0	6.5	0.5	1.0	1.4
	6.0	1.0	2.1	2.8
	5.5	1.9	3.7	5.1
	5.0	3.9	7.8	10.7
6.5	6.0	0.5	1.1	1.5
	5.5	1.4	2.7	3.7
	5.0	3.4	6.8	9.3

Source: Trowbridge and Bassuk, *Trees in the Urban Landscape*, John Wiley & Sons, Inc. © 2004, p. 59.

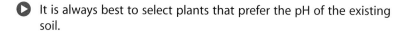 It is always best to select plants that prefer the pH of the existing soil.

Fertilization

A soil test should be conducted to determine existing nutrient levels before any fertilizer is added to the soil. A testing lab should be able to provide recommendations for improvement based on the test results, if necessary. Unless there is a significant nutrient deficiency, there is generally no reason to fertilize a tree that has just been planted.

If fertilization is determined to be necessary, time-release fertilizers that will benefit the tree over multiple years are the more desirable type. A slow-release, low-nitrogen fertilizer that can be applied to the surface is another acceptable approach. The low nitrogen level will keep the tree from pushing new growth instead of developing a healthy root system.

It is best to fertilize beyond the planting hole by incorporating the fertilizer into the top layer of the soil. Fertilizer should not be mixed into the backfill.

Mycorrhizal Fungi

Mycorrhizal fungus is a symbiotic fungus that can help promote root growth. Although this fungus exists naturally in soils, the addition of a mycorrhizal fungus amendment can ensure that there are sufficient amounts available to promote root growth and development. There are mycorrhizal products that are tailored to certain tree species, and applications can be matched to provide the most benefit.

Other root-stimulating soil amendments are available, for which a variety of beneficial results are claimed. These can have some positive effect on root growth, but they are not absolutely necessary for a newly planted tree.

Polymer Gels

Polymer gels are mixed with the soil to improve water-holding capacity. The polymer gel can hold on to an incredible amount of water and make it available to plant roots after the soil around it has dried. This makes it a good amendment for newly planted trees, as it helps minimize water loss and transplant shock.

▶ One pound of a polymer gel can hold up to 50 gallons of water.

Practices to Avoid

- Avoid amending soil and creating a drainage problem by improving the drainage of only the backfill, leaving the plant hole holding water.
- Avoid adding fertilizer to the backfill. The nitrogen level can burn the roots that come into contact with the fertilizer.

Deciduous Tree Planting

Description

Deciduous trees are best planted during their dormant season in the spring before budbreak and in the fall after they have dropped their leaves. This timing allows for root development in the fall and early spring, helping the trees get established before they leaf out and enter the stressful weather conditions of summer. Deciduous trees can be planted at other times, but a higher level of care is required at each stage of the planting and maintenance process. In warmer climates, planting can take place during the winter months. In tropical and subtropical climates, trees can be planted year-round, with special attention given to the amount of water that the tree requires.

It is important to realize that deciduous trees that are supplied balled and burlapped have had their root system reduced by 90 percent or more through the process of digging the plant material from its growing location. The fine roots needed for absorption are easily damaged and can dry out quickly. These trees also experience some shock and stress when transplanted to a new location. With such a significant reduction in the root system, the newly planted trees can suffer from water stress, which is the primary cause of an unsuccessful tree planting.

▶ Container-grown trees experience transplant shock to a lesser degree, as their root system is totally developed within the container.

Site preparation and after-planting care and maintenance are critically important in getting a tree successfully established, by minimizing shock and stress that can slow its growth or cause it to weaken or die.

Assessing Site Conditions

If the information is not already available, a soil sample should be taken and tested for pH, nutrient levels, and organic content. This information is important in deciding what, if any, fertilizer or soil amendments to add at the time of planting.

Check on the location of underground utility lines before digging. Many utility lines are not buried as deep as the required excavation depth for the tree pit.

For additional information, see "Soil Assessment," in Chapter 1, and the related topics in this chapter:

- "Soil Amendments"
- "Site Considerations and Tree Selection"

Acceptable Practices

Digging the Planting Hole

The planting hole is the initial step—and one of the most critical—in the planting process. It is also a step where common mistakes can have serious negative impacts on the long-term health and growth of the tree. The most common mistake made is planting the tree too deep in a tree pit that is too small. This deprives the tree roots of needed oxygen and impairs their ability to spread, limiting their intake of water and nutrients and affecting their ability to anchor the tree. Every effort should be made to plant the tree at the same soil depth at which it was originally grown.

▶ Follow the old adage: "Dig a $100 hole to plant a $10 tree." It is good advice.

The following steps should be taken in order to dig the planting hole properly:

- Be sure that the tree is well watered while the planting hole is being prepared; roots should not be allowed to dry out.
- The center of the planting hole should be marked with a stake. Cut a string that is at least equal in length to the diameter of the root ball, container, or spread of the roots for a bare-root tree (which will result in a tree pit twice the size of the root spread), or preferably 1½ times the diameter of the root ball (which will result in a tree pit three times the size of the root spread). Tie the string to the stake and use

it to mark a circle around the stake (like using a compass) with a can of marking spray paint.

▶ In small-diameter tree pits, where the soil surrounding the hole is compacted or has a heavy clay content, roots can become deformed when reaching this impenetrable barrier. Wherever possible, loosen compacted soil as far from the root ball as practically possible, to give the roots that much room to grow and help the tree get established.

- All vegetation within the circle, and slightly beyond, should be cleared.
- Measure the height from the trunk flare (where the roots spread at the base of the tree) to the bottom of the root ball or container. For a bare-root tree, measure from the root crown (top of the roots) or from the soil level at which it was originally planted (usually indicated by a discoloration in the color of the trunk bark) to the bottom of the roots. This measurement is used to determine the depth of the tree pit.

▶ If the trunk flare is not visible, it may be necessary to untie and remove some of the burlap, and even carefully loosen some soil from around the trunk until the trunk flare is exposed.

- A tarp should be placed alongside the edge of the marked tree pit to keep the soil separated from the surrounding grass or pavements. See Figure 4.71.
- Use a pointed spade shovel to dig in along the edge of the marked circle. If grass or vegetation is growing within the circle, it should be scraped off with a flat-edged shovel and used elsewhere on the site or discarded. It should not be mixed in with the rest of the excavated soil.
- The planting hole should be dug with the spade shovel to the measured depth. If a machine is used to excavate the planting hole, extra care should be taken not to dig the hole too deep. The hole should be saucer-shaped, with the edges having a slight taper. The excavated soil should be placed on the tarp.
- To measure the depth of the planting hole accurately, drive a stake on one side of the tree pit, and secure a string at the level of the surrounding grade. Pull the string across the hole to a point on the other side of the hole at the level of the surrounding grade. The depth of the hole should be measured down from the string level at the center of the hole.
- Trees should be planted so that the top of the root ball is even with, or slightly higher than, the surrounding soil. This is especially critical for trees planted in compacted or wet soils.

Figure 4.71   Planting holes have already been dug prior to delivery of the trees, to minimize the time until the trees can be planted. Tarps on the pavement keep the soil from getting on the pavement or, in this case, migrating into the joints of the pervious concrete pavers.

When planting on steep slopes, dig the planting hole so that the top of the root ball on the uphill side will be even with the soil. The side of the root ball on the downhill side will then be somewhat above the level of the surrounding soil. Soil will need to be added on the downhill side to cover the sides of the root ball and construct a small berm or saucer to hold water.

- Ideally, the tree should sit on the firm base at the bottom of the planting hole. If the planting hole needs to be made deeper, enough soil should be carefully scraped away until the desired level is reached. If the hole has been dug too deep, soil added will need to be compacted to minimize any settling of the tree after backfilling. As some settling is likely, it would be advisable to have the soil compacted 2 to 3 inches higher than the measured height. It is always better to have the tree planted a bit higher, rather than too deep.

- The soil should be loosened around the edges of the tree pit, which will result in a slightly raised flat pedestal in the center of the tree pit, where the tree can sit. The sides of the tree pit should be scarified and soil loosened to allow the roots to grow into the surrounding soil. This is an especially important step with clay soils; the shovel can smooth the surface of a clay pit's sides, creating a barrier that water can't pass through (referred to as "glazing"). The water can become trapped in the tree pit, which can have a detrimental effect on the newly planted tree's survival.

Setting the Tree into the Hole

Before placing the tree in the hole, measure to be sure the depth is correct. The development of tree roots in the top 12 inches of soil is critical, and planting the tree too deep will limit the availability of oxygen to the roots and impair their growth. Setting the root ball just 2 or 3 inches too deep can have a detrimental effect on root growth and development. Having to lift the tree in and out of the hole to adjust the depth can be damaging to the tree, particularly to balled and burlapped trees whose root balls can be damaged by unnecessary handling. See Figures 4.72 and 4.73.

The following steps should be taken in order to set the tree in the planting hole properly:

- The tree should be carefully transported to the planting hole. Lift it by the trunk or container, using straps or chains, and support the branches to prevent damage.
- The container for containerized trees should be removed. This can be made easier by gently pushing the container in on all sides and

Figure 4.72 The depth of the tree ball is measured.

Figure 4.73 The depth of the planting hole is checked and adjusted to the size of the tree ball.

sliding the container off. If the container does not come off easily, it may be necessary to cut it away. Tugging on the trunk while pulling on the container can only damage the tree. The tree should be checked for circling roots, and these should be cut or loosened away with a hand cultivator before placing the tree into the hole.

- Be sure the trunk flare is exposed.
- The tree should be carefully lowered into the planting hole, never dropped.
- Every tree has a "better" side. Position the tree so that it is facing in the direction that is most important. If the tree has the north side marked as the way it grew in the field, it is desirable to plant it with that same orientation.
- To avoid damaging the tree, make any necessary adjustments to the tree's position by lifting or turning from the bottom, not by turning, twisting, pulling, or pushing on the trunk.

Backfilling the Hole

The following steps should be taken to backfill the planting hole properly:

- Before backfilling the planting hole, make sure the tree is still straight.

- Backfill the planting hole with the original soil by working it in with the shovel and tamping it gently and firmly in layers, without compressing the soil too much. Excessive compression can reduce large pore space, which limits the availability of oxygen in the soil.
- Backfilling in layers and adding water to settle the soil will eliminate air pockets without reducing the large pore space.
- Soil peds are acceptable in the backfill.
- In clay soils, the soil should not be pulverized. This destroys the large pore spaces.
- There should be no backfill on the top of the root ball or covering the trunk flare.
- If a bermed ring is to be formed around the planting hole to capture water, the ring should be kept to approximately 3" in height. Consider creating the ring from mulch rather than soil, which may eventually end up covering the root ball area.

▶ **Soil amendments should only be added as needed. Generally, the original soil removed from the planting hole is considered more desirable as backfill for the tree.**

Specific procedures for planting balled and burlapped, containerized, and bare-root trees follow.

Planting a Balled and Burlapped Tree

Balled and burlapped trees are trees that have been field grown and dug from the growing field with the soil around the trunk of the trees kept intact. The root ball is typically wrapped in burlap and tied with twine to prevent the soil from loosening and falling away from the roots. The digging process typically only includes up to 10–20 percent of the tree's feeder roots within the ball, making the other steps in the planting process critical to a tree's survival.

In some cases, the root ball may be wrapped with plastic (usually green or tan) instead of the biodegradable burlap and/or with nylon rope (usually orange) instead of twine. These synthetic materials must be removed completely. Wire baskets used to keep the root balls of larger trees intact will also need to be cut away from the upper portions of the root ball.

It is important that the materials holding the root ball together not be removed until the tree is placed in the planting hole. It is important that the root ball remain tightly wrapped and in contact with the root system. Excessive handling, lifting, or moving of the tree should be avoided to minimize any loosening of the root ball soil and damage to the root system.

The following steps should be followed for a typical planting of a balled and burlapped tree:

- The tree should be carefully lowered into the planting hole by the root ball. See Figures 4.74 and 4.75.
- The trunk flare should be visible and set even with or slightly above the surrounding soil. If the trunk flare is not visible, soil should be carefully removed until it is uncovered. See Figure 4.76.
- The tree should be positioned so that its best side is facing the desired direction. The tree should be centered in the tree pit. See Figures 4.77 and 4.78.
- If the tree has been grafted, the inside curve above the graft should be positioned to face north in order to minimize winter bark injury.
- The tree should be adjusted to be straight and vertical. It is helpful to have another person looking from different angles guide this alignment. See Figure 4.79. When the tree is straight, some soil should be placed around the root ball to prevent shifting and keep the tree vertically aligned.
- With the tree properly positioned in the planting hole, the wrapping materials around the ball can be removed.

Figure 4.74   The tree is lifted by chains attached to the wire basket and held in place vertically by a strap wrapped around the trunk as it is moved to the planting hole.

Figure 4.75 The tree is carefully lowered in place and guided to the center of the planting hole by the planting crew.

Figure 4.76 The tree ball is checked for correct planting depth by laying a 2x4 across the top of the hole over the root ball. In this example, the top of the root ball is set slightly below the top of the pavers. This will result in the top of the tree ball being set an inch or so higher than the surrounding soil.

Figure 4.77 The tree is checked to be sure the trunk is centered in the planting hole.

Figure 4.78 Any slight adjustments to center the tree are made by lifting the tree slightly, and the tree is adjusted by leveraging a 2x4 against the root ball. Adjustments in the planting hole should never be made by rocking, pushing, or pulling against the tree trunk.

Figure 4.79 The tree is checked to be sure it is set vertical. It is helpful to have someone standing away from the tree to help judge when the tree is vertical. Once the tree is vertical, the planting hole should be partially back-filled so that the tree does not shift from vertical.

- As much of the twine should be removed as possible. See Figure 4.80. Twine takes longer to decompose than the burlap, and nylon or other synthetics never decompose, creating the potential for girdling of the tree. It is particularly important to remove any nylon wraps from around the trunk.
- If the tree ball is supported in a wire basket, as much of the wire bas-ket as possible should be removed, using heavy-duty wire cutters or a bolt cutter (Figure 4.81). Because the heavy-gauge metal wire can take 20–30 years to decompose, long-term root development can be affected, and there is the potential to have the wire girdle the roots. Although it is not necessary to remove the portion of the wire under the root ball, if the basket is sufficiently tapered, the bottom can be removed before lowering the tree into the planting hole with the taper still holding the root ball securely. If there is any question as to whether the bottom of the wire basket should be removed, it is best to keep it in place and remove as much of the wire as possible once the tree is set in the planting hole.
- The burlap should be untied at the trunk and cut away from approx-imately the top two-thirds of the root ball. Removing the burlap will facilitate a better interface between the soil from the root ball and the backfill. Until finally decomposing, burlap left in the planting hole

Figure 4.80 With the planting hole partially backfilled to keep the tree from shifting, the twine holding the burlap is cut away.

Figure 4.81 The wire basket is folded back and cut away as low as possible, using long-handled bolt cutters.

can wick away moisture that otherwise would be available to the tree roots. It is acceptable to leave some burlap around the bottom of the tree ball. Because the roots will tend to growth outward horizontally, any material left under the root ball will not be a critical factor in the tree's growth. Therefore, it is not worth disturbing the root ball or alignment of the tree to remove any of these materials from under the root ball. See Figures 4.82 and 4.83.

- Any synthetic wrapping should be removed completely or to the greatest extent possible. It will not decompose and can inhibit root growth.
- Use a multipronged hand cultivator to carefully loosen the root ball soil and gently free the small roots along its outer edge. Any circling roots discovered should be cut and removed.
- Remove any wrapping from around the trunk. Install tree stakes and backfill the tree pit. See Figures 4.84 and 4.85.

Planting a Container-Grown Tree

There is a trend toward growing trees directly in containers rather than ball and burlapping field-grown trees. They are grown in rich organic soils, and because they retain 100 percent of their root system when planted, there is less potential for transplant shock and greater potential for quicker establishment. They are generally available in

Figure 4.82   The burlap is untied and folded away.

Figure 4.83   The burlap is cut away from the top of the root ball and removed. The burlap should not be folded down into the planting hole. Roots are visible near the top of the root ball, and they are loosened as the burlap is being cut away.

Figure 4.84   The tree stakes are pounded into place outside the root ball.

Figure 4.85 The planting hole is backfilled in layers with the soil being gently but firmly tamped into place. The planting hole will be thoroughly watered before the final layer of soil is placed. The tree is set at a height so that the top of the root ball will be just above the surrounding soil and will not be covered with any of the planting mix backfill.

smaller sizes than balled and burlapped trees. In many ways, container-grown trees are easier to handle and plant.

The following steps should be followed for a typical planting of a container-grown tree:

- The tree should be moved and handled by the container only.
- The planting container should be removed by gently pushing in on all sides to loosen the soil from the edge of the container, and then sliding the container off. If the container does not come off easily, it may need to be cut off. Some thinner-walled and fiber containers make cutting an easier approach to removal.
- Container-grown tree roots should be examined carefully, as they often are in a dense network along the outside edge of the container (a tree in this condition is referred to as root bound or pot bound). See Figure 4.86. Minimally, these roots should be gently loosened with a multipronged hand cultivator without tearing them.
- Circling roots, particularly in the upper portions of the soil, will need to be cut. Making slices an inch or so deep from the surface of the soil to the bottom, in three or four places around the soil edges, will

Figure 4.86 Container-grown trees often have a dense network of roots formed along the outside edge of the root ball, against the container, that should be loosened.
Courtesy Dr. Ed Gilman, University of Florida.

break their growth pattern, encourage new root growth that will promote establishment, and prevent tree girdling.

- The tree should be carefully lowered into the planting hole by supporting the roots, not the trunk.
- The trunk flare should be visible and set even with or slightly above the surrounding soil. If the trunk flare is not visible, soil should be carefully removed until it is uncovered.
- The tree should be positioned so that its best side is facing the desired direction.
- If the tree has been grafted, the inside curve above the graft should be positioned to face north, in order to minimize winter bark injury.
- The tree should be adjusted to be straight and vertical. It is helpful to have another person looking from different angles guide this alignment. When the tree is straight, some soil should be placed around the roots to prevent shifting and keep the tree vertically aligned.
- Backfill the tree pit in layers, gently applying pressure to firm the soil and watering thoroughly to settle soil and eliminate air pockets.
- After the planting hole is backfilled, the soil should be firmed by gently applying foot pressure to the soil. Deeply soak the soil around the roots with a thorough, slow watering.

▶ Container trees are usually grown in well-drained soils and can therefore lose their moisture to the surrounding soil. This raises the importance of irrigation after planting.

Planting a Bare-Root Tree

Bare-root trees are dug in the late fall and have all the field soil removed from the roots. They are placed in cold storage to be shipped and planted as early as possible in the spring, while they are still dormant. Bare-root trees are less expensive than their balled and burlapped or container-grown counterparts. However, bare-root trees are generally only available in smaller sizes. It is critical that the roots not be allowed to dry out during the shipping or planting process.

The following steps should be followed for a typical planting of a bare-root tree:

- Bare-root trees should be planted as soon as possible after delivery. If this is not possible, they should be stored in a cool, dark or shady location. The bundles should remain wrapped, and the roots should not be allowed to dry or become frozen. If bare-root trees need to be stored for an extended period of time, they should be "heeled in" by covering the roots and lower stems with soil that must be kept moist. It should be noted that once buds begin to break, there is a significant decrease in survival rate.
- Before planting, unbundle the trees, examine the roots for damage or disease, and prune out any affected roots. Look to see that the roots are not crushed or torn. If the root ends are not cleanly cut, they should be recut, removing any damaged portions of the roots.
- There should be numerous healthy and moist fine roots. Some exceptionally long roots may need to be shortened. See Figure 4.87.
- Keep roots immersed in water to prevent drying. Mixing water with a polymer that is produced to hold moisture and dipping the roots into the mixture can coat the roots completely.
- A cone-shaped mound should be created in the center of the tree pit to help support the roots. The tree should be placed on the mound and the roots gently spread evenly around the planting hole. See Figure 4.88.
- Carefully backfill, gently lifting and lowering the tree to make sure the soil is filling in all around the roots without creating air pockets.
- Water in thoroughly with the planting hole about half-full, to further eliminate any air pockets that might cause roots to dry.
- The upper roots should be kept closer to the soil surface as the planting hole is backfilled.

Figure 4.87 Bare-root trees should have a well-developed fibrous root system.
Photo courtesy of Nina Bassuk, Urban Horticulture Institute, Cornell University.

Figure 4.88 Plant a bare-root tree on a cone-shaped mound, and spread the roots as they naturally would grow.
Photo courtesy of Nina Bassuk, Urban Horticulture Institute, Cornell University.

- After the planting hole is backfilled, the soil should be firmed by gently applying foot pressure to the soil. Deeply soak the soil around the roots with a thorough, slow watering.
- Be sure the tree is set to the correct depth and not planted too deep. A slight discoloration on the trunk will indicate the level of soil at which the tree was originally planted. See Figures 4.89 and 4.90.

▶ The tree needs to be supported as the planting hole is backfilled.

Staking and Guying Trees

In most situations, newly planted trees do not required staking or underground stabilization. The roots should be allowed to develop and strengthen naturally to secure the tree. Trees that are not staked at the time of planting tend to establish more quickly and develop stronger

Figure 4.89   A shovel is laid across the planting hole to check that the tree is being planted at the correct depth with the root collar at the surface.
Photo courtesy of Nina Bassuk, Urban Horticulture Institute, Cornell University.

Figure 4.90 As the tree is being backfilled, soil is worked into place and settled carefully by using the shovel handle.
Photo courtesy of Nina Bassuk, Urban Horticulture Institute, Cornell University.

trunk and root systems. Tree staking or underground stabilization is advisable in the following situations, where movement of the root ball can break new roots growing into the backfill (see Figures 4.91 through 4.95):

- Locations where the tree will be subjected to high winds.
- Relatively sandy soils that may not offer sufficient support.
- Very large trees with top-heavy crowns.
- High-traffic areas (to protect the tree against soil compaction or vandalism).
- Locations where trees may need protection against damage by lawn mowers.

▶ **Bare-root and smaller container-grown trees are likely to benefit from initial staking.**

Staking should be loose enough to allow some tree sway. Flexible tree ties allow for some movement (See Figure 4.95). If only one stake is used, it should be positioned on the side of the prevailing wind.

Support staking and guying should be removed after the first year. If the plant stands erect, remove the stake. If not, repeat the process approximately every few months until sufficient trunk strength develops. Leaving small branches along the lower trunk will also help the

Figure 4.91 Tree staking with two vertical stakes, traditional wire, and rubber hose to protect trunk. One stake should be set on the side of the prevailing winds and the other 180 degrees opposite.

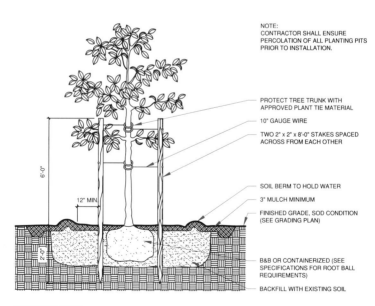

NOTE:
CONTRACTOR SHALL ENSURE
PERCOLATION OF ALL PLANTING PITS
PRIOR TO INSTALLATION.

PROTECT TREE TRUNK WITH
APPROVED PLANT TIE MATERIAL

10" GAUGE WIRE

TWO 2" x 2" x 8'-0" STAKES SPACED
ACROSS FROM EACH OTHER

SOIL BERM TO HOLD WATER

3" MULCH MINIMUM

FINISHED GRADE, SOD CONDITION
(SEE GRADING PLAN)

B&B OR CONTAINERIZED (SEE
SPECIFICATIONS FOR ROOT BALL
REQUIREMENTS)

BACKFILL WITH EXISTING SOIL

6'-0"

12" MIN.

2'-0"

TWO VERTICAL STAKES

Figure 4.92 Vertical staking system detail.
Source: Hopper, *Landscape Architecture Graphic Standards.* Copyright John Wiley & Sons, Inc., 2007.

Figure 4.93 Tree with guy wires and rubber hose attaching to the first group of branches. Guy wires are barely visible and should be marked with high-visibility flagging to prevent injury.

trunk increase in diameter and strength. These branches can be removed once the tree can support itself.

▶ Any stakes supplied with the trees should be removed. The purpose of these stakes is to minimize damage during tree transport. If left in place, they can be detrimental to trunk and lower branches.

Tree Wrapping

Wrapping of the tree trunk is only a consideration in northern climates, to protect trees with sensitive bark against sun-scalding during the first few winters after planting. The tree wrap should start at the bottom of the trunk and wrap up to the second branch, where it should be secured with a tack. The tree wrap needs to be removed in the spring to prevent disease or insect infestation.

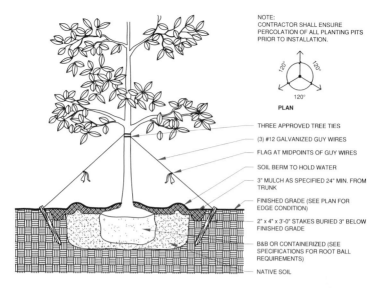

NOTE:
CONTRACTOR SHALL ENSURE PERCOLATION OF ALL PLANTING PITS PRIOR TO INSTALLATION.

120°   120°

120°

PLAN

THREE APPROVED TREE TIES

(3) #12 GALVANIZED GUY WIRES

FLAG AT MIDPOINTS OF GUY WIRES

SOIL BERM TO HOLD WATER

3" MULCH AS SPECIFIED 24" MIN. FROM TRUNK

FINISHED GRADE (SEE PLAN FOR EDGE CONDITION)

2" x 4" x 3'-0" STAKES BURIED 3" BELOW FINISHED GRADE

B&B OR CONTAINERIZED (SEE SPECIFICATIONS FOR ROOT BALL REQUIREMENTS)

NATIVE SOIL

THREE GUY WIRE STAKING SYSTEM

Figure 4.94 Detail using #12 twisted galvanized wire for guying. Guy wires should be equally spaced around the tree at a 60 degree angle to the ground. The detail shows the use of wooden stakes as deadmen to anchor the guy wires, although there are several commercial products available that perform this function.
Source: Hopper, *Landscape Architecture Graphic Standards.* Copyright John Wiley & Sons, Inc., 2007.

Figure 4.95 Polypropylene tree tie straps are replacing the traditional wire and hose for tree staking. They have high tensile strength and are flexible enough to allow some tree sway, which will encourage the tree to develop a healthy trunk and root system. They are easily secured with a traditional knot. They eliminate the risk of having the wire cut through the rubber hose and damage the tree. They should be tied to the tree to eliminate excessive slack but not so tight as to be under tension.

Figure 4.96 These tree stakes and polypropylene tree tie straps were left in place too long. The tree has grown over the straps and they cannot be removed.

Tree Pruning

If high-quality trees are purchased, little pruning should be required. Compensatory pruning to balance root loss is not required and may be detrimental to root growth. Initial pruning at planting should be limited to:

- Removing damaged or broken branches.
- Cutting back or removing co-dominant leaders.
- Removing clustered or competing branches.
- Removing branches with bark inclusion.

The top of the tree or leader should never be pruned, as this can change the characteristic growth habit of the tree. There is no reason to treat cuts with any wound paints. This does not help; it slows the healing process.

Mulch

A layer of mulch reduces moisture evaporation from the soil, which can promote root growth. As mulch decays, organic material is added to the soil that provides an inviting environment for earthworms and beneficial microorganisms.

▶ Hardwood mulch can raise soil pH, which is less desirable for conifers, while conifer mulch can lower pH, which is less desirable for hardwoods. Use conifer mulch for conifers and hardwood mulch for hardwoods.

A three-inch layer of organic mulch such as bark or wood chips can:

- Provide weed control.
- Protect soil from compaction.
- Retain moisture.
- Moderate soil temperature changes.
- Minimize growth of weeds and turf that can compete for moisture and nutrients.

▶ Deeper layers of mulch (greater than 3 inches) can reduce the availability of oxygen in the soil.

Mulch should not cover the trunk at the base of the tree. This could cause bark decay. Leave an area of 12 inches or more clear of mulch around the trunk, with only a thin layer (if any) over the root ball itself. Ideally, the mulch should cover the entire area under the drip line, and if possible twice the diameter for a new tree. The area of mulch around the tree minimizes trunk damage from mowers, as there is no need for them to get that close to the tree. See Figures 4.97 through 4.99.

Where called for (typically, where trees will be watered with a hose or bucket delivering a high volume of water over a short period of time), consider creating a bermed ring around the planting hole from mulch rather than soil. Soil has a tendency to end up covering the root ball over time.

Watering

In addition to initial heavy and deep watering at the time of planting, newly planted trees should be watered at least once a week during the first growing season and more often during dry periods of summer. Regular deep watering that penetrates a minimum depth of at least 12 inches into the soil is more beneficial in promoting root growth than more frequent lighter applications of water. This is particularly important with bare-root planted trees.

Figure 4.97 Trees properly mulched.

Figure 4.98 Mulch should be pulled away from the tree trunk, with only a very thin layer of mulch placed over the root ball.

Figure 4.99 "Volcano mulch" piled onto the trunk—this should never be done.

▶ **Well-drained soils dry out quicker and may need additional water during dry periods.**

Drip irrigation bags (see Figure 4.100) that are loosely tied around the trunk are another approach to ensure the tree is getting enough water. Over the course of the day, the drip irrigation bags slowly release water that penetrates deep into the soil. Drip irrigation bags should be checked and filled every day.

There are also a variety of commercially available polymers that can be added to the backfill to absorb moisture from the soil and release it to the tree roots if the soil dries out.

The soil should be kept moist but not saturated. Overwatering can fill voids and deprive the roots of oxygen. The leaves turn yellow (which usually prompts additional watering) and then fall off.

▶ **Keep turf, groundcover, and weeds away from the root ball. They will compete with the tree for moisture.**

Fertilizer

Fertilizer should not be applied indiscriminately at the time of planting. It can have adverse effects. Before considering a fertilizer application at time of planting, evaluate soil conditions for factors such as:

- Nitrogen (N)
- Phosphorus (P)
- Potassium (K)
- Organic content
- pH
- Soil type
- Drainage

Figure 4.100 Drip irrigation bags are helpful in applying slow, deep watering to newly planted trees.

Trees planted in difficult soil situations, such as some urban environments, may require the soil to be amended. However, the amendments must be a balanced supplement that responds to the existing soil analysis.

▶ An initial "one size fits all" standard application of fertilizers or other soil amendments should be avoided.

Newly planted trees do experience some inherent root loss and related stress. Although mycorrhizal fungi exist naturally in the soil, an application of mycorrhizal fungi can stimulate root growth. Time-release fertilizer packets that release a controlled amount of nutrients over a multi-year period can benefit trees long after the initial planting, and are a better alternative to any standard application of a quick-release fertilizer.

▶ Products are available that are customized to specific soil conditions and specific trees. A detailed analysis of the existing soil characteristics is a critical first step in making the right choice of any amendments to the existing soil.

Practices to Avoid

- Avoid damage to the root ball. Handle trees carefully by lifting and moving them by the root ball or container, never by the trunk or branches.
- Do not leave any synthetic wraps around the root ball or tree trunk; they must be removed completely.
- Avoid having layers of burlap wick away moisture or hamper new root growth. Cut burlap away from the top of the root ball and remove it from the planting hole, rather than just folding it down around the root ball.
- Avoid the most common mistake of planting a tree too deep. The root flare must not be buried in the soil. It is always better to err on the side of planting a tree an inch or two higher than to risk bark decay caused by a buried root flare.
- Avoid having the soil around the tree dry out. Newly planted trees need to be watered regularly for at least a growing season after planting. Irrigation bags can be helpful in keeping the soil deeply watered.
- Do not backfill the tree pit with removed grass or other vegetation.
- Do not apply a layer of mulch deeper than 3 inches; it can reduce the availability of oxygen to the roots. Avoid mulch volcanoes (the misguided practice of piling mulch high onto the trunk) at all costs. Use only a thin layer of mulch over the tree ball to allow water and air to penetrate to the root ball more easily.
- To avoid trunk decay and bark and root diseases, do not place mulch in direct contact with the tree trunk. Roots can grow up into the mulch around the trunk, which can result in girdling roots that can kill the tree.
- Use caution when considering mulching on wet soil; it can keep the soil excessively wet.
- Do not use plastic sheeting under the mulch for weed control. Plastic should not be used because it interferes with the exchange of gases between soil and air, and prevents water infiltration, inhibiting root growth. Use a geotextile landscape fabric that is porous and allows water and air to pass through freely.
- Do not prune without a specific reason to remove any branches. Reducing leaf area places additional stress on a newly planted tree.
- Do not automatically add fertilizer at planting. Fertilizer is unnecessary unless warranted by a detailed soil analysis.

Evergreen and Conifer Tree Selection and Planting

Description

Evergreen trees retain most of their foliage, typically needles, through the winter season. Therefore, they can provide year-round interest, color, texture, and environmental benefits.

Conifers are gymnosperms that bear cones. Although not specifically defined as evergreen or having needles, this is most often the case.

Evergreen trees will drop needles on an annual basis, which is a natural process. Different species retain their needles for varying lengths of time (anywhere from two to over ten years) before dropping the oldest needles, generally those located closer to the trunk.

Assessing Site Conditions

If the information is not already available, a soil sample should be taken and tested for pH, nutrient levels, and organic content. This information is important for deciding what fertilizer or soil amendments, if any, need to be added at the time of planting.

Although many of the site assessment factors for planting deciduous trees apply to evergreens and conifers, the following are typical of these trees:

- Most evergreen trees and conifers prefer full sun; some will tolerate partial shade.
- Most evergreen trees prefer an acid soil, a pH lower than 7. If the site has a higher pH, limit choices to evergreen trees or conifers that are more tolerant of this condition.
- There are evergreen trees and conifers that are suited to a broad range of different soil types; match plant choices to the site's soil type.
- Evergreen trees and conifers can have a broad range of water preferences; match water requirements to existing conditions, and group evergreen trees and conifers with similar water needs together.

Trees planted on slopes will likely receive less water than those planted on flatter sites.

- In addition to choosing plants from the applicable hardiness zone, look for possible microclimate conditions that can affect evergreen trees and conifers, such as exposed locations subject to high winds.
- Be aware of conditions that create broad temperature fluctuations in the course of a day, such as a warm, sunny, sheltered location that can quickly plunge below freezing when the sun is blocked or sets. These temperature extremes call for hardy evergreen trees and conifers that are not susceptible to winter dieback or burn.

Check on the location of underground utility lines before digging. Many utility lines are not buried as deep as the required excavation depth for the tree pit.

For additional information, see "Soil Assessment" in Chapter 1, and the related topics in this chapter:

- "Soil Amendments"
- "Site Considerations and Tree Selection"
- "Deciduous Tree Planting"

Acceptable Practices

Plant Selection

The criteria for selection of evergreen trees and conifers are largely the same criteria outlined in the other sections of this chapter for deciduous trees. Because evergreen trees and conifers retain their foliage during the winter, the following are unique design characteristics to consider during plant selection:

- Evergreen trees and conifers can provide year-round screening of undesirable views or frame desirable views and vistas.
- Evergreen trees and conifers can be planted in groups to block prevailing winter winds.
- Evergreen trees and conifers have a variety of color, textures, sizes, and shapes that can perform a number of design functions in the landscape.

Planting

The procedures outlined in the section "Deciduous Tree Planting" are applicable to the planting of evergreen trees and conifers. The same emphasis on the preparation of the planting hole, setting the tree into the hole, and backfilling should be observed.

Evergreen trees and conifers are best planted in the fall or early spring. Planting in the fall allows the trees to become acclimated to the new site conditions with less stress while their need for water and sunlight lessens as they prepare for dormancy during winter. Already planted, they are ready to benefit from spring conditions as soon as the ground begins to thaw. Planting in the early spring allows the trees to become acclimated and benefit from the spring rains before the drier, hotter conditions of summer stress their systems.

▶ Planting evergreen trees and conifers in the summer places a great deal of stress on the trees. Special attention should be paid to irrigation and keeping the soil moist if planting at this time of year is unavoidable.

Care and Maintenance

Fertilizer should not be applied indiscriminately at the time of planting. It can have adverse effects. Before considering a fertilizer application at time of planting, soil conditions need to be evaluated for presence of nutrients and soil pH. Evergreen trees or conifers that exhibit a loss of a healthy green color may benefit from the application of a balanced fertilizer or a fertilizer that balances the nutrient content of the existing soil based on test results.

Watering is critical during the first year after planting. In hot, dry weather, water should be applied slowly and in sufficient quantity to allow for deep penetration into the soil, which will encourage deep root growth. Deep watering in the fall before the ground freezes is important in preventing drying and winter burn. In areas that do not freeze, evergreen trees and conifers will benefit from additional watering during the winter months, which can typically be dry and windy.

Some species of evergreen trees and conifers may require initial protection from winter sun and wind. Be aware of where these species may be subjected to these conditions, and call for adequate protection during the winter months.

Evergreen trees and conifers generally benefit from a layer of mulch to help keep the soil moist and moderate temperature change. A layer of organic matter will replicate the conditions of the forest where the evergreen's and conifer's own needles provide a natural mulch, and other forest material provides organic matter.

Practices to Avoid

- Avoid planting sensitive evergreen trees or conifers in microclimate conditions to which they are not suited.
- Do not add fertilizer at planting unless warranted by a detailed soil analysis.
- Avoid summer planting of evergreen trees and conifers. The heat and dryness of summer place undue stress on these trees, adding to the typical transplant shock a plant experiences.

References

ALSO IN THIS BOOK

See also "Soil Overview," "Soil Assessment," and "Designed Soil Mixes" in Chapter 1.

OTHER RESOURCES

American Association of Nurserymen (AAN). *American Standard for Nursery Stock* (ANSI Z60.1-1996). The American Association of Nurserymen, Washington, DC: AAN, 1996.

American Nursery & Landscape Association (ANLA), formerly the American Association of Nurserymen, 1250 I Street N.W., Suite 500, Washington, DC 20005. Phone: 202-789-2900, Fax: 202-789-1893.

Gillman, Jeff, and Carl Rosen, Tree Fertilization: A Guide for Fertilizing New and Established Trees in the Landscape. www.extension.umn .edu/distribution/horticulture/ dg7410.html.

Gilman, Dr. Ed. *Illustrated Guide to Pruning*, Third Edition. Florence, KY. Delmar Publishers, 2011.

Good, George L., and Richard Weir III. *The Cornell Guide for Planting and Maintaining Trees and Shrubs*. Ithaca, NY: Cornell Cooperative Extension, 2005.

Hopper, Leonard. *Landscape Architectural Graphic Standards*. Hoboken, NJ: John Wiley & Sons, Inc., 2007.

International Society of Arboriculture. www.isa-arbor.com.

National Invasive Species Council, www.invasivespecies.gov, accessed 2010.

National Plant Board. *Safeguarding American Plant Resources*. Washington, DC: USDA, July 1999.

Professional Landcare Network (PLANET), 950 Herndon Parkway, Suite 450, Herndon, VA 20170. Phone: 703-736-9666 or 1-800-395-2522,

Fax: 703-736-9668. PLANET was created on January 1, 2005, when the Associated Landscape Contractors of America (ALCA) and the Professional Lawn Care Association of America (PLCAA) joined together. Of particular interest is PLANET's *Guide to Interior Landscape Specifications*, 5th edition, 2003.

Trowbridge, Peter, and Nina Bassuk. *Trees in the Urban Landscape*. Hoboken, NJ: John Wiley & Sons, Inc., 2004.

United States Department of Agriculture. www.usda.gov.

University of Florida. Environmental Horticulture. http://hort.ifas.ufl .edu.

Urban, James. *Up By Roots*. Champaign, IL: International Society of Arboriculture, 2008.

Chapter 5

Shrubs and Groundcovers

Shrub Selection and Planting

Shrub Selection and Planting

Description

Shrub planting can serve a number of different aesthetic, environmental, and psychological functions in the landscape. The selection of appropriate shrubs should match function with the existing or proposed conditions of the site.

Assessing Site Conditions

The conditions of the existing site and the way any proposed site design changes will affect those conditions are important areas to assess before selecting a plant that will survive, thrive, and serve the function for which it has been selected over the long term. Some important site conditions that should be noted as part of an initial site assessment include:

- Soil type
- Drainage
- Water availability
- Sunlight
- Winds
- Slope
- Relationship of the new planting to other site features
- Existing vegetation and ecosystems that need to be protected

Soil assessment is the most critical part of the site assessment process. If the information is not already available, a soil sample should be taken and tested for pH, nutrient levels, and organic content. This information is important in deciding what fertilizer or soil amendments, if any, need to be added at the time of planting. Soil texture should be determined, as it has a close relationship to drainage. Soil bulk density should be assessed, particularly looking for evidence of compaction and damage to the soil's structure.

Soil drainage should be checked by performing a percolation test. Shrub roots need oxygen to develop and grow. In poorly drained soils, pooling water fills the voids in the soil structure, preventing oxygen from reaching the roots. Sandy soils have large pore spaces but poor water retention capacity. Depending on the results of the percolation test, the soil may need to be amended before shrub planting. Shrub selection should be matched with water availability. Shrubs that tolerate wet conditions should be selected for low-lying areas or poorly drained soils. Shrubs planted on slopes may have less water available to them. Drought-tolerant shrubs should be selected for areas where there may not be rainfall for extended periods, or where the soil is particularly sandy. It is advisable to group shrubs with similar water requirements together, to prevent incompatibility.

Shrubs are available that tolerate shade, partial shade, and full sun. Assess the sunlight conditions of the existing site as well as any changes the proposed site development may cause.

The shrub planting location's relationship to other site features, such as trees, buildings, fences, and walks, among others, will factor into plant selection. In addition to assessing existing conditions, evaluate the changes that any proposed design may create. Consider where existing or proposed trees will cast shade, and select appropriate shade-tolerant shrubs. Shrubs should be selected whose mature spread will leave a compatible distance from the fence, walk, or building where they are being planted. Shrubs exposed to prevailing winds will tend to dry more quickly. Some shrubs require protective shade to prevent leaf scorch or desiccation. The south sides of a building will generally be a more sheltered microclimate, which can allow the planting of less hardy shrubs, although the warming winter sun can cause damage to the bark of some plants. The warming sun during the day and the extreme cold of the winter nights can affect the hardiness and survival of sensitive shrubs.

The site assessment should consider protection of existing plant communities, diversity, and wildlife habitat. Valuable existing vegetation should be preserved and integrated into the design whenever possible. In addition to protecting these valuable resources, the assessment should look for opportunities for restoration and improvement.

Invasive plant species that threaten the existing ecosystem should be identified, and a plan to manage or eliminate them should be developed and implemented before any new construction or planting is undertaken.

See these related topics for additional information:

- "Soil Overview," in Chapter 1
- "Soil Assessment," in Chapter 1
- "Soil Amendments," in Chapter 4

Acceptable Practices

Selection

Shrubs can provide a varied number of important design functions:

- Tall evergreen shrubs can provide a year-round screen.
- Shrubs can reduce energy consumption and urban heat island effects.
- Selection of shrubs or combinations of shrubs can provide interest (flower, berries, leaf color, bark color, branching, fragrance) in all four seasons, not just a flowery show for a few weeks in the spring.
- Shrubs can be positioned to create intimate spaces or hidden gardens.
- Shrubs increase the psychological size of an open space.
- Shrubs add interest to blank building walls.
- Shrubs can be used to create a focal point or frame a view.

There is increased interest in selecting native plants that are naturally adapted to local soils and climates. Once established, native plants result in lower costs, have fewer problems, and require less care and maintenance than nonnative plants. All shrubs selected should be noninvasive species that are nursery grown or legally harvested from another site.

Where applicable, shrub criteria should include selection of fire-resistant plant species planted with appropriate spacing in locations that are in compliance with local fire management practices.

Planting Time of Year

Generally, early spring and fall are the best times of the year to plant shrubs. Planting in early spring allows the plant to get established before shoot growth and the dry, hot periods of summer. Planting in fall gives the plant time to get established before the dormant season of winter (in some geographical areas) as well as the full spring period when the ground begins to thaw. Some specific planting guidelines for planting times are:

- Bare-root material must be planted early in the spring before buds break and growth begins.

- Container-grown plant material can be planted any time of the growing season. Because all of the plant's roots are within the container, transplant shock is minimized.
- Balled and burlapped plant material can be planted any time of the growing season. Because the digging and balling process removes some of the plant's roots, additional watering and care are required if planting during the late spring or summer.

▶ Any evergreen shrubs, particularly broadleaf evergreens, need to be planted early enough in the fall to allow the roots to get established before the winter.

Planting

Be sure the shrubs are well watered in their root balls or containers, and that bare-root material is being properly stored before planting. The planting hole should be dug at a depth equal to the height of the root ball or container, and minimally two to three times as wide (see Figure 5.1). Do not dig the planting hole deeper or fill the bottom with loose soil, which can result in the plant sinking lower or leaning as this loose soil becomes compacted over time. The width of the hole is a critical factor for the depth of root growth and development. Scarify the sides of the planting hole to create a transitional interface to help

Figure 5.1   The planting hole should be dug at least twice as wide as the container and at the proper depth.

Figure 5.2 Scarify the sides of the planting hole with the shovel to improve the interface and promote root growth beyond the planting hole.

the roots penetrate to the soil beyond the planting hole (see Figure 5.2). Planting hole sides that are smoothed and slickened by a shovel can create a barrier that will inhibit root growth. The bottom of the hole should be moistened before planting.

The following steps should be taken in order to plant a shrub properly:

- For a balled and burlapped shrub, place the shrub into the hole and check that the top of the root ball is level with the surrounding soil level. Remove any twine, and cut back the top third of the burlap. The root ball should be handled carefully and disturbed as little as possible. Any plastic wrapping must be removed completely.
- For a container shrub, remove the plant from the container by turning it upside down and gently tapping on the bottom and sides of the container. The plant should slide right out. If not, the container sides should be gently squeezed and tapped from the bottom again, until the plant slides out easily (see Figures 5.3 and 5.4). Inspect the condition of the roots. Often they will be matted and circling the perimeter. If this is the case, use a hand cultivator or other tool to gently loosen the roots before placing the shrub into the planting hole.. The more tightly root bound the root ball is, the more the roots should be loosened and disturbed (see Figure 5.5). Shrubs in fiber pots should have the tops of the pot broken away so that

Figure 5.3 Gently pushing down around the container perimeter will loosen the plant from the container.

Figure 5.4 When the container is turned upside down, the shrub should slide out easily.

Figure 5.5   Roots matted along the outside a container-grown shrub will need to be loosened and disturbed using a hand cultivator.

root growth will not be inhibited. Place the shrub into the planting hole with the top of the root ball level with the surrounding soil (Figure 5.6).

- For bare-root shrubs, make a mound in the middle of the hole and spread the roots in the planting hole so that they are evenly and naturally spaced. Add soil and backfill the hole, then water thoroughly to settle the soil and eliminate air pockets, gently firming the soil until the soil is at the correct level.

▶ **In sites that have poor drainage, consider planting the shrub an inch or two higher than the surrounding soil level, and slightly slope the backfill away from the plant.**

Backfill the planting hole with the soil that was removed, gently but firmly compacting the soil, as shown in Figures 5.7 and 5.8. Clods of soil should be broken up, as they can create air pockets. With the planting hole about half-full, water to settle the soil and eliminate air pockets. Unless soil tests have determined that any soil amendments are necessary, backfilling with the original soil is recommended. The planting hole should not be completely modified with new soil or soil amendments, as this can prevent roots from spreading into the existing soil beyond the hole, and can create a problem by letting water accumulate at the bottom of the planting hole and preventing it from

Figure 5.6 Place the shrub into the planting hole and check for correct depth. The root ball of the shrub should be set level with or slightly higher than the adjacent soil level.

Figure 5.7 Backfill about halfway, gently tamp soil, and water.

Figure 5.8 The planting hole should be completely backfilled, the soil gently tamped, creating a shallow basin, and watered. Add soil if the watering creates a drop in soil level.

draining away into the adjacent soil. Fertilizer should never be added to the backfill or placed into the planting hole at time of planting.

▶ If the shrub planting is on a slope, forming a berm on the downhill side of the slope will help catch runoff and direct it down to the plant's roots.

Planting shrubs in massed beds rather than individual holes provides the plants' roots with a larger area in which to develop before having to penetrate into the soil beyond. The shrub bed should be carefully backfilled in a similar manner to filling individual planting holes, gently firming soil and watering to eliminate air pockets.

After planting, the newly planted shrub(s) should be watered, eliminating air pockets and keeping the plant roots moist. If the soil level drops after watering, some additional soil or mulch can be added to bring the level back up to the top of the root ball. The soil should be kept moist during the first transitional year, especially during periods of drought. A temporary low ring of soil around the planting hole will help catch water and direct it down to the root zone during this initial period of establishment.

Adding a two- or three-inch layer of mulch will help the soil retain moisture, moderate temperature changes, and help control weed

Figure 5.9 A layer of mulch placed over a porous landscape fabric helps keep weeds down and soil moist. No mulch should be spread directly over the root ball.

growth that could compete with the shrub for water and nutrients. See Figure 5.9. A porous landscape fabric placed under the mulch layer ensures that weeds will not penetrate, but that water and air will still be allowed to pass through freely.

▶ Plastic sheets should not be used under mulch.

Maintenance

Watering

For the first weeks after planting, shrubs require routine watering and should be monitored closely to prevent the soil from drying and the plant wilting. Many initial problems experienced after planting are attributable to improper watering. During hot, dry periods, this may mean the plants need to be watered daily. The greatest demand for watering will be during a plant's first summer. Shrubs should be watered right up until the ground begins to freeze. Slower applications of water, which allow deep penetration into the soil, will encourage desirable deep root growth. Shrubs in a well-drained sandy soil will require more watering than those planted in a clayey soil. As the roots develop, watering may be done less frequently.

▶ Short, frequent watering should be avoided, as it promotes development of a shallow root system that makes the shrub more susceptible to environmental stresses.

Fertilizer

Fertilizer is generally not needed for newly planted shrubs unless a soil test reveals a specific deficiency. Over time, organic material worked into the soil or a surface application of a slow-release balanced fertilizer may benefit the shrubs planted.

Avoid applying fertilizers with nitrogen in the early fall, as this may stimulate new shoot growth that may not harden off in time before winter. Consider fertilizers with phosphorous and potassium, which help plants prepare for winter.

Pruning

Newly planted shrubs rarely need pruning. As the shrub grows, some minor pruning of small branches may be necessary, to allow more light into the shrub canopy, to cut rogue branches that have grown unusually long, or to remove dead branches. Any major pruning should be done in the late winter or early spring before the branch twigs begin to show new growth. The exception would be flowering shrubs that generally should be pruned after they flower, so that they can set new flower buds for the following year.

Regular pruning helps maintain the desired plant form, promotes plant health, and stimulates new growth. It should be viewed as a process that takes place over several seasons, not as a one-time radical procedure. A shrub's specific growth habit, flowering, or fruiting characteristics must be considered before pruning; not all shrubs should be pruned in the same way. Basic pruning skills and proper tools are required.

Some specific pruning techniques and objectives are:

- Heading involves cutting back small branches just above the bud or branch node. This type of pruning helps maintain the plant's form and encourages new growth below the cut.
- Thinning involves cutting a branch (usually the oldest or tallest) at its place of origin, from a main stem or lateral branch. This type of pruning creates a more open plant form that has improved air circulation, discourages fungal diseases, and encourages side branch growth without pushing excessive top growth.
- Renewal pruning is gradual pruning done on an annual basis that removes select oldest or tallest branches and shortens longer branches to maintain a shrub's desired form.

- Rejuvenating pruning is performed on shrubs that have become overgrown and require the removal of $1/3$ of the tallest and oldest branches (usually at or close to ground level), to encourage the growth and development of new shoot growth. Returning a shrub's shape and form may require two or three years, in order to avoid shocking the plant.

▶ **Pruning should preserve the natural shrub form and framework. Proper shrub selection should not require extensive pruning to keep its desired size, shape, form, and design function in the landscape. A properly pruned shrub should not look as if it has been pruned at all.**

Winter Care

Evergreen shrubs can suffer from winter burn caused by the effects of the wind and sun. A screen of burlap staked to the south to protect against the sun and to the north/northwest to protect against the winter winds (or whichever direction the prevailing winter winds come from) will help to prevent shrub damage. It is best to select the hardiest of shrubs for locations that are exposed to these winter conditions and to locate more sensitive shrubs in sheltered locations.

In some areas, winter damage from animals may be a problem. This may call for fencing or other barriers to prevent animals from damaging shrubs. Animal repellents that are sprayed onto branches and foliage are available if physical barriers are not practical. Repellent may need repeat applications during the course of the winter.

Practices to Avoid

- Avoid incompatibility between shrubs and planting location by performing a thorough site assessment and soil test.
- Avoid planting broadleaf evergreens in the late fall; they will not have time to acclimate before winter, increasing the chance that they may not survive or may suffer extensive damage.
- Do not dig the planting hole deeper than the root ball or fill the bottom with loose soil; this can result in the plant sinking lower or leaning as this loose soil becomes compacted. If the hole is dug too deep, backfill and compact the soil to provide the shrub with a firm base.

- Avoid backfilling the planting hole with completely modified or new soil. This can create drainage problems and inhibit root development into the adjacent soil.
- Do not mix fertilizer in with the backfill; this can burn and kill the shrub roots.
- Avoid air pockets; firm and water the soil in layers as the shrub is being backfilled.
- Do not place plastic sheets below mulch; it prevents water penetration and air exchange that are critical to root development.
- Avoid frequent, superficial waterings after planting. This encourages roots to develop closer to the surface, where they can be more vulnerable to periods of drought and early freezing temperatures.
- Avoid nitrogen applications to evergreen shrubs in late fall. It can encourage new shoot growth that will not have adequate time to harden off before winter.

References

ALSO IN THIS BOOK

See "Deciduous Tree Planting" in Chapter 4 of this book, as many of the same principles that apply to tree planting also apply to shrub planting.

OTHER RESOURCES

Hopper, Leonard J. *Landscape Architectural Graphic Standards*. Hoboken, NJ: John Wiley & Sons, Inc., 2007.
Sustainable Sites Initiative, www.sustainablesites.org/.

Chapter 6

Turf

Considerations and Objectives

Considerations and Objectives

Description

Overview

Turf can be an integral part of a landscape. It can provide functional, aesthetic, and recreational benefit. Initial planning for a turf area includes consideration of environmental and cultural requirements. The quality of turf area is directly related to proper preparation and establishment. This includes the following factors:

- Selecting the appropriate seed for the region and purpose.
- Soil preparation.
- Planting.
- Care and maintenance during the establishment period.

Introduction to Environmental Perspectives

Following is an overview of environmental perspectives.

Grasses and the Ecosystem

Turf areas provide an outdoor surface that is relatively safe, resilient, easily trafficked, and aesthetically pleasing. But turf areas must be managed to persist, and the level of management required is influenced by regional succession patterns, site conditions, and grass species. Grasses are often aggressive, serving as pioneer species. Exotic grasses often compete effectively against native herbaceous materials, and establishment of turf in and near forests can be damaging to the forest ecosystem.

Humid Regions

In humid regions where succession favors forest landscapes, grasslands are temporary, occurring in disturbed areas. To maintain grass landscapes in these regions, management practices must repeatedly reset the succession clock.

Dry-Temperate Regions

In dryer regions, grasslands and savannas are favored and persist for extensive periods. Fire is responsible for maintaining grassland quality and diversity. In these regions, grass landscapes are most easily maintained when composed of diverse native species.

Arid Regions

In arid regions, some native grasses occur, but plant density can be low. Human landscapes tend to prefer high-density turfs, which require greater water inputs than natural precipitation will support. Minimize the use of turf in arid regions to conserve water and maintain the natural regional ecosystem.

Hybrids versus Natives

Most turfgrasses used in North America today are hybrids developed from exotic species and selected for low cutting height. Low-cut turfs have similarly short root structures. By comparison, many native North American grasses grow tall and have correspondingly deep root structures. Generally, the taller grass is allowed to grow, the deeper its roots penetrate. Greater root depth reduces irrigation and fertilizer requirements, reduces storm water runoff, and improves infiltration characteristics, soil quality, and drought resistance.

Lawns were initially composed of multiple species, but following the advent of selective herbicides, they have been more typically defined by a hybrid turfgrass monoculture. Monocultures are by nature unsustainable and require regular management to maintain them. When actively and properly managed, turfgrass monocultures do produce relatively uniform lawns. Mixtures of native grasses and some mixtures of hybrid turfgrasses may reduce management requirements.

Expectation of a weed-free uniform turf is unrealistic, even if the turf is composed of native grass. Some percentage of weeds will always occur. Turf uniformity is affected by a number of conditions that influence the level of competition between a turfgrass and other grasses and forbs: shade, moisture levels, soil composition, soil compaction, nutrient levels, wind patterns, use characteristics, and management practices.

Definitions of Key Terms

- *Lawn* — A turf area commonly kept between ¹⁄₂ inch and 4 inches in height.

- *Greensward* — A mixed grass and wildflower area kept between 5 and 7 inches in height.
- *Meadow* — A mixed grass and wildflower area often exceeding 12 inches in height.
- *Blend* — A combination of multiple varieties of the same grass species.
- *Mixture* — A combination of multiple grass species.
- *Top-dressing* — A surface application to existing turf, usually composed of sand or soil.
- *Overseeding* — Applying a cool-season temporary grass to existing warm-season turf.
- *Sprigging* — The establishment of turf by planting live vegetative stolons or rhizomes.
- *Plugging* — The establishment of turf by planting regularly spaced sod chunks.

Grass Growth Habit Types

Grasses can be divided into four growth habit types (see Figure 6.1):

- Bunch-type grasses tend to form small clumps and spread actively by seed.
- Stoloniferous grasses spread by surface stolons. Nodes along the stolon root into the soil and start new grass shoots.
- Rhizomatous grasses spread by lateral rhizomes under the soil surface. Nodes on the rhizome send new grass shoots up through the surface of the soil.
- Rhizomatous stoloniferous grasses spread by both means, and stolons may move both above- and belowground.

Assessing Site Conditions

Overview of Turf Planning Objectives

Choosing to specify turf is just like any other design choice made in the planning process. The fact that turf is ubiquitous in the human landscape does not necessarily mean that it is the right or best choice. The program, the environmental conditions, and the long-term management capabilities of the client all must be evaluated before selecting turf.

Turf as a Pavement Alternative

Turf can be a green alternative to pavements; it is living, is pervious, reduces glare and noise, and can capture and eliminate pollutants.

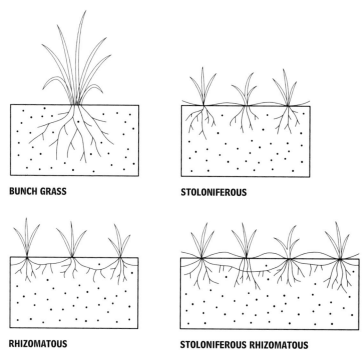

BUNCH GRASS

STOLONIFEROUS

RHIZOMATOUS

STOLONIFEROUS RHIZOMATOUS

GRASS GROWTH HABITAT TYPES

Figure 6.1 Grass growth habit types.
Source: Hopper, *Landscape Architecture Graphic Standards.* Copyright John Wiley & Sons, Inc., 2007.

Replacing impervious pavement with even a standard type of lawn significantly improves hydrological processes on a site.

Turf does, however, require more intensive management than most pavements, especially turf receiving active use. If turf is to be used in inclement weather, soil structure and management guidelines should be carefully planned at the design stage. Initial installation costs are generally lower for turf than for pavements, but costs can vary depending on site conditions, base design, irrigation systems, and drainage requirements. Regular management activities and water costs are ongoing expenses most pavements do not require.

Turf used with cellular pavers can combine the benefits of structural support with the pervious and living qualities of a turf. Using a stoloniferous turf may reduce the need for reseeding or replanting if cells become vacant due to traffic damage.

"Reinforced turf" is a term representing a variety of systems designed to enable turf to withstand more intensive uses, often without relying

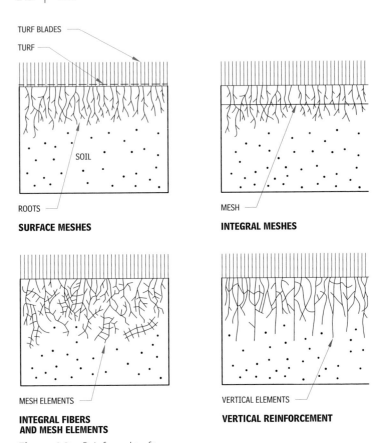

Figure 6.2 Reinforced turf types.
Source: Hopper, *Landscape Architecture Graphic Standards.* Copyright John Wiley & Sons, Inc., 2007.

on a visible structural component. Four general approaches include reinforcement by: surface meshes, integral meshes, integral fibers or mesh elements, and vertical reinforcement. Figure 6.2 illustrates the placement of these reinforcing members within the turf profile. For the most reliable surface, the base should be a high-sand base installed with subsurface drainage lines.

Lawn Alternatives

Greenswards are turfs composed of taller grasses and low wildflowers. Such mixed turfs were common through the 1800s and into the early twentieth century. A greensward should be maintained at 5 to 7 inches in height to encourage short herbaceous species. String trimmers may be necessary to achieve the appropriate cutting height, as most lawn mowers will not adjust that high. Mowing may not be required more than five or six times annually. Greenswards will accept light and infrequent traffic, and are suitable where a little unkempt-ness is acceptable. Converting an existing lawn to a greensward can be facilitated by modifying mowing practices and by introducing desired low-growing annuals and biennials.

Meadows are tall grasslands requiring only an annual cutting of between 8 and 12 inches in height after the second hard frost and before the spring thaw. To convert an existing lawn or greensward to a meadow, Sauer (1998) recommends mowing only five times during the initial conversion year, and thereafter reducing mowing frequency by one cutting per year for each of four subsequent years. A combination of native grasses and wildflowers appropriate to your region should be added over time, and hand removal of problem exotics may be neces-sary until the meadow is established. Periodic reseeding of wildflowers may be required. Meadows are "wild" in character, and the designer should determine the appropriateness of a meadow within the context of the local landscape.

Overview of a Plan for Environmental Responsibility

Choices made by the designer during the design process will influence the way the owner uses and impacts natural resources. Sustainability begins in design. Define clear design objectives, evaluate site suitability, plan for the establishment period, and specify long-term management objectives.

Defining Clear Design Objectives

Clear design objectives are essential to determining the proper soil base structure and turf composition. Programming should define the desired turf functional requirements, environmental sensitivity, and aesthetic qualities. Define functional requirements by activity needs, rather than by landscape component—for example, a 10,000-square-foot passive play area rather than a 10,000-square-foot turf area. Specify the activity level by both activity type and frequency of use, according to Table 6.1, "Turf Type Functional Suitability."

Consider local landscape standards dictated by ordinance or covenant, as well as the proposed turf setting (urban, suburban, or rural) before selecting an appropriate turf type. Where standards limit the type of turf component, consider minimizing turf area. Define aesthetic quali-ties in terms of turf uniformity, texture, color, and seasonal qualities. Lowering uniformity requirements increases turf options.

Table 6.1 Turf Type Functional Suitability

	Wildlife Habitat/Utility Corridors	Buffer/Filter Strip Greenway Edges	Passive Activities	Leisure Play	Athletics/Golf	Vehicular Applications
Meadow	+	+	*	-	-	-
Greensward	*	+	+	*	-	-
Turf lawn	-	-	+	+	*	-
Turf:high-sand base	-	-	+	+	+	*
Turf in open-celled pavers	-	-	*	-	+	+
Reinforced turf	-	-	+	+	+	+

Notes:
+ Good
* Fair
- Poor

Evaluating Site Suitability

To determine site suitability for turfgrass, evaluate regional, seasonal, and site-specific conditions. See "Turf Region Considerations" in this chapter, and Figure 6.3.

As part of a site suitability evaluation, regional conditions can be addressed by the following:

- Where heavy winter use of dormant warm-season turfgrasses is anticipated, overseed with a winter annual grass to protect the turf and soil surface from damage.
- Consider improving the soil structurally to limit compaction.
- In regions where dry periods correspond to heavy-use events, maintain a regular irrigation program so that the turf can withstand and recover from damage.

▶ No special treatment is needed where turf uses will be light and infrequent.

Table 6.2 provides details of turf species characteristics.

Figure 6.3 and Table 6.3 provide details of turf species characteristics.

Turf Region Considerations

- *Sun/Shade* — Grasses generally perform best in full sun within their appropriate region. Some cool-season grasses cannot withstand full sun in southern regions without heavy irrigation, but are suitable for light-shade areas. Shade-tolerant turfs can generally withstand up to four hours of shade. Turf is not a reliable option where insufficient sun is available. Turfgrass grows most aggressively during the morning hours; therefore, it is the morning sun that is most beneficial, both for growth and for drying of the turf, which limits disease.
- *Wind* — The most desirable site receives active airflow during the morning hours to dry the turf surface. A lack of airflow allows moisture to remain longer on the turf and can facilitate disease. Good surface ventilation can reduce cold pockets and minimize premature greening in early spring. Planning for airflow can reduce future turf management problems: Thin nearby tree stands and selectively remove lower tree limbs to improve ventilation on existing turf.
- *Soil characteristics* — Investigate the site's soil structure thoroughly before selecting a turf. Soil permeability and porosity are critical to turfgrass success and are a function of the particle sizes of soil components. Where clay soils predominate, permeability and porosity are generally low; clay soils can retain significant water for extended periods of time, but may also release that water reluctantly. In wet

Table 6.2 Turf Species Characteristics

	Compaction Tolerance	Wear Resistance	Heat Tolerance	Cold Tolerance	Drought Tolerance	Shade Tolerance	Disease Resistance	Salt Tolerance	Texture	Color	Notes	Growth Habit
Alkaligrass												
Puccinella distans	−	*	*	+	*	*	−	+	Medium fine	Medium green	Native	Bunch
Bahiagrass												
Paspalum notatum	−	+	+	−	+	*	+	−	Coarse	Medium	—	Bunch
Creeping Bentgrass												
Agrostis palustris	*	*	−	+	−	*	*	+	Medium fine	Medium green	—	Stoloniferous
Bermudagrass												
Cynodon species	+	+	+	*	+	−	*	+	Fine	Medium green	—	Stoloniferous Rhizomatous
Annual Bluegrass												
Poa annua	+	−	−	+	−	−	+	—	Medium	—	—	Bunch with stolons
Rough Bluegrass												
Poa trivialis	−	−	−	+	−	−	+	*	Medium	Lt-med green	Wet tolerant	Stoloniferous
Kentucky Bluegrass												
Poa pratensis	*	*	*	+	*	−	+	*	Medium	Dark green	—	Rhizomatous

Species									Texture	Color	Native	Growth habit
Buffalograss												
Buchloe dactyloides	—	-	*	*	+	-	—	—	Fine	Medium green		Stoloniferous
Centipedegrass												
Eremochloa ophiuroides	—	*	*	-	+	*	*	-	Medium coarse	Yellow green	—	Stoloniferous
Chewings Fescue												
Festuca rubra var. *commutata*	-	-	-	+	*	+	-	*	Fine	Dark green	Insect resist.	Bunch, but tillers aggressively
Creeping Red Fescue												
Festuca rubra	—	*	-	+	*	+	-	—	Fine	Dark green	—	Rhizomatous
Fine Fescue/Hard Fescue												
Festuca longifolia	*	*	-	+	*	+	-	*	Fine	Dark green	Insect resist.	Bunch
Sheep Fescue												
Festuca ovina	-	-	-	+	*	+	-	—	Fine		—	Bunch
Tall Fescue												
Festuca arundinacea	+	*	*	+	+	+	-	*	Coarse	Medium green	—	Bunch, but does spread by tillers

Continued

Table 6.2 *Continued*

	Compaction Tolerance	Wear Resistance	Heat Tolerance	Cold Tolerance	Drought Tolerance	Shade Tolerance	Disease Resistance	Salt Tolerance	Texture	Color	Notes	Growth Habit
Seashore Paspalum												
Paspalum vaginatum	-	+	*	*	*	-	+	+	Medium coarse	Dark green	Waxy leaf	Stoloniferous Rhizomatous
Perennial Ryegrass												
Lolium perenne	+	+	-	+	+	+	+	*	Medium	Medium	Insect green	Bunch resist.
St. Augustine Grass												
Stenataphrum secundatum	-	-	+	-	*	+	-	+	Coarse	Lt-med green	Rapid grower	Stoloniferous Rhizomatous
Zoysiagrass												
Zoysia species	*	+	+	*	+	*	*	*	Medium fine	Medium green	—	Stoloniferous Rhizomatous

NOTES

+ Good

* Fair

- Poor

Sources: Beard, James B., 1982, and Lofts Seed, Inc. (not dated).

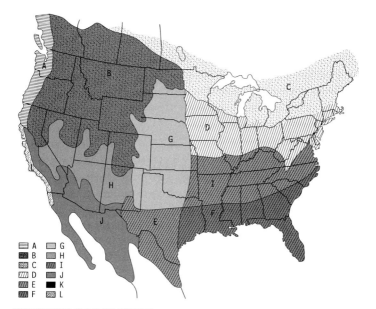

TURF REGIONS OF NORTH AMERICA

Figure 6.3   Turf regions of North America. Specific turf regional compatibility can be found in Table 6.3.
Source: Hopper, *Landscape Architecture Graphic Standards*. Copyright John Wiley & Sons, Inc., 2007.

periods and in low areas, clay soils can become anoxic, killing the turfgrass; subsurface drainage may be necessary. Where sands or gravels predominate, the soil is high in porosity, enabling rapid infiltration and drainage, but it can be droughty and is often low in fertility. Soil conditioners can improve soil characteristics, but weigh modifications against environmental and economic cost.

- *Sand-based systems* — Since the 1960s, sand-based turf systems have grown in popularity for golf course and sports field construction. The Texas-USGA profile, the California variant of that profile, and other similar systems capitalize on the inherent porosity of various sands to control soil moisture and provide uniformity in the turfgrass base. The Texas-USGA method, as shown in Figure 6.4, is the most thoroughly documented system. High-sand bases provide a compaction-resistant soil for active-use turfs and a rapid-use capability following precipitation events, but require an actively managed cultural program to coordinate frequent irrigation, fertilization, and other cultural practices.

- *Hydrology* — Evaluate local climatic information and weekly precipitation rates before determining lawn size and turfgrass composition. Most nonnative turfgrasses are aggressive consumers of soil moisture and require ample water to maintain health and vigor.

Table 6.3 Turf Regional Compatibility

	A	B	C	D	E	F	G	H	I	J	K	L
Alkaligrass	*											
Bahiagrass (Argentine)					*							
Bahiagrass (Pensacola)					*							
Creeping Bentgrass	*	*	*	*	*	*	*	*	*	*		
Bermudagrass					*				*	*	*	
Kentucky Bluegrass	*	*	*	*	*		*	*				
Buffalograss							*					
Carpetgrass						*						
Centipedegrass						*						
Fescue (Creeping Red)	*		*	*	*		*	*		*		
Fescue (Kentucky 31)	*		*	*	*		*	*		*		
Fescue (Tall)	*	*	*	*	*		*	*				
Perennial Ryegrass		*	*	*	*		*	*				*
St. Augustine Grass						*					*	
Seashore Paspalum						*			*	*	*	*
Zoysiagrass					*	*			*	*	*	

Notes
* Suitable zone for species.
Sources: www.lawngrasses.com and Lofts Seeds, Inc.

In regions where precipitation is lacking during the growing season, local water conservation issues may preclude the use of turfgrass. Plants native to a site are adapted to the site water balance and flourish without irrigation inputs.

- *Irrigation* — Irrigation is needed to establish most turf. Once turf is established, irrigate it thoroughly and deeply to encourage deep root growth. Shallow, frequent watering produces turf with poor root structure and low drought tolerance. Water from several sources may be available; seek alternatives to standard potable sources, surface water bodies, or wells. For small areas, cisterns can be used to store rainwater for later use in irrigation. Some areas permit the use of treated effluent and "gray water." In coastal areas, certain turf cultivars can withstand the use of salt water for irrigation. Where salt water is used or where irrigation is performed in arid regions, periodic flushing of the soil must be performed to remove salt accumulations.

- *Drainage* — Site areas that do not drain well are not suited for turfgrass without making soil modifications, installing subsurface drains,

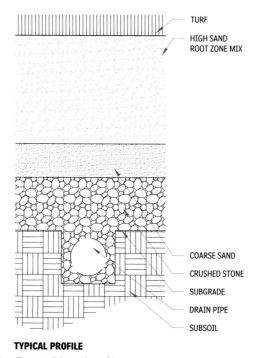

TURF

HIGH SAND
ROOT ZONE MIX

COARSE SAND

CRUSHED STONE

SUBGRADE

DRAIN PIPE

SUBSOIL

TYPICAL PROFILE

Figure 6.4   Texas-USGA soil profile.
Source: Hopper, *Landscape Architecture Graphic Standards.* Copyright John Wiley & Sons, Inc., 2007.

and/or altering site grading. Surface runoff, subsurface drainage, and water infiltrating into groundwater from turf areas can contain nutrients and chemicals, which may pose a human and environmental hazard. Consider proximity to local potable water supply sources, particularly streams and shallow wells, before selecting turf sites. Provide adequate natural buffers around intensive turf areas.

- *Nutrition* — Proper nutrition is essential for the establishment and management of turf areas. Soil surveys can provide a general suitability guideline during master planning, but on-site soil testing should be conducted prior to detailed site design. Use existing soil fertility as a guide to sustainable turfgrass design. Soils that retain nutrients better can reduce fertilizer requirements, yielding high-quality turf at a lower cost to the client. Where poor soil nutrient conditions prevail, consider reducing turf area or selecting grasses appropriate for site conditions. Nutrient competition from tree roots can be controlled by root pruning nearby trees. Contact a local arborist to determine site- and species-specific root pruning practices.

Site-Specific Conditions

Visual Site Assessment

Any conditions that might interfere with the turf installation should be noted, including rocks, stumps, large surface roots, or other debris on the site. These situations should be addressed in the construction documents. Location of utility lines should be noted, particularly any existing irrigation lines and heads. These should be called out for marking during installation, to prevent damage.

Note the types of weeds that are growing on the site and the extent of coverage. Extensive weed cover may require control with a herbicide prior to turf installation, as tilling them into the soil will not necessarily eliminate them.

Soil Assessment

Soil assessment is an important part of turf installation preparation. A soil analysis that will determine type of soil, existing nutrient levels, and pH should be performed before any soil modifications are considered. Soil drainage characteristics and level of compaction should also be determined.

A testing laboratory will analyze soil samples for pH, lime requirement, and plant nutrients. A laboratory analysis and report will typically recommend the amount of dolomitic limestone needed to raise the pH level, if required; how much organic matter to incorporate; and how much and what nutrient mix of fertilizer may be beneficial.

▶ Soil tests should be performed well in advance, as some soil modifications, such as pH adjustment, need to be made prior to turf installation.

Poor drainage, damaged soil structure, and overcompaction can be addressed with the addition of organic matter to the soil. Organic matter will also increase aeration, enhance water-holding capacity, and minimize leaching of plant nutrients. The incorporation of uniform-particle sand will contribute to soil structure and improve infiltration and aeration, especially if the existing soil texture is clayey.

▶ See the sections "Soil Overview," "Soil Assessment," and "Designed Soil Mixes" in Chapter 1.

Acceptable Practices

Overview of a Plan for Establishment

Proper planning for the establishment period is critical for achieving a successful turf and minimizing repairs. The more intensely used the turf will be, the more important the establishment period becomes. If turf is put into use prior to completing establishment, damage to the turf and soil profile can occur. Turf can be replanted, but soil structure repair requires extensive work.

Overview of Soil Preparation

Soil should be thoroughly cultivated to a minimum depth of 2 to 3 inches, regardless of the turf planting method. Remove all rocks, sticks, and other debris, and rake smooth. Adjust soil nutrients prior to planting. Roll seeds into the soil to maximize seed-soil contact.

Overview of Soil Nutrient Adjustment

Adjust soil nutrient levels prior to planting, on the basis of lab soil tests. Local golf course turf managers are good sources for specific nutrition guidance. Fast-acting limes can be incorporated prior to planting, but use slower-acting limes after germination to limit foliar burn. Evaluate and supplement macro- and micronutrients to achieve a balanced nutrient content. Phosphorus must be present during turf establishment, and 50 to 70 parts per million (ppm) is recommended.

Overview of Seed

Timing is critical for good turf establishment. Seeding of cool-season turfs can occur in both fall and spring, but fall seeding produces the most mature root and shoot system prior to summer heat stress. Late summer and early fall seeding benefit from warm soil temperatures that encourage quick germination, less competition from weeds, cooler fall temperatures that reduce stress on early growth, and more predictable precipitation patterns. Early heat following spring seeding can result in a poor turf stand, and immature plants increase reliance on irrigation.

Warm-season grasses, such as Bermudagrass should be seeded or sprigged in late spring once the daily low and high temperatures add up to 150 degrees. Buffalograss establishes slowly from seed, and may require repetitive seeding to develop a solid stand. Typical seeding rates are shown in Table 6.4, "Turf Seeding and Sprigging Rates."

Table 6.4 Turf Seeding and Sprigging Rates

	No. of Seeds/lb (approx.)	Seeding Rate: lb./acre	Seeding Rate: lb/1,000 sf	Golf Greens Sprigging Rate: bushels/1,000 sf[1]	Lawn Sprigging Rate: bushels/1,000 sf[2]
Alkaligrass	2,000,000	130 to 175	3.0 to 4.0	n/a	n/a
Puccinella distans					
Bahiagrass	272,400	160 to 320	3.7 to 5.3	n/a	n/a
Paspalum notatum					
Creeping Bentgrass	6,135,810	20 to 45	0.5 to 1.0	8 to 12	5 to 8
Agrostis palustris					
Bermudagrass	2,072,510	40 to 65	0.9 to 1.5	6 to 10	2 to 4
Cynodon species					
Annual Bluegrass	—	—	—	n/a	n/a
Poa annua					
Rough Bluegrass	2,092,240	45 to 65	1.0 to 1.5	n/a	n/a
Poa trivialis					
Kentucky Bluegrass	1,391,510	45 to 65	1.0 to 1.5	n/a	n/a
Poa pratensis					
Buffalograss	38,900	45 to 80	1.0 to 1.8	—	2" plugs on 6" centers
Buchloe dactyloides					
Centipedegrass	874,759	20 to 35	0.5 to 0.6	—	2 to 4
Eremochloa ophiuroides					

Species					
Chewings Fescue	408,600	150 to 200	3.4 to 4.6	n/a	n/a
Festuca rubra var. commutata					
Creeping Red Fescue	408,600	150 to 200	3.4 to 4.6	n/a	n/a
Festuca rubra					
Fine Fescue/Hard Fescue	530,000	175 to 260	4.0 to 6.0	n/a	n/a
Festuca longifolia					
Sheep Fescue	530,000	120 to 170	2.8 to 3.9	n/a	n/a
Festuca ovina					
Tall Fescue	206,570	300 to 390	6.9 to 9.0	n/a	n/a
Festuca arundinacea					
Seashore Paspalum	n/a	n/a	n/a	5 to 14	5 to 10
Paspalum vaginatum					
Perennial Ryegrass	240,620	300 to 390	6.9 to 9.0	n/a	n/a
Lolium perenne					
St. Augustine Grass	450,000	20 to 45	0.5 to 1.0	—	3 to 10
Stenataphrum secundatum					
Zoysiagrass	1,006,652	90 to 135	2.1 to 3.1	6	2 to 4
Zoysia species					

Notes:
One bushel of sprigs = one square yard of dense turf sod.
[1] Golf green rates are stated for species only where specific references were found.
[2] Sprigging rates represent acceptable lawn establishment rates; higher rates will produce faster results.
Sources: Beard, James B., 1982, and Lofts Seed, Inc.

▶ The finer the seed, the lower the rate of application.

Overview of Sprigs and Plugs

Sprigging and plugging are less expensive than installing solid sod, and generally produce a reliable turf faster than seeding. Apply sprigs of both stoloniferous and rhizomatous turfs to prepared soil at the general rates shown in Table 6.4. Proper irrigation is the key to successful sprig establishment. Once sprigs are rooted, perform regular mowing and vertical cutting or slicing to develop a dense turf. Sprigs can be broadcast or planted in rows. Plugs are typically installed in a regular grid pattern.

Sod

Sod is the means to instant lawn. While it is initially more expensive than seeding or sprigging, it is the most reliable method for producing a high-quality turf and minimizes initial management expenses. Sod is available for most turfgrasses, although local selections may be limited. Most growers contract to grow sod of a desired cultivar, blend, or mixture.

Soil-free sod is a sod product that is essentially a mat of bare-root turf, grown on a mesh or fibrous-type material to provide a structure. Soil is removed by washing, or a nonsoil medium is used. This results in a very light product, increasing load quantity and decreasing labor demands. With proper cultivation, soil-free sod reduces the potential for layering in the turf profile, which can impede air, water, and nutrient movement.

Turfgrass Species

Selection of the appropriate species is critical in the successful establishment of a turfgrass area. Factors to consider include:

- The geographical area, climate, and microclimate conditions.
- The intended use and the level of performance required.
- The anticipated level of management and maintenance.

A seed mixture is a combination of two or more species of grass. A blend is three or more cultivars of the same species. Seed mixtures or blends of grass seed will better withstand a range of different conditions, responding and adapting to changing conditions (drought, disease, insect infestations, drainage conditions, etc.). It is usually desirable to introduce genetic diversity into the turfgrass area by using a seed mixture or blend.

Seed Quality

Selection of high-quality seed is important in establishing a high-quality turfgrass stand. Low-quality seed produces a thin stand that is vulnerable to weed invasion, disease, pests, and adverse environmental conditions.

The quality of a seed is dependent upon its purity, viability, and their combined result, identified as pure live seed. Purity is the percentage by weight of pure seed of the identified species or cultivar in a lot of seed. Viability is the percentage of seed that is alive and will germinate under laboratory conditions. Pure live seed is determined by multiplying percentage of germination by the percentage of purity and dividing by 100.

▶ **A seed with a purity of 96 percent and a germination percentage of 85 percent will have a pure live seed value of 81.6 percent.**

High-quality seed is usually more expensive, but less seed is needed for good turf establishment than with a poor-quality seed. The best measure to determine value and the amount of seed needed for a specific area is to compare the pure live seed value between mixes. To determine how much seed is required to plant, divide 100 by the pure live seed percentage. In the previous example, 100 divided by 81.6 equals approximately 1.2. Therefore, 1.2 pounds of seed would be needed for each pound specified in the seed mixture. A poor quality of seed would have a lower pure live seed value, and when divided into 100 would result in a larger ratio factor, thus requiring more seed to be applied for the same size area.

▶ **As a rule of thumb, good-quality seed mixes have a purity percentage over 90 percent and a germination rate over 85 percent.**

Other factors that contribute to the quality of a seed mix are:

- *Crop* — The percentage by weight of seeds that are grown as a cash crop (hay or pasture grasses). High-quality seed mixes should have a crop percentage as close to 0.00 percent as possible. A crop percentage over 0.5 percent should not be accepted.
- *Weed* — The percentage by weight of weed seeds. A weed is defined as any seed not included in the pure or crop percentage. Any seed mix with a weed content of over 0.3 percent should not be accepted.
- *Noxious weed* — The number of seeds per pound or ounce of weeds that are considered undesirable. Seed mixes with noxious weed seeds should be avoided.

- *Inert* — Percentage by weight of material in the seed mix that will not grow. The lower the inert percentage, the better the quality of the seed mix. Seed mixes with inert percentages over 8 percent should not be accepted.
- *Date tested* — Indicates when the lot was tested for viability and purity. Germination rates can decline over time, and seed with a test date over a year old should be avoided.

▶ By law, seed mixture containers must be labeled with the name and address of the labeler responsible for the contents, lot number, turfgrass species and cultivar (from highest percentage to lowest), origin, purity, percent germination, weed seed content, and date tested.

Seed mixes are inspected and certified by regulatory agencies. Certified seed mixes are an assurance that the seed matches the information provided on the label.

▶ "VNS" (variety not stated) on a label indicates that there is seed in the mix that has no cultivar name. This indication is generally associated with lower-quality seed mixes.

Site Preparation

Rough Grading

After any other construction activities have been completed, the site can be prepared for turf installation. All construction debris, large rocks, tree stumps, and unwanted vegetation should be removed.

If there is extensive perennial grass weed coverage, control with a nonselective systemic herbicide, such as glyphosate, should be considered at this early phase. Allow enough time for the herbicide to be effective before grading operations begin. A repeat herbicide application may be required in some cases. There is usually a 4–8 week period between applications and a 7-day period after the final application during which the soil should not be disturbed.

If extensive grading is required, existing topsoil should be stripped and stockpiled for later distribution over the site. Utility lines and irrigation pipes and heads should be clearly marked, and existing trees should be protected. If the soil has been compacted by heavy construction equipment, consider calling for the soil to be broken up by a ripper attachment, which will help during the rough grading process.

Rough grading involves shaping the subsoil parallel to and below the desired finished grade of the surface (to allow for the placement of topsoil). The subsoil grade should be free of any depressions and slope away from any structures. On sloping sites, the grading plan should include swales to channel the water away from and around structures. Although rough grading can be accomplished using a number of different pieces of construction equipment, large tire tractors that spread the machine's weight over a larger area, or lighter equipment such as a skid steer, are best to prevent overcompaction of the subsoil.

Irrigation

If required, a properly designed irrigation system that delivers water uniformly over the entire area of turf should be installed after rough grading. This allows the system to be installed at the correct depth below finished grade, with the trenches backfilled and properly firmed during finished grading, prior to the installation of turf. The irrigation system should be pressure tested for leaks and proper operation before trenches are backfilled. Final adjustments to sprinkler head heights are made after fine grading.

▶ Mark sprinkler head and valve locations with flags to prevent damage during final grading operations.

Local code requirements, necessary permits, and required inspections should be checked prior to installation and compliance ensured during the design and installation phases.

▶ See Chapter 8, "Irrigation and Water Use Efficiency."

Spreading of Topsoil

After rough grading has been completed, topsoil should be spread evenly across the site, bringing the level of the soil to the desired finished grade. It is desirable to mix the topsoil into the top 2 or 3 inches of the subsoil to facilitate drainage at the interface of the two soils. Typically, a minimum of 6 inches of firmed topsoil will be sufficient for good turf establishment. Any depth less than 4 inches will require increased irrigation levels and will not support high-quality turf growth.

If soil tests determine that organic matter or sand should be added to amend the soil, it should be spread evenly and worked into the topsoil. If more than a 2-inch depth of organic matter needs to be added, a 2-inch layer should be incorporated first, followed by another layer of organic matter worked into the topsoil.

If soil tests determine that fertilizer or lime is required, it can be added to the topsoil layer. Because a surface application of phosphorus and potassium does not move into the soil fast enough to benefit the new turf, it should be incorporated into the topsoil layer. Phosphorus, potassium, and lime, if necessary, can be spread evenly over the top-soil and tilled into the top 4–6 inches. Nitrogen has a tendency to leach out of the topsoil before the turf can be established, and is best applied on the surface at time of seeding.

A rototiller is most commonly used to incorporate amendments and fertilizer into the soil. Tilling is most effective when the soil is moist, but not wet. The tilling should produce a loose, crumbly soil texture with small clods ranging from $1/8$ to $3/4$ inch. Excessive tilling can pulverize the soil, turning it into a powdery mix and destroying its structure.

▶ **A soil with a texture of loam or sandy loams with a pH of 6.0–7.0 provides the best conditions for high-quality turf establishment.**

Fine Grading

The last step of fine grading firms and smoothes the soil surface before seeding or sodding. This is accomplished mechanically on larger sites by pulling a steel mat or roller over the site, enough to firm the soil but not compact it. Any large stones should be removed. After the soil is firmed, a landscape rake, harrow, or steel mat is run over the surface to smooth out any high spots and fill any depressions, producing an even, smooth surface. For smaller sites, soils can be firmed by rain or hosing and after the soil has dried, hand-raking with a grading rake.

Starter Fertilizer

After finished grading is complete, a starter fertilizer should be lightly worked into the topsoil surface just prior to seeding or sodding. Recommended rates of application for the starter fertilizer selected should be followed.

Starter fertilizers are low in nitrogen (the first number in fertilizer analysis) but high in phosphate (the second number in fertilizer analysis) and include potassium (the third number in the fertilizer analysis), which will encourage good root growth and turf establishment. Typical ratio examples of starter fertilizers include 18-24-6, 5-10-5, and 20-27-5.

Selection of Seed or Sod

A high-quality turfgrass can be established by seeding or sodding, if the site is prepared properly. Each method has its own advantages and disadvantages.

Establishing a turfgrass area from seed includes the following advantages:

- Initially less expensive (cost of seed and labor).
- Greater variety of cultivars available.
- Greater flexibility in addressing varying site conditions by planting different mixtures for parts of a site that may be in shade or sun, subject to high traffic or intense use, etc.

Establishing a turfgrass area from seed includes the following disadvantages:

- Best planted at specific times of the year, usually late summer/early fall.
- Needs daily watering during germination and initial establishment.
- Takes longer to become established and develop into a good stand of thick, full turf.
- Newly seeded areas need to be protected from use for periods from 2 to 3 months.
- Weed growth can be a problem.
- Heavy rains can wash seed away.

Establishing a turfgrass area from sod includes the following advantages:

- Immediate impact.
- Provides immediate erosion control on slopes.
- Provides immediate turf cover on high-traffic areas.
- Less opportunity for weed growth.
- Can be installed at almost any time of the year.

Establishing a turfgrass area from sod includes the following disadvantages:

- Initially more expensive (cost of sod and labor to install).
- Less diversity of turf cultivars.
- Generally requires more irrigation to establish and can be less drought tolerant.

▶ Not all warm-weather grasses can be planted by seeding. Some require vegetative propagation, which includes sodding, sprigging, or plugging.

Seeding

The seed should be spread evenly over the properly prepared site, using a drop spreader and applying the seed at one-half the recommended rate in one direction and then going over the same area again, perpendicular to the first seeding direction. The seed should be applied within the recommended rate range. If the area may be subjected to heavy use, or if seed is not being applied at the best time of year, an application rate that is closer to the high end of the recommended range may be of benefit.

▶ The recommended seeding rates should not be exceeded. This leads to seedling competition and a weakened stand of turf susceptible to disease, not to a thicker turf.

The seed should be very lightly raked to ensure good contact with the soil. The seed should not be buried deeper than half an inch. A light covering of straw mulch or wood fiber placed over the surface will hold in moisture and minimize erosion. The entire site should be lightly rolled to firm the soil.

For larger areas, a cultipacker seeder pulled by a tractor creates small grooves in the soil, drops the seed into the grooves, and firms the soil, all in a single pass.

On slopes where erosion may be a concern, burlap, cheesecloth, or thin netting should be staked over the seeded area. The seed will be able to sprout through the protective covering, which will degrade over time and not need to be removed.

Irrigation is critical to seed germination and even coverage. Minimally, the area should be watered twice a day, in the morning and in the evening. Another midday watering to prevent the soil from drying out is advisable. Water should be provided as a fine spray so that the area is thoroughly moistened with no puddling, and seeds are not uncovered. After two weeks and seed germination, watering can be transitioned to one longer watering in the morning to encourage deep root growth.

Hydroseeding involves mixing seed, water, fertilizer, and mulch in a large tank and pumping the mixture through a hose or gun onto a prepared soil surface. The mulch in the mixture reduces evaporation, keeping soil moist, resulting in excellent germination rates and turf establishment. The tank is mounted on a truck or trailer that is moved across the site. As the tank is moved, the operator sprays the area by moving the hose or gun back and forth until the entire area is evenly covered. The mixture is usually tinted so that any missed or thin spots are easily visible. The hydroseeding method is usually used on large sites, long linear sites such as highway embankments, or hard-to-access slopes, for stabilization.

The turfgrass should be ready to mow after about a month, when the first few blades of grass reach about 2 inches. After mowing, reseed any bare or thin spots. It is usually recommended that a balanced fertilizer be applied (10-10-10 for example). After three or four mowings, the mower height can be set to a standard mowing height of approximately 3 inches.

▶ It may take several mowings before a full, dense stand of turfgrass is developed.

Sod

Sod should be purchased from reputable growers, and information on the grass species and cultivars contained in the sod should be evaluated for their suitability. It is advisable to choose sod that is grown in soil similar to that of the site where it is to be installed. The compatibility of the soil types minimizes the creation of an interface that could hamper root development and water infiltration. Although sod can be installed at any time of year, spring and fall are best because of the lower temperatures. Sod installed in the summer will require more irrigation.

Before final grading, the thickness of the sod should be determined so that the sod will be at the proper elevation after being installed. The thickness of the sod will vary, depending on the species of grass, from $\frac{1}{4}$ inch up to 1 inch (or sometimes even thicker). This thickness needs to be compensated for in the final grading process, and the sod supplier should be called for this information, to verify the thickness of the sod that will be delivered.

▶ Thinner sod is easier to handle but also dries out more quickly, making adequate irrigation critical to establishment.

Sod is usually delivered in rectangular strips and folded on pallets (although large rolls are available for mechanized installations for extremely large installations). See Figures 6.5 through 6.7. The sod should be inspected upon delivery for the following:

- Sod should be a uniform, deep green color without any yellowing.
- Sod should be evenly moist but not wet.
- Sod should not have cracked or dried edges.
- Feel the sod on the interior of the pallet. If it is warm, this could indicate that the sod has been on the pallet for some length of time and is already beginning to decompose.
- Sod should be free of weeds.
- Sod should be free of visible evidence of insects and disease.

▶ If the sod fails to meet any of these criteria, it should be rejected.

Figure 6.5 Sod is available in rectangular strips or rolls that are loaded on pallets for delivery.
Courtesy of Jim Novak – Turfgrass Producers International.

Figure 6.6 Sod being harvested in rectangular strips.
Courtesy of Jim Novak – Turfgrass Producers International.

Figure 6.7 Sod being harvested in large rolls that are for mechanized installations on large projects.
Courtesy of Jim Novak – Turfgrass Producers International.

If possible, the sod should be stored in a shady location until it can be laid. Sod stored on a pallet can deteriorate quickly, and if it cannot be installed within 24 hours after delivery, it should be taken off the pallet, laid flat, and watered thoroughly until it can be laid.

The sod should be installed with the following steps:

- If the soil is dry, lightly moisten the soil before the sod is laid.
- The sod should be started along a straight edge with full pieces.
- The sod should be laid out so that the ends of the individual pieces of sod are staggered, similar to a running bond brick pattern (see Figure 6.8). This will involve cutting the second and third rows of sod to keep the end seams from lining up.
- All edges of the sod should be in contact with the adjacent pieces of sod, as exposed edges can dry out quickly.
- The sod should not be stretched, but instead be laid loosely and pushed into the edge of the adjacent piece of sod. Stretched sod will shrink later, leaving gaps between the pieces and exposed edges that will dry out.
- If the area is sloped, sodding should start on the lower part of the slope, working up toward the top. On steep slopes, the sod may need to be secured with stakes (which will need to be removed later) or with biodegradable sod staples.

Figure 6.8   Sod is laid out in a staggered pattern so that the end seams do not line up.
Courtesy of Central Sod Maryland.

- Any trimming necessary should be done with a sharp, stiff knife. Using a 2×4 or other straightedge will result in cleaner, more even cuts.
- Avoid leaving a narrow piece of sod along the edge. If the dimensions require a narrow piece, consider installing it next to a full piece that is placed along the outer edge.
- After the sod is in place, it should be lightly rolled to ensure good sod-to-soil contact.
- After rolling, the sod should be thoroughly watered immediately. If the area to be sodded is very large, consider having the sod rolled and watered in sections, while the balance of the area is being sodded. It is critically important that the sod not be allowed to dry out. A deep watering will eliminate air pockets that could dry the roots on sections of sod, resulting in some sections yellowing.
- Edges and corners have a tendency to dry out more quickly and may need additional hand watering to ensure that these areas are watered thoroughly.
- Keep foot traffic off the sodded area until it has become well established.

▶ Check to see that the sod has been watered thoroughly by lifting an edge and sticking your finger a few inches into the soil. Thorough watering should result in moistened soil to a depth of 4–6 inches.

After installation, the sodded area should be kept thoroughly and consistently moist. Watering intervals will depend on weather conditions. In cooler weather, this may be once every couple of days; in warmer weather, at least once daily, with perhaps even a midday watering if conditions warrant. If the new sod begins to look wilted or turn yellow or brown, it can be returned to a healthy green color by adequate watering. After two or three weeks, the sod should be established to a level at which thorough watering can be scheduled at a more normal once or twice a week.

▶ **Watering deeply but less often encourages deep root growth. Frequent shallow watering encourages roots to grow near the surface, which is detrimental to turf establishment.**

Initial mowing should be done after two or three weeks, with the mower height initially set to 3 inches. Check to see that the sod is knitted to the soil below by gently pulling up on an edge. If it pulls up easily, wait to mow; if it offers resistance, it is beginning to root into the soil below. Measure the lawn so that the initial mowing does not remove more than one-third of the blade height. Use of a mulching mower that returns the clippings to the surface can provide nutrients to the sod as they decompose.

The sod can be fertilized after four to six weeks, using a balanced fertilizer (such as a 10-10-10). Herbicides, weedkillers, or crabgrass control chemicals should not be used for the first year after sod installation. They can interfere with root growth and inhibit turf establishment.

Sprigs

Sprigging is commonly used to plant warm-season grasses such as Bermudagrass or zoysiagrass. Sprigs are individual pieces of stolon, rhizome, or stem, without any soil attached, that are planted in furrows or small holes. They are usually produced by cutting or pulling sod apart into individual pieces, or they can be purchased by the bushel. Each sprig should have two to four nodes from which roots can develop.

Sprigs are perishable and should be planted within 24 to 48 hours after being harvested. They should be kept moist and in shaded conditions until planted. Sprigging is usually done in May, when warm-season grasses begin to green up, and after the soil has been properly prepared.

Sprigs are most commonly planted by creating furrows 1–2 inches deep and 6–12 inches apart, and planting the sprigs approximately 4–6 inches apart. The closer the spacing, the quicker the turf will fill in.

The sprig should be covered with soil, leaving the foliage portion of the sprig exposed on the surface. Each sprig should be tamped or the area lightly rolled to firm the soil.

Alternate methods of planting sprigs include placing the sprig on the surface and pressing it into the soil with a notched tool. Sprigs can also be planted by spreading them evenly over the soil surface, covering them with a thin layer of soil or compost, and rolling to firm the soil. This method, called "stolonizing," is a quicker alternative to placing individual sprigs. Stolonizing fills in more rapidly, but the rate of mortality is higher, and it therefore requires a higher number of sprigs to be planted.

Watering is critical, as the sprigs are planted very shallow and the soil dries out quickly. Light, frequent waterings, twice a day if conditions warrant, are recommended so that the roots are not allowed to dry out, and the sprigs can become established. This may take up to a month or longer.

Fertilizing after approximately four weeks with a fertilizer high in phosphorus can promote root growth, hasten establishment, and lead to the sprigs filling in faster. Patience is required, as it may take a while for the sprigs to grow and fill in the spaces between them for a uniform, dense turf stand.

Plugs

Plugging is the vegetative propagation of turfgrasses by planting plugs or small sod pieces of approximately 2-to-4-inch-diameter circles or block-shaped squares at regular intervals over the site. Plugs can be cut from pieces of sod, and some varieties are available commercially and sold in trays.

Plugging is generally done in May, when warm-season grasses begin to green up, and after the soil has been properly prepared.

Plugs are planted by making small holes with a trowel or bulb planter, approximately 6–12 inches apart. The closer the planting holes, the quicker the grass will fill in the spaces between. For larger installations, special machines are used for planting plugs. After the plugs have been planted, the area should be rolled to ensure good plug-to-soil contact.

Watering is critical, and the plugs should be watered immediately after planting. Light, frequent waterings, twice or three times a day if conditions warrant, are recommended so that the roots of the plugs are not allowed to dry out. Although plugs can take longer to fill in than sprigs, they tend not to dry out as quickly.

Fertilizing after approximately four weeks with a fertilizer high in phosphorus can promote root growth, hasten establishment, and lead to the plugs filling in faster. Mulching will help retain moisture, prevent erosion, and discourage weed establishment.

Post-establishment Care

The care a turf area receives after planting can determine whether or not establishment will be successful. Careful attention to some basic procedures during the first two months after installation will help ensure that the turf planting will be successful.

- Limit traffic over the new turf. The seedlings are very sensitive and have very limited tolerance.
- Initial frequent watering to keep the soil surface moist for the first few weeks should be followed by more thorough watering to keep the soil moist down to a depth of about 2 inches, encouraging deep root growth. The seedlings should not be subjected to moisture stress. If the soil surface is allowed to dry out, the seedlings can die. Adjust watering schedules to account for rainy or overcast days.
- The turf should be mowed on a regular basis. It is better to remove shorter lengths of grass blades frequently than to remove longer lengths infrequently. No more than one-third of the overall grass blade length should be removed at one time (see Figure 6.9). Allowing the clippings to remain will add nutrients back into the soil.
- An application of fertilizer should be considered after four weeks. Seed and sod will benefit most from a balanced fertilizer. Sprigs and plugs will benefit most from a fertilizer higher in phosphorus, to promote root growth.
- Avoid the use of herbicides in the first two months after planting. New turf seedlings are very sensitive, and establishment can be negatively impacted.
- Mulching can help aid establishment by helping to retain moisture, moderate soil temperatures, keep seeds from being washed away, and prevent soil erosion. Straw evenly distributed at a rate of approximately 80–100 pounds per 1,000 square feet (slightly higher for steep slopes) is a common mulching method. Excess straw should be removed after the turf is established. Hydromulching with wood fibers or chopped recycled newspaper at a rate of 30–40 pounds per 1,000 square feet is another mulching alternative. Recycled newspaper pellets are also available, some with fertilizer mixed in.

▶ Do not exceed recommended rates for mulching. Thicker mulching can shade and smother new seedlings. If the turf begins to yellow, excess mulch should be removed.

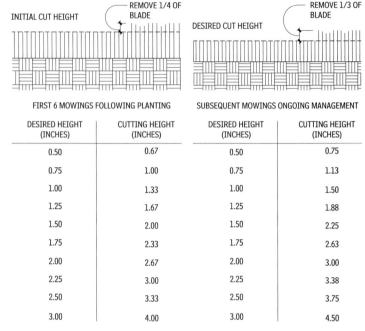

FIRST 6 MOWINGS FOLLOWING PLANTING

DESIRED HEIGHT (INCHES)	CUTTING HEIGHT (INCHES)
0.50	0.67
0.75	1.00
1.00	1.33
1.25	1.67
1.50	2.00
1.75	2.33
2.00	2.67
2.25	3.00
2.50	3.33
3.00	4.00

SUBSEQUENT MOWINGS ONGOING MANAGEMENT

DESIRED HEIGHT (INCHES)	CUTTING HEIGHT (INCHES)
0.50	0.75
0.75	1.13
1.00	1.50
1.25	1.88
1.50	2.25
1.75	2.63
2.00	3.00
2.25	3.38
2.50	3.75
3.00	4.50

TURF MOWING HEIGHTS

Figure 6.9 Mowing heights during turf establishment.
Source: Hopper, *Landscape Architecture Graphic Standards.* Copyright John Wiley & Sons, Inc., 2007.

▶ Before mowing or fertilizer application, the turf should be checked to see if it is established enough to tolerate foot traffic without being damaged. After a few steps are taken onto the turf, the blades should move back to an upright position. If not, wait— damage to the turf should not be risked. Use of a lightweight mower for the first few mowings can be less damaging.

Overview of Management Objectives

Management practices vary based on turf type and species. Consequently, establishing management objectives during the design process improves the likelihood for long-term turf success, and can minimize the overuse of irrigation, fertilizers, pesticides, and herbicides. Management demands and costs are least for meadows, moderate for greenswards, and high for active-use turf.

Proper management practices for an established lawn include cultivation, irrigation, mowing, fertilization, pest control, disease control, weed control, top-dressing, overseeding and reseeding, and traffic control. Table 6.5, "Management Practices," indicates appropriate management

Table 6.5 Management Practices

Activity	Initial Establishment Period	Ongoing Management
Cultivation	Aerate during the first year to maintain aggressive growth and to avoid sod-layering problems. Perform slicing to encourage lateral growth and improve stem and root density.	Cultivation is recommended twice per year on golf courses; similar practice should be employed on active-use turfs, less often on other turfs. Cultivate to reduce compaction, reduce soil layering, encourage thatch reduction, spur deeprooting, and improve soil air-water exchange. Coring is a most reliable method for long-lasting soil improvement. Slicing and spiking are short-term in effects, but spur lateral growth and improve soil-seed contact if performed following overseeding. High-pressure injection uses water or air to create small channels deep into the soil.
Irrigation	Seed and sprig installations: Implement an irrigation program for the first 2–3 weeks that will achieve initial root establishment by keeping the soil moist in the $1/4''$–$1/2''$ range. For high-sand greens, a typical irrigation schedule might be as follows: 6 minutes every 2 hours from 6:00 A.M. to 11:00 A.M.; 4 minutes every hour from noon–6:00 P.M.; one 6-minute application from midnight–6:00 A.M. After 70% to 80% germination or when rooting of sprigs has begun, shorten run-times without reducing start times for the next 10 to 16 days. After this period, reduce the number of start times and begin deeper	Use irrigation to manage active-use turf, turf subject to use during low-rainfall periods, and turf established on highly porous soils. Apply irrigation to achieve deep watering without runoff. Apply water evenly and at rates specifically designed for the turf and soil conditions. Surface pooling is indicative of improper application rates or of soil compaction. Reduce water application rates and/or cultivate the soil to improve infiltration. Overwatering results in poor turf quality, nutrient leaching, disease-prone conditions, extra expense, and wasted resources.

Continued

Table 6.5 *continued*

Activity	Initial Establishment Period	Ongoing Management
	watering. Adjust the program based on soil composition and weather conditions.	
Mowing	Mow based on grass height, not based on turf density. The first 6 mowings should not remove more than $1/4$ of the turf blade. See Figure 6.9 for a guide to mowing height and desired height. Contact a local turf specialist for initial turf height for specific cultivars. Use mulching mowers.	The higher turf is maintained, the deeper and better its root structure. Determine mowing height for specific cultivars from local turf specialists. Never remove more than $1/3$ of the grass blade length. See Figure 6.9 for a guide to mowing height and desired height. Keep mower blades sharp to reduce disease potential. Use a reel-type mower on thick grasses such as zoysia and all grasses that are cut very short. Avoid mowing when the soil and turf are moist; vary mowing patterns to limit compaction due to wheel action. Use mulching mowers or compost-collected clippings.
Fertilization	Prior to planting, make sure soil pH and nutrients are in proper balance for the specific turf. Correcting pH can be accomplished more rapidly prior to planting than afterward. Phosphorus is recommended at 50–70 ppm for establishment.	Follow a fertilization program based on regular soil testing rather than reacting to visually apparent turf conditions. Soil-test annually for clay-based soils, more often for sand-based soils. Strive for optimum fertility levels without generating growth surges. Monitor soil pH to maintain proper minor element availability. Use slow-release and organic fertilizers as much as possible, and avoid weakening the turf with excessive or insufficient nitrogen. Maintaining good potassium

		levels has been shown to make turf more traffic-tolerant.
Pest control	Only apply pesticides if the infestation is excessive.	Integrated pest control programs recognize that insects are always present, but a healthy turf can resist insect damage and recover quickly from minor infestations without the use of chemicals. Large overpopulations of damaging insects are of concern, but do not apply pesticides unless the specific infestation has been properly identified. Environmental stress symptoms can resemble insect damage. Pesticides should be a last resort, because they kill beneficial insects as well. Some "green" pesticides are now available, as are biological controls using beneficial insects.
Disease control	Only apply fungicides if necessary. Use fungicide-treated seed when possible.	Diseases are best controlled by a strong cultural management program. Most diseases are caused by fungi that enter plants through wounds. Wounds most frequently occur from mowing, but traffic impacts and insects are secondary causes. Keeping blades sharp and mowing heights high reduces the likelihood of fungal infection. Excessive moisture due to overwatering, soil compaction, and shade can encourage fungal growth. Fungicides are available for specific infections and for preventative measures, but the specific disease must be determined.

Continued

Table 6.5 *continued*

Activity	Initial Establishment Period	Ongoing Management
Weed control	Only spray herbicides if necessary. Immature turf can be sensitive to herbicides. When installing turf by seed, seed at the proper rate to provide sufficient competition against weeds.	Weed control is an issue in all turfgrass. However, depending on the type of turf, weed definition may change. A good turf management program can help limit some weeds, but most must be managed by herbicides. Organic "green" pesticides are now available. Apply herbicides when weeds are young and actively growing. Once seed heads form, herbicides have little effect, become a wasted expense, and demonstrate environmental irresponsibility.
Top-dressing	Apply top-dressing to even out turf surfaces. On high-sand bases, top-dress prior to aerification to limit rutting until the turf is established. Use a drag mat after aerification cores dry to blend soil and limit layering.	Apply top-dressing to even out turf surfaces, repair damaged turf, and control thatch build-up. An application of sand or soil mix is most typical. Try to match the character of the existing soil to reduce the potential for layering. Top-dressing bunch-type grasses should be done at seeding times, while stoloniferous and rhizomatous grasses can receive incremental applications throughout the growing season. Application of crumb rubber from recycled tires as a top-dressing (0.05–2.0 mm diameter at 17.8 and 35.7 tons per acre) was found to reduce surface hardness, reduce turfgrass wear injury, and beneficially raise soil temperatures in a northern climate. It is unclear if the soil

		temperature effect is acceptable in southern climates.
Overseeding and reseeding	Overseeding of warm-season turfs during the establishment period should be avoided. Overseeding increases management requirements and can negatively impact spring growth of immature turf.	Overseeding can be performed for functional and aesthetic reasons. Overseed/reseed bunch-type grasses regularly to maintain turf quality. Usually, cool-season grasses are best seeded both fall and spring. Of the warm-season grasses, Bahia in particular will benefit from reseeding to maintain a thick turf. In the South, cool-season grasses are often overseeded onto dormant warm-season grasses for aesthetic reasons. Annual or perennial ryegrass is commonly preferred. Unless the area is heavily trafficked and will benefit functionally, overseeding simply creates off-season management requirements.
Traffic control	Do not allow turf to be trafficked except for management purposes until establishment is complete. Traffic impacts on immature turf will reduce turf quality and damage soil/root structure. Alter mowing patterns regularly to minimize damage.	Traffic control is important in areas subject to high use. Compaction and wear, particularly during stress periods can severely damage turf. Reroute pedestrians using movable barriers (posts and ropes) or by adding potted plants, sculptures, or bollards along busy sidewalks to control major traffic flows. Where turf areas are intended for pedestrian traffic, design them to be broad so that traffic will be spread out, or provide alternative routes that can be opened or closed as needed.

practices for the establishment period and for ongoing turf management. Follow LEED guidelines to minimize negative environmental impacts associated with turf and especially those impacts due to poor management practices.

Practices to Avoid

- Avoid excessive tilling. It can pulverize the soil, turning it into a powdery mix and destroying its structure.
- Avoid poor-quality seed. Low germination, weed seeds, and poorly adapted species will cause problems later.
- Seed should not be buried or covered with soil.
- Avoid overwatering; floating seeds can wash away, resulting in uneven cover.
- Apply enough water to moisten the top half-inch or so of the profile, but avoid overwatering, saturating the area, and possibly washing away seeds.

References

ALSO IN THIS BOOK

See Chapter 1, "Soils," and Chapter 8, "Irrigation and Water Use Efficiency."

OTHER RESOURCES

Beard, James B. *Turf Management for Golf Courses*. New York: Macmillan Publishing Company, 1982.

Hopper, Leonard J. *Landscape Architectural Graphic Standards*. Hoboken, NJ: John Wiley & Sons, Inc., 2007.

Sauer, Leslie Jones, and Andropogon Associates. *The Once and Future Forest*. Washington, DC: Island Press, 1998.

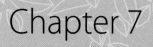

Chapter 7

Planting in Difficult or Special Situations

Tree Planting in Paved Areas

Description

Traditional designs in which trees are regularly spaced in small openings within paved areas generally result in poor tree performance, as shown in Figure 7.1. This is because such designs generally do not provide adequate soil for root growth and ignore the fact that trees must significantly increase trunk size every year. As well, competition for space, both

Figure 7.1 This tree and the empty tree pit in the background represent the unfortunate outcome of planting small trees in individual tree pits in a dense urban environment.

at ground level and below, is intense in urban areas. Smaller trees planted in dense urban environments are also more susceptible to vandalism.

Assessing Site Conditions

Obstacles to Healthy Tree Growth

Trees grow poorly in urban areas unless the soil beneath and adjacent to hard surfaces supports root growth. Root growth is the critical factor for successful design execution. The system has to be specially designed to accommodate tree root growth.

Rarely in the urban environment will there exist the typical soil horizon profile diagrams we are familiar with. However, there will be soil that has not been highly disturbed and may still provide favorable root conditions, water holding, and nutrient supply. These remnant soils may be on the surface or buried under paving or layers of fill. Remnant soils generally have their B and C horizons intact and often do not have root-limiting bulk densities. Locating these soils and identifying their degree of disturbance is critical at the early stage of soil analysis, so that they can be protected as much as possible during construction. See Figures 7.2 and 7.3.

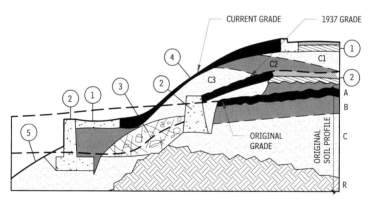

Figure 7.2   Urban soil profiles A, B, C, and R. Original soil horizons may be graded and/or compacted. Remnant and buried topsoil may be encountered, C1–C3 are fill soils of various types, bulk density levels, and consistencies from heavy clays to sands. Expect soil interfaces between different soils. (1) Existing impervious surfaces. (2) Buried impervious surfaces and structures. (3) Buried trash and debris, which may be unstable organic trash or compacted rock and gravel. (4) Eroded topsoil layer and exposed fills. (5) Exposed original subsoil with low organic content.
Courtesy of James Urban/ISA.

Figure 7.3   Remnant soil. (1) New topsoil. Note sharp interface between topsoil and fill material below. (2) Fill soil. Note lack of structure and fine roots. (3) Buried remnant topsoil. Note thick roots and angular structure preserved in the soil. (4) Original B horizon soil with strong structure and gradual transition between topsoil and subsoil. (5) Trash piled into excavation, if not removed, will become a part of the urban soil profile.
Courtesy of James Urban/ISA.

When roots encounter the soils that are densely compacted to support pavements and other infrastructure, they change direction or continue growing in contorted shapes close to the trunk and near the surface. This leaves the tree susceptible to a host of problems associated with abnormal root growth—drought conditions, heaving pavements, and general instability.

Compacted soils have high rates of runoff, with little water infiltration that is needed by tree roots for proper growth and root development. Therefore, even in situations where there may be adequate amounts of rainfall, very little may be finding its way down to where it can be absorbed by the tree roots.

▶ Compaction is the enemy of growth and storm water management.

Trees need significant soil volumes of low-compacted soil with suitable pore space, drainage, and organic matter to provide for healthy long-term growth. The amount of soil required for trees of different sizes is shown in Figure 7.4. As the graph indicates, a large tree needs more than 1,000 cubic feet of soil to reach the significant size that we as designers envision on our plans.

Areas of pavement provide difficult conditions and obstacles to healthy tree growth that must be overcome. However, these areas have the greatest need and stand to benefit the most by the storm water management and heat island mitigation that a healthy urban tree planting can provide. Therefore, we should look to find ways to provide large volumes of noncompacted soils with adequate drainage and aeration that can not only be used in our tree pit openings but also extended under the adjacent pavements. See Figure 7.5.

Regulations and Restrictions

There are usually state, county, or local regulations that place restrictions on where trees can be planted, particularly concerning street tree planting. Regulations control how close a tree can be planted to an

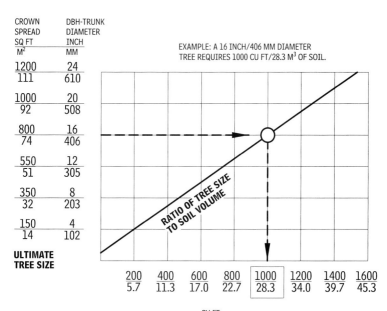

Figure 7.4 Tree size to soil volume relationship.
Courtesy of James Urban/ISA.

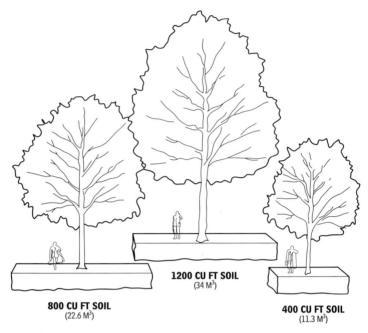

800 CU FT SOIL
(22.6 M³)

1200 CU FT SOIL
(34 M³)

400 CU FT SOIL
(11.3 M³)

TREE SIZE – SOIL VOLUME

Figure 7.5   Tree size and life expectancy will respond proportionally to increases in soil volume.
Courtesy of James Urban/ISA.

intersection, vehicular curb cut, utility pole, traffic sign, streetlight, and so forth. These regulations should be checked prior to any preliminary site visit or development of a planting plan along a public right-of-way.

Some municipalities may also restrict tree planting to an approved list of trees. Check for restrictions on which tree species are acceptable before developing a planting plan.

Acceptable Practices

Species Selection

In addition to the normal criteria considered when selecting which tree species to specify (see "Site Considerations and Tree Selection," in Chapter 4), tree species that are more suitable for planting in a paved urban or suburban situation have the following characteristics:

- Trees that do not have a prominent root flare that can lift sidewalk or curbs.

- Trees that tend to have a deeper root system.
- Trees that do not have messy fruits or flowers that can create a maintenance or safety problem.
- Trees that can tolerate the use of road deicing salts.
- Trees that require little maintenance.

Soil Volume

The soil provides many resources for the tree, primary among them being water, oxygen, nutrients, and a medium for root growth. When soil volume is limited, tree growth suffers because so much of the top growth of the tree is dependent on what the roots can deliver, and that in turn depends on the size of the resource pool of soil. It is possible to grow trees in quite small containers as long as water, nutrients, and oxygen are supplemented, which is not easily done in urban areas. However, we are beginning to learn that roots not only are the conduits of resources to the tops of the trees but also produce growth factors necessary for shoot growth. Roots must grow themselves in order to produce these growth factors. Moreover, only new white roots efficiently take up nutrients. Therefore, if root growth is restricted, top growth will also be restricted, even if water and nutrients are plentiful in the soil (Hawver 1997).

Areas of dense urban development leave little room for tree roots to develop. Large areas of pavement, competition with foundations and utilities for space belowground, and extensive soil compaction and disruption limit the amount of soil available for trees.

In paved areas where room for root growth may be constrained and the open area around the tree is limited, the following tree growth characteristics need to be considered (see Figure 7.6):

- *Crown growth* — The tree crown expands every growing season at a rate of 6 to 8 inches per year. Once the crown reaches a competing object, such as a building or another tree canopy, the canopy growth in that area slows and then stops. Eventually, the branches on that side of the tree die. As the canopy expansion potential is reduced, the overall growth rate and tree health are also reduced.
- *Trunk growth* — The tree trunk expands about $^1/_2$ to 1 inch per year. As the tree increases in size, the lower branches die and the trunk lengthens. Tree trunks move considerably in the wind, especially during the early years of development, and are damaged by close objects.
- *Trunk flare* — At the point where the trunk leaves the ground, most tree species develop a pronounced swelling or flare as the tree

matures. This flare grows at more than twice the rate of the main trunk diameter and helps the tree remain structurally stable. Any hard object placed in this area, such as a tree grate or confining pavement, will either damage the tree or be moved by the tremendous force of this growth.

- *Zone of rapid root taper* — Tree roots begin to form in the trunk flare and divide several times in the immediate area around the trunk. In this area, about 5 to 6 feet away from the trunk, the roots rapidly taper from about 6 inches in diameter to about 2 inches. Most damage to adjacent paving occurs in this area immediately around the tree. Keeping the zone of rapid taper free of obstructions is important to long-term tree health. Once a tree is established, the zone of rapid taper is generally less susceptible to compaction damage than the rest of the root zone.

- *Root zone* — Tree roots grow radially and horizontally from the trunk and occupy only the upper layers (12 to 24 inches) of the soil. Trees in all but the most well-drained soils do not have taproots. A relationship exists between the amount of tree canopy and the volume of root-supporting soil required (see Figure 7.4). This relationship is the most critical factor in determining long-term tree health. Root-supporting soil is generally defined as soil with adequate drainage, low compaction, and sufficient organic and nutrient components to support

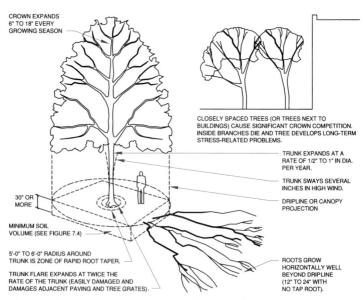

Figure 7.6 Tree structure — parts and growing characteristics.
Source: Hopper, *Landscape Architecture Graphic Standards.* Copyright John Wiley & Sons, Inc., 2007.

the tree. The root zone must be protected from compaction both during and after construction. Root zones that are connected from tree to tree generally produce healthier trees than isolated root zones.

Typical Situations

Tree Pits between Sidewalk and Street

The traditional street tree pit is one of the most common tree plantings, as well as one of the most challenging to a tree's survival. Very rarely are the openings in the pavement large enough to provide the water and air necessary for tree health and growth (see Figure 7.7). The compacted soils to support the adjacent curbs and sidewalks create a barrier that stops roots from growing beyond the soil within the tree pit, limiting growth and contributing to early decline.

Trees planted in these situations rarely live longer than 10 to 12 years, with the tree experiencing a visibly painful decline during those last

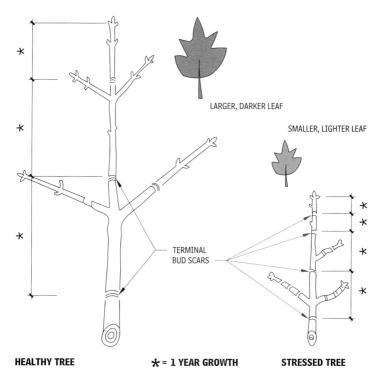

LARGER, DARKER LEAF

SMALLER, LIGHTER LEAF

TERMINAL BUD SCARS

HEALTHY TREE   ✱ = 1 YEAR GROWTH   STRESSED TREE

Figure 7.7 Comparing the incremental yearly growth distance on twigs can help an observer estimate the stress level and growth rates of the trees.
Courtesy of James Urban/ISA.

Figure 7.8   A mature tree's roots have lifted the sidewalk, creating a tripping hazard as they seek out soil in the turf area on the other side of the walk.

few years. Trees that miraculously live longer often develop root systems that lift the adjacent pavements, as shown in Figure 7.8, leading to a later decision to cut the roots rather than leave a potential tripping hazard. Either scenario prevents the tree from achieving a mature canopy and will usually result in the need for a regular cycle of tree replacement. The sequence of photos in Figures 7.9 through 7.12 documents this situation.

If a traditional tree pit in a paved area is the only alternative for tree planting, the following techniques can improve the tree's chances for survival and increase longevity:

- The larger the pavement opening can be made—backfilled with an uncompacted planting mix or amended soil—the better. The greater volume of soil conducive to root growth will increase survival rate and ultimate canopy growth (see Figure 7.4).
- Unit pavers installed on a flexible base can be used to prevent the soil within the tree pit areas from becoming compacted, and to allow water and air to infiltrate down to the root system. Unit pavers can extend the walking surface of the adjacent pavement, allowing the tree pit opening to be made larger without creating a tripping hazard, benefiting both tree and pedestrian. As the tree grows in size, the unit pavers can be removed to make the opening larger to accommodate trunk growth.

Figure 7.9   The planting of a new street tree in an individual tree pit (approximately 400 cubic feet of planting soil available) cut into the sidewalk between the street and a raised planter.
Courtesy of James Urban/ISA.

Figure 7.10   The tree at 12 years appears to be relatively healthy.
Courtesy of James Urban/ISA.

Figure 7.11   The tree at 16 years shows signs of branch dieback and decline as the tree's roots run out of soil volume.
Courtesy of James Urban/ISA.

Figure 7.12   The tree at 25 years has died. The trees farther down the block, whose roots have access to soil in planted areas on the other side of the sidewalk, continue to survive.
Courtesy of James Urban/ISA.

- Consider the use of a mechanical root barrier to direct roots down and away from adjacent paved areas. (See the section "Alternate Strategies" in this chapter.)
- Provide opportunities for the tree root system to grow underneath the adjacent pavements, utilizing a controlled engineered approach that accommodates root development and protects the structural integrity of the pavement. (See "Alternate Strategies.")

▶ If street trees are to be planted between the sidewalk and street, with the intent that they survive and thrive, one of the alternate strategies for tree planting in pavement should be considered.

Adjacent Unpaved Areas

"Plant the easy places first." —James Urban

It is better to provide large open areas for tree planting than to provide small openings in the pavement that constrain root growth and tree

Figure 7.13 Planting street trees in a wide planting strip between the street and sidewalk provides roots with a large soil volume and allows water and air infiltration, providing these trees with a better chance to survive and mature. Complemented by the trees planted on the opposite side, a pleasant tree-lined walk with overlapping canopies is created.

development. Large unpaved areas lend themselves to soil modification if necessary and provide trees with adequate soil volumes for root development and long-term, healthy canopy growth.

In existing landscapes, look for places with large, open areas where lawn or other existing vegetation is already growing, indicating healthy, uncompacted soil. During design development, look for opportunities to create large, open areas within paved spaces for tree planting, as shown in Figures 7.13 and 7.14. Equally important is to call for these areas to be protected during construction from compaction that could destroy soil structure. See Figures 7.15 through 7.17.

Highways and Parkways

Trees planted along major roads are usually planted in large enough open areas that special attention to creating adequate soil volumes for root growth is not required. Because trees planted in these areas receive little maintenance or watering and are often open and exposed to sun and wind, trees that are drought tolerant should be considered. Tree selection criteria should include tolerance of salt and salt spray from the use of deicing agents, if applicable. Trees with thicker bark will be less susceptible to damage from larger mowers and weed wackers.

Figure 7.14 Large planting areas are created adjacent to the walkway, allowing trees to thrive and mature.

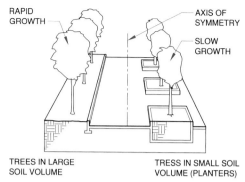

Figure 7.15 A good growth comparison diagram between trees planted in an easy place and trees planted with the more difficult constraints of a traditional tree pit. If visually symmetrical trees are desired, then symmetrical soil volumes are required to produce similar crown sizes.
Source: Hopper, *Landscape Architecture Graphic Standards.* Copyright John Wiley & Sons, Inc., 2007.

Median Strips

Trees considered for planting in median strips between traffic lanes should be drought and salt tolerant. Trees with upright habits are more appropriate than trees with lower and/or spreading branching habits, as these can block signage and traffic control devices. Median

Figure 7.16 A good comparison of the different growth rates of the same species of tree. One row of trees was planted in a continuous open area, and the other row in individual tree pits within the pavement.
Source: Trowbridge and Bassuk, *Trees in the Urban Landscape,* Fig. 3-31b. Copyright John Wiley & Sons, Inc., 2004.

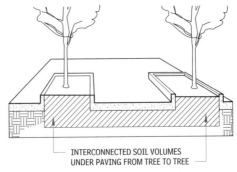

INTERCONNECTED SOIL VOLUMES
UNDER PAVING FROM TREE TO TREE

Figure 7.17 The interconnection of soil volumes from tree to tree has been observed to improve the health and vigor of trees.
Source: Hopper, *Landscape Architecture Graphic Standards.* Copyright John Wiley & Sons, Inc., 2007.

strips that are slightly raised with a curb along the edge restrict traffic, and the tree pit openings can be relatively large. Where pavement is desired, unit pavers that allow water and air to infiltrate to the roots are a good alternative. See Figures 7.18 through 7.23.

Parking Areas

Parking areas are large paved areas that would benefit greatly from healthy tree and shading canopies. They also have inherent challenges

Figure 7.18 The trees planted in wide median strips of lawn and shrubs fare better than their counterparts planted in median strips that are paved.

Figure 7.19 Trees planted in median strips paved with concrete have the same obstacles to survival as a street tree in an individual tree pit between the sidewalk and curb. These trees have a high mortality rate and need to be replaced regularly.

Figure 7.20 Trees planted in median strips paved with unit pavers generally do better than those in concrete. However, how well they do still depends on the uncompacted soil volumes below the pavers. At first glance, these trees seem to be doing moderately well.

Figure 7.21 However a closer look shows that they are experiencing branch dieback and nutrient deficiency (evidenced by the color of their leaves). They are actually in a state of decline.

Figure 7.22 These trees, planted in median strips with unit pavers, have survived and grown quite well. The unit pavers allow water and air to infiltrate down to the soil.

Figure 7.23 New trees that are being planted in this median are clustered together, and the pavers have been replaced with mulch. The shared soil area is wider and longer than the area available to trees planted in individual tree pits. This should increase their chances for survival.

to tree establishment and growth. It is best to avoid planting trees in singular, small openings in the pavement; trees rarely do well in these highly constrained situations. It is best to create larger islands or planting strips where trees have adequate soil volumes for root development. See Figures 7.24 through 7.28. Any parking location where a tree is to be planted should account for vehicle overhangs to prevent trees from being damaged from contact with car bumpers.

Alternate Strategies

Planting Trees between the Sidewalk and Street

Long, linear, open planting strips are better suited to tree planting than the typical 5′ x 5′ sidewalk cutout. As seen in Figure 7.29, the open area provides an adequate volume of uncompacted soil that

Figure 7.24 Trees planted in tiny openings in the paved area of a parking lot are easily damaged and will not grow a large enough canopy to provide any meaningful shade.

Figure 7.25 Trees planted in larger islands will develop large enough canopies to provide shade and contribute toward mitigating the heat island effect of large asphalt-paved surfaces. These trees are grouped two to an island and are able to share the soil volumes available.

Figure 7.26 These parking lot islands frame out the parking space and provide enough planted area for two trees and groundcover planting. Vertical rods indicate corners of curb so that trees are not damaged during snow removal.

Figure 7.27 Creating larger parking lot islands and clustering trees can provide adequate soil volumes for healthy tree growth, encouraging canopy development that can have a meaningful impact on mitigating heat island effect.

Figure 7.28 This large planted median between parking rows allows for mature tree growth and provides a site amenity for the staff at this corporate campus.

Figure 7.29 Planting trees in open planting strips helps increase chances of survival and positive growth. In this case, the planting strip is twice as wide as the sidewalk (not the other way around).

will allow water and air to infiltrate down to promote healthy root development.

Where it may not be practical to leave the entire planting strip open, either because of maintenance concerns or heavy pedestrian traffic, installing a unit paver on a sand base is a good alternative. Pervious pavers have distinct openings installed on a base of No. 8 stone with No. 9 stone swept into the joints to ensure water and air infiltration.

Root Barriers

Mechanical root barriers that direct tree roots to grow down and away from adjacent paved areas can be considered. They can be installed in a surround application that lines the entire perimeter of a tree pit and uncompacted backfill. They can also be installed in a linear application (see Figure 7.30) that directs root growth away from adjacent pavements and curbs on two sides. This approach can be especially effective when used in conjunction with interconnected tree pits. Roots are

Figure 7.30 Root barrier installed in a linear application directs roots growing in the planting strip down away from pavement.
Courtesy of Deep Root Partners, L.P.

encouraged to grow in the planting mix between the tree pits but are directed away from curbs and sidewalks.

▶ Root barriers perform best in existing or amended soils that are well drained and have good aeration.

Interconnected Tree Pits and Soil Volume

Trees that are planted in tree pits that are connected to each other can benefit by sharing the volume of soil between them for root development. Although it may not be practical to leave these areas between the tree pits unpaved in every situation, an alternative unit paving that allows water and air to infiltrate is a good compromise. See Figures 7.31 and 7.32.

Excavating and backfilling between tree pits with a planting mix or amended soil will encourage root growth beyond the immediate tree pit soil. A linear application of a root barrier to discourage lifting of sidewalks or curbs will help keep root growth within the interconnected soil path.

Cluster Planting

Planting trees in clusters, rather than individual tree pits, allows a group of trees to share and benefit from an increased soil volume. The

Figure 7.31 These trees are planted in connected tree pits that are backfilled with a planting mix and paved with permeable concrete pavers.

Figure 7.32 The permeable concrete pavers have a distinct joint space between them. The joints are swept with a No. 8 or 9 stone that allows water and air to permeate to the planting soil below.

area to be shared needs to be larger than the area that would be available to individually planted trees, to provide enough soil volume to benefit the root development of all the trees that are planted.

This strategy can lead to more successful tree planting in large paved areas such as parking lots and urban plazas. A cluster of healthy trees will have more design impact and environmental benefit than trees in declining health that are planted individually in pits 30 feet apart (see Figures 7.33 and 7.34).

Structural Soils

Typically, soils under pavements are densely compacted to support the weight of the pavement and whatever pedestrian or vehicular loads are placed on it. Compaction destroys soil structure and eliminates large pore spaces. Roots cannot penetrate densely compacted soils, which gives rise to the inherent conflict of growing healthy trees in paved areas. Structural soils are designed to support pavements as well as provide the required pore space that allows for the water infiltration and aeration required for root growth.

Structural soils are typically a very specifically engineered blend (approximately 80 percent stone and 20 percent soil) of larger

Figure 7.33 Trees clustered in open planted areas benefit from increased soil volumes. These trees provide more of an impact along the street side-walk than trees planted in individual tree pits along the curb.

Figure 7.34 In this example, trees are planted in open planted areas, where possible, and in tree pits in unit pavers when necessary. The trees in the individual pits are not doing quite as well as the trees clustered in the larger planted areas.

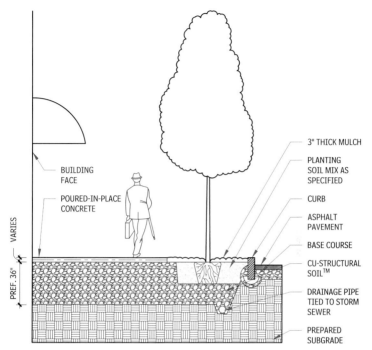

Figure 7.35 Detail of a typical structural soil installation. Structural soil is supporting the concrete pavement between the curb and the building face, providing the tree roots additional room to grow under the pavement.
Courtesy of Nina L. Bassuk, Urban Horticulture Institute, Cornell University.

angular stone (approximately 1 inch), a high-quality soil mix (clay loam), and hydrogel. The large stone supports the pavement through stone-to-stone contact, which distributes the load over the subgrade. The void spaces between the stone are filled with a high-quality soil mix. The hydrogel is added as a tackifier to prevent the segregation of soil during mixing and installation. Typically, structural soils are installed at depths of between 24 and 36 inches. See Figures 7.35 and 7.36.

When the structural soil is compacted for pavement support, the soil mix in the voids remains loose and uncompacted. The roots grow between the voids and into the soil mix. This allows the roots to penetrate beyond the tree pit and grow under adjacent pavements supported by the structural soil (see Figure 7.37). This increases the soil volume available for root development. Research indicates that the trees are deep-rooted and do not lift the sidewalks or curbs supported by the structural soil.

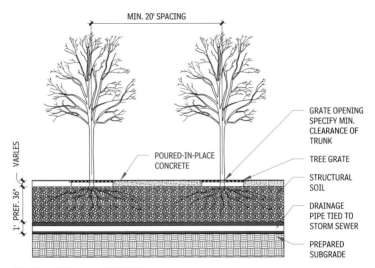

TYPICAL STREET TREE PLANTING

Figure 7.36 Structural soil installation elevation showing the structural soil supporting the pavement between tree openings, encouraging root growth under the pavement.
Courtesy of Nina L. Bassuk, Urban Horticulture Institute, Cornell University.

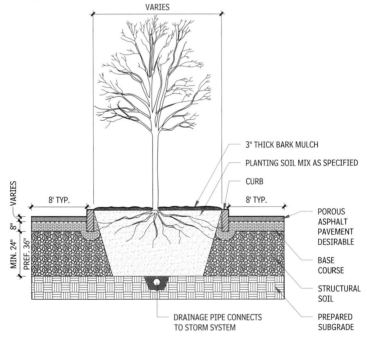

BARE ROOT TREE IN TYPICAL PARKING LOT ISLAND

Figure 7.37 Detail showing how structural soil can be used to support the parking lot pavement and at the same time encourage root growth beyond the confines of the parking lot island.
Courtesy of Nina L. Bassuk, Urban Horticulture Institute, Cornell University.

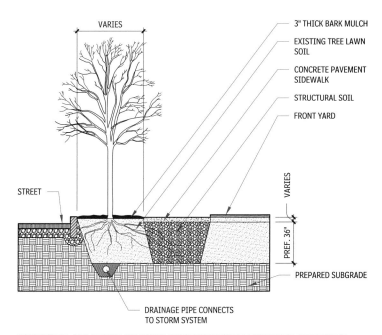

VARIES

3" THICK BARK MULCH

EXISTING TREE LAWN SOIL

CONCRETE PAVEMENT SIDEWALK

STRUCTURAL SOIL

FRONT YARD

STREET

VARIES

PREF. 36"

PREPARED SUBGRADE

DRAINAGE PIPE CONNECTS TO STORM SYSTEM

STRUCTURAL SOIL BREAK-OUT ZONE FROM NARROW TREE LAWN TO FRONT YARD

Figure 7.38   Structural soil can be used to provide a break-out opportunity for roots to grow from a narrow planting strip adjacent to the street curb under the sidewalk in order to access the soil volume available in the front lawn. Courtesy of Nina L. Bassuk, Urban Horticulture Institute, Cornell University.

The use of structural soil is a good alternative to expanding the available volume of soil for trees planted in parking areas, plazas, or any large expanse of pavement. Structural soils can be particularly effective in encouraging root growth under pavements to areas where they can access large volumes of good soil (see Figure 7.38). A typical example is a street tree planted between the curb and a sidewalk constructed over a structural soil blend. The tree roots can be interconnected or grow under the sidewalk to access the larger soil area of a lawn or planted area between the sidewalk and building. See Figures 7.39 through 7.42.

Modular Cell System
The modular cell system is preengineered to support pavements and create large spaces under pavements that are filled with a planting soil mix that remains loose and uncompacted. The system provides 95 percent of the space within the cells for a planting soil mix that is conducive to root growth and development.

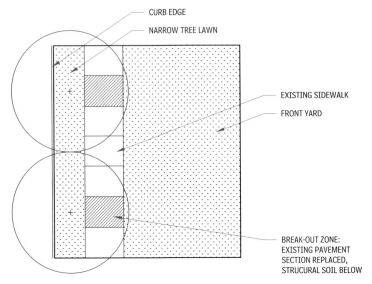

PLAN VIEW OF RETROFITTED STRUCTURAL SOIL BREAK–OUT AREA

Figure 7.39 A plan view where one flag of an existing sidewalk is removed, the existing soil beneath is replaced with structural soil, and the concrete flag replaced. The structural soil provides roots with a path to the planting soil of the front yard.
Courtesy of Nina L. Bassuk, Urban Horticulture Institute, Cornell University.

Figure 7.40 Structural soil is being installed between the sidewalk and curb, providing a connection between tree pits.
Source: Trowbridge and Bassuk, *Trees in the Urban Landscape.* Copyright John Wiley & Sons., 2004.

Figure 7.41 The area between trees is completed with the installation of unit pavers over the structural soil.
Source: Trowbridge and Bassuk, *Trees in the Urban Landscape.* Copyright John Wiley & Sons., 2004.

Figure 7.42 These *Pyrus calleryana* "Chanticleer" trees planted in a plaza space utilizing CU-Structural Soil are doing very well. Trees that are both alkaline soil tolerant and moderately to highly drought tolerant make the best candidates for use with a structural soil mix.
Courtesy of Nina L. Bassuk, Urban Horticulture Institute, Cornell University.

The system is compatible with concrete, asphalt, porous asphalt, porous concrete paving, and modular brick and concrete pavers. Each paving type must include an appropriate base course between the paving and the deck, from 4 inches for concrete to 12 inches for modular pavers. An airspace provided under the deck allows water to move under the pavement and pool above the soil, while keeping roots growing in the upper soil layers from lifting the sidewalk. The airspace can receive rainwater either from infiltration through pervious pavers above the cells or by channeling surface water from inlets, drains, and roof leaders into the airspace.

The cell structures are set on a 4-inch gravel subbase (see Figures 7.43 and 7.44). This subbase acts as the foundation for the cells (see Figures 7.45 through 7.47) and as a drainage course to remove water from the soil. The modular cells can be stacked one, two, or three units high, depending upon space, budget, and site needs.

The increased soil volumes under the pavement provide for good root development and healthy tree growth. See Figures 7.48 through 7.56. The ability for the soil to have increased water storage capacity and pollutant removal rates makes the cell system an integral part of a good storm water management system.

Figure 7.43 The aggregate subbase is laid out over compacted subgrade of excavation.
Courtesy of Deep Root Partners, L.P.

Figure 7.44 The aggregate subbase is leveled and compacted.
Courtesy of Deep Root Partners, L.P.

Figure 7.45 Using 2"x3" lumber as spacers to achieve the desired 1"–3"
spacing between cells, the modular cells are laid out and spiked into place.
Courtesy of Deep Root Partners, L.P.

Figure 7.46 Two layers of the modular cells are laid out. The workers are standing in the space where the trees will be planted.
Courtesy of Deep Root Partners, L.P.

Figure 7.47 Zip ties are used to attach a geogrid to the perimeter of the cells to keep the soil within the frames during installation.
Courtesy of Deep Root Partners, L.P.

Figure 7.48 Soil is loaded into the frames in 8" lifts.
Courtesy of Deep Root Partners, L.P.

Figure 7.49 Modular cells are filled with planting soil mix. Strongbacks sticking up from the frames help hold the posts in place during installation.
Courtesy of Deep Root Partners, L.P.

Figure 7.50 Strongbacks are removed and the decks are snapped and screwed on.
Courtesy of Deep Root Partners, L.P.

Figure 7.51 With all the decks secure, the area is ready for the final lift of backfill and compaction.
Courtesy of Deep Root Partners, L.P.

Figure 7.52 The area around the cells is backfilled and compacted.
Courtesy of Deep Root Partners, L.P.

Figure 7.53 A geotextile fabric is laid out over the decks, and the fabric is cut out for the tree openings.
Courtesy of Deep Root Partners, L.P.

Figure 7.54 The aggregate base course is laid over the geotextile fabric.
Courtesy of Deep Root Partners, L.P.

Figure 7.55 The aggregate layer is brought up to the desired grade and compacted, ready for the installation of pavers.
Courtesy of Deep Root Partners, L.P.

Figure 7.56   The installation of unit pavers over the aggregate base and setting bed, site amenities, and, of course, the planted trees complete the streetscape installation.
Courtesy of Deep Root Partners, L.P.

Practices to Avoid

- Avoid soil compaction in areas to be planted—before, after, and during construction.
- Avoid planting trees in small, disconnected tree pits with small volumes of available soil that inhibit root development.
- Avoid damage to the tree trunk and root flare by providing enough room for growth and development.
- Avoid tree trunk damage from vehicles in parking areas by remembering to account for vehicle overhangs in the design.
- Planting trees in raised planters can add soil volume (see Figure 7.57). Avoid building up soil around the trunks of existing trees; this will kill the tree (see Figure 7.58).
- Avoid planting trees crooked. On slopes, trees should always be planted truly vertical. See Figure 7.59.

Figure 7.57 Planting trees in raised planters can provide additional soil volume for roots.
Source: Trowbridge and Bassuk, *Trees in the Urban Landscape.* Copyright John Wiley & Sons., 2004.

Figure 7.58 Raised planters built around existing trees damage the trunk, keep air and water from reaching the roots, and eventually kill the tree.

Figure 7.59 Trees should be planted with the trunk truly vertical. This tree was planted perpendicular to the slope of the ground and is leaning right from the start.

Green Roofs

Description

The term "green roof" has taken on ecological and social significance beyond its seemingly simplistic description. "Green roofs," as commonly understood, have become a panacea for the reduction of pollution and heat islands, for large-scale mitigation of storm water runoff, and for maximum utilization of urban land.

"Green roof," today, is often used as an umbrella term for a number of greening systems built over a structural decking that serves as a roof to that specific portion of the structure. As a "roof garden," "eco-roof," "extensive green roof," or "intensive green roof," the system acts and is perceived as a roof or lid. As a "roof garden," "over-structure-open-space," or "intensive green roof," the system may either serve as a roof or a grade-level floor.

This ambiguity and confusion of terminology is exacerbated by current jargon derived from European usage of "extensive" and "intensive," two words used within the fabrication, supply, and, now, the design industry. These terms, which may seem counterintuitive to English speakers, describe the depth of growing medium and level of effort required to maintain the "green roof."

- *Extensive* is loosely used to describe a system that typically has a very shallow depth of soil or growing medium. It is not irrigated, it is expected to require minimum maintenance, and it is not intended to be accessed for use as a garden or open space.
- *Intensive* is loosely applied to those systems that have a greater depth of soil or growing medium, which allows for a greater diversity in size and type of vegetation. This diversity usually implies a need for supplemental irrigation and, overall, a more intensive level of maintenance.

A disadvantage to using "extensive" and "intensive" as blanket terms is that neither clearly reflects the expected purpose or use of the system, or adequately conveys design requirements to construct and maintain the appropriate components to support its use. A terminology-driven, rather than use-driven, approach to the design and construction of "green roofs" can lead to further confusion and inaccuracy in design, documentation, and client expectations.

Thus, for clarity, in this discussion, terms are defined as follows:

- "Living green roof" is used to describe a thin-profile system where the growing medium is less than 8 inches and where the primary use is to effectively satisfy storm water management requirements in lieu of conventional storm water engineering methods.
- "Landscape over structure" describes a system where the growing medium is greater than 8 inches and, based on programmatic requirements, may be designed to accommodate its use as accessible open space. The combined depth of component parts may exceed several feet, and related systems required to support the uses often become more complex.

"Living green roof" and "landscape over structure" should not be compared with one another. Rather, large-scale ecological and social benefits can be recognized in the appropriate application of either, as well as their combined use to reduce storm water runoff, bind dust and pollutant particulates, reduce energy consumption, improve visual quality of conventional roofs, and provide valuable beautiful, comfortable, usable open space. The selection of the most suitable application should be defined by varied use and design goals.

Assessing Site Conditions

Rooftops are inherently stressful environments, particularly for planting, as they are subject to heat, accelerated evapotranspiration, and desiccating and potentially damaging winds. Tops of roofs, and the structural decking supporting them, essentially become the floor of living green roofs and landscapes over structure. See Figure 7.60.

Basic to building a successful living green roof or landscape over structure are:

- Structure to support it.
- Waterproofing to protect what is below.
- Protection board to protect the waterproofing.
- Drainage systems to remove, direct, release, or retain water.

Planting requirements include:

- Insulation from thermal fluctuation.
- Sources for water and aeration.

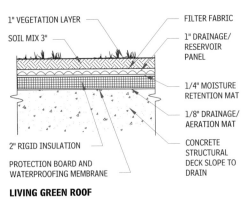

Figure 7.60 Living green roof typical detail.
Source: Hopper, *Landscape Architecture Graphic Standards.* Copyright John Wiley & Sons, Inc., 2007.

- Selection of plants that can survive and flourish in an artificial environment.
- Growing medium, of suitable depth, in which the plants can gather nutrients and establish and maintain their root systems.

Each project will gain more specificity during each subsequent design phase, but there are several key issues that should be considered very early in the project. The client should be made aware of the proper resolution of these issues, as they can have enormous programming, aesthetic, and cost implications. Among the most significant considerations are determining the structural support system and coordinating interior and exterior finished elevations in relationship to the top of the structural slab or deck. Many interrelated factors will affect how these are determined and resolved, and all require extensive, early design coordination among the landscape architect, architect, and structural, civil and mechanical, electrical, and plumbing engineers.

Following is a broad overview of the critical issues requiring early design decisions and coordination:

- Program and expected use of finished interior and exterior surfaces.
- Resultant structural requirements and structural slab configuration.
- Subsurface drainage requirements.
- Drain locations.
- Waterproofing requirements.
- Minimum and optimum slope requirements for structural slab.
- Surface materials, profile of system, and constituent components.
- Surface grading and drainage requirements.

Other early considerations might include requirements for:

- Height limitations for bottom of structure (floor-to-floor requirements).
- Mechanical, electrical, or plumbing plenum or conduit locations.
- Venting size, direction of flow, noise level, location, and surface expression.

If it is determined that planting is a part of the program, key issues to be addressed should include:

- Whether the planting is a living green roof, a larger-scale landscape, or both.
- The plan limits of each type of planting.
- Horticultural requirements.
- Microclimate considerations such as wind and effect of rapid soil temperature fluctuations.
- Expected planting profiles (low-growing drought-resistant plants, ground covers, shrubs, flowering and understory trees, large-caliper trees).
- Maximum depth and weight of root balls or box sizes.
- Soil or growing medium type, depth, and weight.
- Saturation and evaporation rate of soil type.
- Irrigation requirements.
- Insulation requirements.

Early consideration for coordination of other site elements might include requirements for:

- Site walls or stairs
- Fountains
- Other special site features

▶ To successfully implement living green roofs and landscapes over structure, the planning and design considerations, and coordination required in documentation and construction, necessitate early and continuous collaboration among numerous design disciplines, the owner, and contractors.

Acceptable Practices

Overview of the Application of Landscapes over Structure

Depending on the amount of vegetation, most of the same ecological and environmental benefits may be derived from the construction of landscapes over structure as from living green roofs. The greater the density and coverage of the vegetation, the greater the capacity of a landscape over structure to intercept, absorb, and slow storm water runoff. Likewise, the collateral benefits of more vegetation on the Earth's surface are also derived from landscapes over structure.

Depending on use and the ultimate physical expression of the design, landscapes over structure, like any built landscape, can take many forms and have the potential for a wide range of ecological, aesthetic, and social benefits.

Horticulturally, with a growing medium typically greater than 12 inches, landscapes over structure can support a greater diversity in size and type of vegetation. Greater size and diversity of plants usually require a deeper soil profile, supplemental irrigation, and a more complex infrastructure to support and sustain plant growth in an artificial environment.

Based on intended and expected use, the structural system required to sustain the additional weight of growing medium, vegetation, site elements, and potential live loads is significantly more substantial in complexity of design, size, and cost than that required to support a living green roof.

Overview of a Living Green Roof

The depth of growing medium required for a living green roof is typically 3 to 6 inches. Typically, irrigation is not employed, so the vegetation, which must survive in shallow soil and, often, harsh, dry conditions, is usually composed of low-growing, horizontally spreading, water-storing plants. Most often, but not exclusively, the majority of plants are selected from various species of *Sedum*. *Sedum* is a genus with hundreds of species, typically succulent plants that can store water in their leaves and stems for extended periods of droughty conditions.

The dominance of their use in the overall plant selection of living green roofs has led to the additional misnomer of "sedum roofs." As with most successful planting plans, the selection of plants for living green roofs should include a matrix of plant genera and species that provide adequate horticultural diversity and that are suitable to the environment. The limited maintenance required for such a plant mix might include initial hand-watering during the installation and adaptation period and occasional weeding, fertilizing, and spot repair.

The overall thin profile of the components of a living green roof generally weighs 12 to 15 pounds per square foot. Usually, structural upgrading of standard decking is not required, because the added weight of the profile is about the same weight of stone ballast applied to protect and preserve the waterproofing membrane of a conventional roofing system. A living green roof, therefore, can be employed when, structurally, no additional weight can be added to the deck. Because generally there is little or no additional cost to provide increased structural support, it can also be a cost-effective way to provide a visual amenity and greater environmental quality.

Since each application of a living green roof will have specific design requirements, it is imperative that a structural engineer review and approve proposed designs to ensure the structural capacity for the weights of the proposed growing medium when saturated. Likewise, any potential for unintentional live loads must be evaluated. Although living green roofs are not intended or designed to be physically accessible for use as an open space amenity, clear demarcation of restricted use should be incorporated into the overall design.

Figures 7.61–7.69 show the step-by-step installation of a tray system green roof.

Figure 7.61   The roof surface is prepared for the laying out of the trays.
Courtesy of LiveRoof, LLC.

Figure 7.62   For smaller-scale buildings, the plant trays can be lifted to the roof by crane.
Courtesy of LiveRoof, LLC.

Figure 7.63   The laying out of planting trays over the prepared roof surface begins in a corner.
Courtesy of LiveRoof, LLC.

Figure 7.64 As the installation continues, the desired plant color pattern is marked out.
Courtesy of LiveRoof, LLC.

Figure 7.65 The installation continues with the correct species and color of plant to match the marking on the roof.
Courtesy of LiveRoof, LLC.

Figure 7.66   The planting trays are placed tightly up against each other.
Courtesy of LiveRoof, LLC.

Figure 7.67   Trays are cut to custom-fit around roof obstacles and perimeter edges.
Courtesy of LiveRoof, LLC.

Figure 7.68　In this specific system, "elevator" strips allow the plants to grow above the edge of the tray and are removed during the installation. This not only allows the edge of the tray to be hidden but also allows the plant roots to grow together in the shared soil between adjacent trays. This is a nice feature in the winter, so the individual trays will not be visible.
Courtesy of LiveRoof, LLC.

Figure 7.69　Initial watering to help get the plants established is important.
Courtesy of LiveRoof, LLC.

Design Considerations

The Structural Support System

The primary supporting element of any living green roof or landscape over structure is the structural deck or slab. Typically it spans the joists and beams that sit atop columns. The structural support system is generally determined by the program of interior use below it and by the amount of weight it must support above it.

The deck can be composed of a number of structural materials and systems, such as plywood sheathing, metal, or concrete. The primary finished deck, or structural slab, referred to here is concrete. However, often in living green roofs of a relatively small scale, or in retrofit conditions, other decking systems and surfaces may include metal decking or even wood decking.

Deck Construction and Positive Slope

Decks or slabs constructed with low-slope or even no slope characteristics are particularly susceptible to the accumulation of water if proper construction techniques for adequate deck or slab drainage are not considered and implemented. Excess water can lead to deterioration of inert components, such as waterproofing, insulation, and concrete, which can lead to the progressive collapse and ultimate failure of the entire system. Excess water in the dynamic, or living, components can lead to anaerobic conditions in soils or growing media, which can cause toxic soils and disease, or even death, of the plants.

The slope, or gradient, of the deck should be a minimum of 1 percent. For poured-in-place concrete decks, preferably, the gradient should be a minimum of 2 percent, to account for concrete creep (or sag) over time.

Attaining adequate positive slope may be accomplished in a number of ways. Sometimes, if the required floor-to-floor height can accommodate it, the columns can be incrementally shortened to achieve the required slope. This allows the beams and deck to slope consistently and at the same thickness. If the column heights cannot be adjusted to accommodate the slope, the top of the deck itself will need to slope from a given high point, causing the thickness of the slab to increase at these points.

A topping slab may also be utilized, whereby an additional layer of concrete, sometimes reinforced, is applied to the top of the cast-in-place concrete deck and is sloped in the direction of the predetermined location of the deck drains. Both the topping slab and the increased thickness of the slab can increase the complexity of construction and the weight of the slab, which will be of concern to the structural engineer. The loss of depth to finished grade will be of concern to the landscape architect.

▶ A topping slab, depending on the location and type of the water-proofing membrane and insulation, may act as a "working slab" or "waste slab," which protects the waterproofing membrane or other components from damage during construction.

Proper Elevation Relationships

Establishing finished floor elevations in relationship to the top of the structural slab and the exterior elements is critical, as this will have direct impact on the survival of the planting and the ability to construct suitable paving systems and other site elements. It will also affect the ability to use and maintain the site in the manner intended.

Often, to have accessible ingress to and egress from a finished floor elevation, the required tolerance may be a half-inch or less. If the top of a structural slab is set too high, it will be very difficult to attain the proper relationship between the interior and the exterior use. Exterior paving systems, for example, can be adversely affected if significant adjustments must be made to the paver thickness, setting bed, insulation, and subdrainage components, to accommodate positive flow away from the interior finished floor elevation. As another example, for living green roofs, there may be local requirements to establish and accommodate a "freeboard" for controlling high-intensity storms. Without proper coordination of finished interior and exterior elevations, this may not be achieved. See Figures 7.70–7.72.

For projects with significant planting, even if the structural deck has been designed to allow for the weight of large-caliper trees and saturated soil, the top of slab, finished floor, and finished grade elevations must be properly coordinated; otherwise, the allowable depth for the soil and root balls can be severely impacted, limiting selection and growth of large-caliper trees.

System Components

Overview

When designing a system for over-structure construction, selecting and specifying the most appropriate components may be the most overwhelming task. It is crucial to determine not only how the system must function as a whole, but also how it must perform both initially and over the life of the project. For each component within that

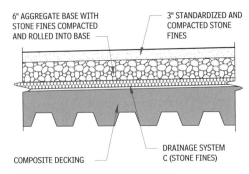

STONE FINES PAVING OVER COMPOSITE STRUCTURAL DECKING

Figure 7.70 Stone fines paving over structure, typical detail.
Source: Hopper, *Landscape Architectural Graphic Standards.* Copyright John Wiley & Sons, Inc., 2007.

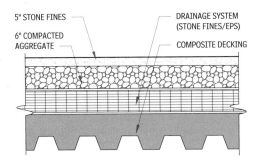

STONE FINES OVER EPS FILL ON COMPOSITE STRUCTURAL DECKING

Figure 7.71 Stone fines over insulation, typical detail.
Source: Hopper, *Landscape Architectural Graphic Standards.* Copyright John Wiley & Sons, Inc., 2007.

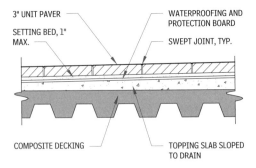

UNIT PAVERS OVER COMPOSITE STRUCTURAL DECKING

Figure 7.72 Unit pavers over structure, typical detail.
Source: Hopper, *Landscape Architectural Graphic Standards.* Copyright John Wiley & Sons, Inc., 2007.

system, it is essential to understand its function, performance, and compatibility with other components within the system. Additionally, the selection of components can be complicated by the fact that sometimes the same component, and same product, might be used for more than one function in a system, but in different locations. An example of this is drainage matting, which is used under the insulation to facilitate drainage across the top of the slab, but might also be used just below the soil or growing medium as aeration matting.

To assist in this determination, it is helpful to understand (1) the properties of constituent materials, (2) the technical properties for each material's proper, sustained performance, (3) whether a product is commercially available or has to be custom-fabricated (4) whether there are measurable standards and requirements for a product (5) where a product can be found (6) whether there are similar products of equal quality (7) whether there are particular attributes that need to be specified for a product's successful installation and performance, and (8) whether there are new and better products available.

At a minimum, the following information should be assessed for each of the components:

- Function
- Physical properties
- Physical limitations
- Relationship to other components

Waterproofing Membranes

The primary purpose of waterproofing is to keep unwanted water and moisture out of the structure below. Since the waterproofing is the primary protective element of the slab and of the structure below, its selection installation and protection are paramount to the success and longevity of any additional components or systems over the structure. Additionally, because, typically, the waterproofing is at the bottom of the system, it is difficult to access once the remaining components are installed. The failure of a waterproofing membrane can lead to the unraveling and failure of a living green roof or an entire landscape over structure.

Some of the primary considerations of subsequent installation and maintenance that may affect the selection of the waterproofing membrane are the potential for:

- Excess moisture in the concrete deck, causing vapor expansion, leading to rupture and excess vapor below deck.
- Thermal expansion or movement causing cracking or tearing.

- Mechanical damage during construction.
- Mechanical damage during subsequent installation of surface or subsurface elements (footings, irrigation, electrical conduit, new drains or new cores, plants with large root balls, etc.).
- Leakage at seams, drains, flashing, or penetrations for utilities (see Figures 7.73 and 7.74).

Although industry and generic definitions of roofing types may vary, these major roofing types for low-slope roofs are generally recognized:

- Built-up membrane
- Single-ply membrane
- Hybrid or composite membrane
- Fluid-applied membrane

▶ For a more detailed understanding of waterproofing membranes and roof types as applicable to the topic of living green roofs and landscapes over structure, see *Landscape Architectural Graphic Standards* (Wiley 2007).

Waterproof Membrane Selection
Because of the importance of this primary protection, systems with increased longevity are preferred. Replacing entire waterproofing systems becomes more complicated over structure. Failure leads not only to interior damage to the building but to the erosion or corrosion

Figure 7.73   Hotmopping of rubberized asphalt membrane.
Source: Weiler and Scholz-Barth, *Green Roof Systems*, Fig. 6-16. Copyright John Wiley & Sons, Inc., 2009
Photo copyright Jeffrey L. Bruce & Co.

Figure 7.74   Flood testing of a waterproofing membrane. Water is allowed to pond 2 inches deep for a period of 48 hours. If any leaks are detected, the membrane should be repaired and flood tested again.
Source: Weiler and Scholz-Barth, *Green Roof Systems*, Fig 6-18. Copyright John Wiley & Sons, Inc., 2009.
Photo copyright Jeffrey L. Bruce & Co.

of the reinforcement and slabs. Mass replacement operations can be prohibitively expensive, are often met with resistance, and are often performed without replacing the system as originally designed.

Any of these systems may be used if the waterproofing membrane is protected from exposure and mechanical damage by protection board, insulation, or other components above it. A significant measure of membrane protection from exposure is inherent in covering the membrane with plants, paving, or other site elements.

The selection should be made in coordination with the architect, landscape architect, structural engineer, waterproofing consultant, supplier, and owner. Considerations should include:

- Size and complexity of the deck configuration.
- Assigned use below deck.
- Programmed use and maintenance above deck.
- Accessibility to the membrane.
- Ability to protect the membrane.
- Climate, availability of materials, construction expertise.
- Cost.

Many proprietary waterproofing systems are installed by the manufacturer's approved and certified contractors, who are familiar and experienced with the product and construction methods. Required accessory products such as drain bodies and flashing systems are usually custom-designed for the waterproofing installation and supplied by the manufacturer. This helps ensure proper installation and protects the viability of the warranty.

▶ The selection of the components above the waterproofing, often supplied by the waterproofing manufacturer as a proprietary system, should not automatically be specified on the basis of the manufacturer's waterproofing warranty alone.

Root Barriers

Root barriers are intended to prevent damage from root penetration or perforation. Usually, root barriers are simple polyethylene sheets, but they can also be polypropylene geotextile fabrics or a chemically inert "antirot" granular-surfaced, fabric-reinforced sheet installed as part of the waterproofing membrane. Sometimes a root barrier is also incorporated into a drainage matting. Root barriers should contain no substances harmful to plant growth.

It is important to ensure that the root barrier is chemically compatible with the waterproofing membrane system. The location of the root barrier is typically directly over or part of the waterproofing membrane, or, depending on the membrane, over the protection board. Polyethylene root barriers should not be placed over polystyrene insulations. Although the insulation is hydrophobic, water vapor can still be transmitted, and the root barrier could form a vapor barrier.

For both the root barrier and the protection board, if a plastic or polyethylene sheeting is used, it is necessary to ensure that it is not affected adversely by solvents released from curing membranes. Also, recently, fabricators have been providing nonbituminous, or bitumen-resistant products, as the bitumen is organic and a "food source" for bacteria. Microbial activity can lead to deterioration and ultimately easier penetration for roots.

▶ Selection of the root barrier, by the landscape architect or architect, should be made in consultation with the waterproofing manufacturer, installer, and the project's independent waterproofing consultant.

Protection Board

Protection of the waterproofing membrane is extremely important for both horizontal and vertical surfaces, in building living green roofs and landscapes over structures. Since there will be continual activity once the membrane is installed, through the construction process and even during maintenance and repair operations, it is very susceptible to damage, and immediate protection is required.

Protection boards may be made of any material that protects the waterproofing membrane itself, but it should be durable and non-deteriorating, such as semi-rigid sheets of cement board or mineral-reinforced membrane, which is often part of the waterproofing system.

If a plastic or polyethylene sheeting is used, it is necessary to ensure that it is compatible with adjacent components. Also, if any paving system is to be installed directly over this, it is very important not to use any material that can act as a "slip sheet." This is also applicable to thin polystyrene boards used as protection boards.

Insulation

Thermal insulation helps to keep a building warmer in the winter and cooler in the summer. In winter, it reduces the loss of interior heat or penetration of cold air through the exterior surfaces of the building. Likewise, in warmer seasons or climates, it helps keep the heat out and cool air in. Its efficacy is measured by its R-value.

In building and waterproofing systems, the insulation material most commonly used is extruded polystyrene boards, ranging in thickness from 1 to 5 inches. Its placement in relationship to the top of slab and waterproofing can vary. If it is placed below the structural deck and waterproofing membrane, some condensation can occur, compromising interior finishes and potentially leading to cracking of the structure and rupture of membrane. Above the deck, it can be placed above or below the membrane; condensation will be minimized and some thermal efficiency may be realized. See Figures 7.75 and 7.76.

Generally, the preferred location is above the membrane, often referred to as an inverted or protected membrane system. When the insulation is placed above the membrane, there is less chance of condensation. Condensation can increase thermal fluctuation and, below the membrane, increase the potential for vapor blisters and membrane rupture. Additionally, moisture can travel under the insulation, making it more difficult to locate and repair any leak.

Other advantages to placing the insulation above the membrane are that it is easier to get proper coverage of the waterproofing membrane directly over the deck than over the insulation; additionally, the insulation over the membrane can serve as another layer of

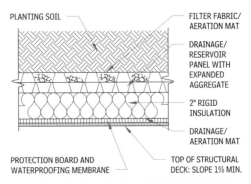

PLANTING SOIL

FILTER FABRIC/
AERATION MAT

DRAINAGE/
RESERVOIR
PANEL WITH
EXPANDED
AGGREGATE

2" RIGID
INSULATION

DRAINAGE/
AERATION MAT

PROTECTION BOARD AND
WATERPROOFING MEMBRANE

TOP OF STRUCTURAL
DECK: SLOPE 1% MIN.

DRAINAGE SYSTEM B: PLANTER DEPTH LESS THAN 24"

Figure 7.75   Polystyrene rigid insulation board placed over waterproofing membrane and protection board (typical detail).
Source: Hopper, *Landscape Architectural Graphic Standards.* Copyright John Wiley & Sons, Inc., 2007.

Figure 7.76   Installation of drainage board over extruded polystyrene insulation board, protection board, and waterproofing membrane.
Source: Weiler and Scholz-Barth, Green Roof Systems, Fig. 6-23. Copyright John Wiley & Sons, Inc., 2009.
Photo copyright Jeffrey L. Bruce & Co.

protection. The disadvantages are that the insulation in this location can impede drainage, and, if it becomes saturated for long periods of time, it can lose its thermal resistance.

Thermal fluctuation can affect vegetation when roots freeze, thaw, and refreeze. This can be exacerbated in winter, when heat emitted from the structure below heats up the soil, or by sunlight striking the vertical surfaces of raised planters. Not only are the freezing and thawing of plant roots detrimental to the vegetation, but they can also expand and potentially crack rigid walls containing large, raised planting beds. Therefore, it is important to insulate the sides of raised planters as well as the bottom.

Insulation Materials Used as Lightweight Fill over Structure

Often in landscapes over structure, a change in elevation of the top of structural deck is needed to reflect architectural use below, or additional depth to the top of structural deck is required to accommodate the depth of root ball and growing medium. The area of fill required between finished grade and top of deck can be significant.

Every additional unit of load can increase the deck thickness and beam and column size, which can result in adding to building footprint and height, construction time, materials, and, ultimately, cost. Polystyrene products, which are lightweight, easy to handle, and readily available, offer an attractive alternative. Polystyrene is a petroleum-based product, which, when used in geotechnical applications, is generically referred to as "geofoam" or "geoblock." These terms are sometimes also used when referring to the use of large blocks of polystyrene, in contrast to the thin board insulation.

The fabrication process of geofoam is either by expansion or extrusion of polystyrene, resin beads, or pellets, thus providing two commonly known products: XPS (planar, extruded polystyrene boards) and EPS (block-molded expanded polystyrene).

- XPS, usually produced as rigid boards, is formed in an extrusion process that includes additives, heat, and pressure. XPS boards are most commonly used for insulating the roof decks for living green roofs and deck slabs for landscapes over structure. As an extruded foam product, XPS provides a very dense and hydrophobic insulation. The boards are usually produced in 24" x 96" or 48" x 96" lengths and widths, and in thicknesses of 1 to 4 inches, although they may be custom fabricated in larger sizes. Typically, one person can handle these sheets of 4 feet by 12 feet, which can be easily cut in the field to fit planters or around drains. XPS is also available in tapered boards that can be used, in some instances, to provide the slope required for drainage, without having to build up the concrete topping slab. Both flat and tapered boards are available with chamfered grooves in the bottom, to further facilitate drainage.
- EPS blocks are made by exposing the polystyrene resin to steam, heat, and pressure, softening, expanding, fusing, and finally molding

them into large blocks. EPS blocks are available in larger sizes than commonly available for XPS. Fabricated in blocks of 4 feet by 8 feet by 30 inches or greater, EPS is often used as lightweight fill in over-structure construction where large areas of fill are required. The blocks can be shop-fabricated in compliance with shop drawings or easily field-cut. Although slightly more cumbersome for one person to handle, like XPS, the EPS blocks are lightweight and easy to install.

Both EPS and XPS are suitable alternatives to soils or other fill. Both are lightweight, easy to handle, and easily field-cut. Shipping and installation costs are typically the same. Both, however, have specific material characteristics—such as R-value, density, and compressive strength—which may make one more suitable as fill than the other. Often, EPS is cited as having a higher absorption rate than XPS, and absorption of moisture could decrease thermal effectiveness. However, neither material's rate of absorption would affect its compressive strength or deformation properties. The selection of either XPS or EPS, when used as structural fill, should be done in collaboration with a structural engineer. See Figures 7.77 through 7.79.

Figure 7.77 EPS blocks for lightweight fill over structural deck.
Source: Weiler and Scholz-Barth, *Green Roof Systems*, Fig. 6-24. Copyright John Wiley & Sons, Inc., 2009.
Photo copyright Jeffrey L. Bruce & Co.

Figure 7.78   EPS blocks can be easily cut in the field with a hot wire.
Source: Weiler and Scholz-Barth, *Green Roof Systems*, Fig. 6-25. Copyright John Wiley & Sons, Inc., 2009.
Photo copyright Jeffrey L. Bruce & Co.

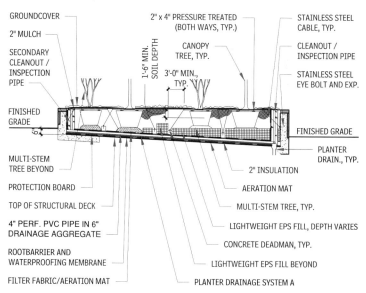

MULTI–STEM AND CANOPY TREE PLANT SECTION

Figure 7.79   Multi-stem and canopy tree planting using EPS as a lightweight fill material.
Source: Hopper, *Landscape Architectural Graphic Standards.* Copyright John Wiley & Sons, Inc., 2007.

Drainage Materials

Adequate drainage is essential for the success of living green roofs and landscapes over structure. There must be ways to collect, detain, direct, and distribute water throughout the entire system. Living green roofs are intended to detain the initial minutes of rainfall from the most frequently occurring storms—those categorized as 2–5 year. Water beyond this significant absorption capacity must be released, as must excess water in a landscape over structure. Standing water in soil leads to the depletion of oxygen and the creation of anaerobic conditions, as well as deterioration of inert components and potential systemwide failure.

One material is clean, free-draining crushed stone, deep enough to accommodate a conventional underdrainage system of laterals and mains. However, crushed stone, when saturated, can become quite heavy, so the structural slab must be sized to accommodate it.

Alternatively, lightweight aggregates, such as expanded clay, balled clay, expanded shale, or other ceramic products are fabricated according to standard grades and are more consistent in composition and the distribution of particle size. They are an attractive alternative to crushed stone, because they are much lighter, and consistency in particle size lessens the potential for compaction. The disadvantage is that they typically are much more costly. The cost of lighter aggregate needs to be weighed against the additional costs of the structure to support the heavier crushed stone.

Drainage mats and panels are an attractive alternative to several inches of drainage aggregate, as they are lightweight, have a thin profile, and can be combined with other component functions such as reservoirs and aeration panels. However, depending on use, required performance, depth and extent of growing medium, and the overall system of components, they should not be considered automatically as a substitute for an adequate system of drainage, which may require a thicker layer of drainage aggregate and a system of laterals and mains. Rather, drainage mats can augment the drainage system— serving as a "belt and suspender" component. See Figure 7.80.

A common type of drainage panel is a webbed plastic mat (see Figures 7.81 and 7.82), fabricated in sheets or panels, often only an eighth of an inch thick. These sheet mats are also available with a geotextile or filter fabric attached. Although this may be attractive as a very thin profile, particularly when loads and depths are restricted, it should not be used in areas under paving, as it can interfere with the interlocking qualities required at the setting bed.

A number of products are available that combine the functions of both a drainage mat and a water retention or reservoir mat. The most

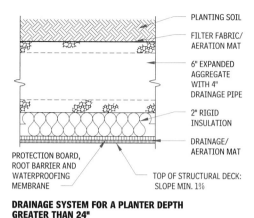

PLANTING SOIL

FILTER FABRIC/
AERATION MAT

6" EXPANDED
AGGREGATE
WITH 4"
DRAINAGE PIPE

2" RIGID
INSULATION

DRAINAGE/
AERATION MAT

PROTECTION BOARD,
ROOT BARRIER AND
WATERPROOFING
MEMBRANE

TOP OF STRUCTURAL DECK:
SLOPE MIN. 1%

**DRAINAGE SYSTEM FOR A PLANTER DEPTH
GREATER THAN 24"**

Figure 7.80   Drainage system for planter areas.
Source: Hopper, *Landscape Architectural Graphic Standards.* Copyright John Wiley & Sons,
Inc., 2007.

Figure 7.81   Placing drainage matting over deck for a living green roof.
Source: Weiler and Scholz-Barth, *Green Roof Systems*, Fig. 6-22. Copyright John Wiley & Sons,
Inc., 2009.
Photo: Atlantis, Australia.

common of these is high-density polyethylene molded into a waffle of
cups and domes (see Figure 7.83). As "cups" on the top side, these retain
water. As "domes," they form drainage channels on both the top and
bottom. See Figures 7.84 and 7.85. Some mats also have tiny holes in
the tops of the domes (see Figure 7.86), which direct excess water back
to the main drainage system and allow for ventilation and evaporation.

Figure 7.82　Drainage mat installed above root barrier layer.
Source: Weiler and Scholz-Barth, *Green Roof Systems*, Fig. 6-34. Copyright John Wiley & Sons, Inc., 2009.

Figure 7.83　Installation of EPS drainage and reservoir panel over water-proofing membrane and protection board.
Source: Weiler and Scholz-Barth, *Green Roof Systems*, Fig. 6-35. Copyright John Wiley & Sons, Inc., 2009.

Figure 7.84   Drainage and reservoir panel as cones (pegs up).
Source: Weiler and Scholz-Barth, *Green Roof Systems*, Fig. 6-32. Copyright John Wiley & Sons, Inc., 2009.

Figure 7.85   Drainage and reservoir panel as cups (pegs down). Notice location of channels and drainage perforations.
Source: Weiler and Scholz-Barth, *Green Roof Systems*, Fig. 6-33. Copyright John Wiley & Sons, Inc., 2009.

Figure 7.86 Drainage and reservoir panel close-up. The panel is filled with lightweight aggregate and covered with filter fabric to facilitate drainage and capillary movement of water.
Photo by George Soukas.

Typically, the panels are fabricated as large as 3 feet by 6 feet and in thicknesses of 1 to 3 inches.

Moisture Retention Mats

More recently, moisture retention mats have been marketed as a way to help retain moisture and nutrients for use by the vegetation layer above. Although their composition varies among manufacturers, most often they are made of polypropylene fibers stitched through a polyethylene sheet (see Figure 7.87). In living green roofs and landscapes over structure, they are most commonly placed below the drainage/reservoir mat. Their inclusion should consider depth and type of growing medium, supplemental irrigation availability, and composite drainage system. The product selection may be based on limitation of depth of overall drainage system profile, compressive strength, and moisture flow and retention rate of mat.

Aeration Mats

Adequate drainage also increases the ability of the soil or growing medium to keep air moving through it, thereby keeping the soil healthy and allowing pore space for root growth and development,

Figure 7.87   Layers of a living green roof include this water retention fabric. Photo by George Soukas.

and lessening the potential for the soil to become anaerobic. Additionally, beneficial air may be incorporated into the soil by combined use of materials that are usually associated with drainage components.

Some mats facilitate both drainage and aeration, and are the same as, or similar to, the products described previously, but used in different locations. The most common are noncrushable panels, fibers, or formed cones, which allow air to be incorporated into the system, forming an "aeration mat."

Aeration mats and drain panels may also be incorporated on vertical surfaces of walls and planters, both to relieve hydrostatic pressure and to increase the air, the soil, and root production.

Filter Fabrics
Filter fabrics are a type of geotextile, which are synthetic cloths used below grade to stabilize soil or facilitate and promote drainage. For application in living green roofs and landscapes over structure, the filter fabric is intended to keep the fines of a soil mixture or growing medium from migrating into the drainage layer.

Typically, they are made of polypropylene fibers and are either woven or nonwoven. A woven fabric is produced from a number of filaments and strands, whereas a nonwoven filter fabric is more uniformly manufactured. Nonwoven fabrics are typically used in planting applications where the water flows in only one direction—in this case, from soil to drainage medium.

Numerous products and types of filter fabrics are available, and the selection may ultimately be based on differentiation of pore space, strength, weight, resistance to rot, and deterioration from ultraviolet light, which can affect their permeability and flow rate.

▶ The key measurements of the physical and mechanical properties of filter fabrics are tear strength and resistance, puncture strength, permeability, and flow rate.

Irrigation and Water Storage

Because living green roofs and plantings within landscapes over structure are required to grow within an artificial environment, the basic needs of plants—a nutrient source, found in the growing medium, and water—have to be incorporated into the system.

Since water over a structural deck does not migrate in the same way as water in terra firma, it is also necessary to supply supplementary water. In many natural systems, groundwater may be available, and the water table may fluctuate greatly during different seasons. Once the required amount of supplemental water is determined, the design and components of the system are similar to those of conventional systems. A major consideration in the design of the irrigation system, however, is the coordination of the mechanical, electrical, and plumbing systems.

Practices to Avoid

- In new construction, avoid coordination conflicts with the building process. Coordinate work of skilled trades, protection of materials, construction sequence, and climate and timeframe issues with the construction manager as early in the construction process as possible.
- Avoid elevation conflicts by confirming the accuracy of the survey. Elevation and horizontal distance tolerances in green roof construction are very limited. Small differences can result in significant consequences.
- Avoid roof leaks by protecting the waterproofing membrane during all phases of construction.

- Monitor installation of the concrete slabs carefully to ensure installation at the correct elevation, with the correct slope and proper location of any drainage structures of other utilities.
- Be sure that all drainage component layers are installed in the correct order and in the proper orientation, to avoid drainage problems later. Once covered with soil, this system is costly to modify if correction is required.
- Avoid seasonal planting problems by factoring when specified plants will be available, the seasonal planting hazard constraints, or planting in extreme weather conditions.

Xeriscape

Description

The goal of xeriscaping is to create a visually attractive landscape with water-efficient plants. Over 50 percent of a homeowner's water consumption in the warmer months is devoted to watering the landscape. By implementing the fundamental principles of xeriscape, this amount can be reduced substantially without any loss of beauty or function in the landscape.

Assessing Site Conditions

Using an accurate plan of the site, conduct a site inventory, noting the orientation of the sun, prevailing winds, soils, drainage patterns, existing plants, and any site challenges and potentials. Create a schematic layout design showing general functional areas, along with a water use schematic (see Figure 7.88), which zones the site into areas of high, medium, and low water use. Grouping plants of similar water needs together is paramount to successful xeriscaping.

Most soils can have their capability to absorb and retain water enhanced through soil amendments. An analysis of the site's soil will indicate the structure, texture, and water-holding characteristics. Amending the soil with organic material (such as compost) will increase the capability of the soil to support xeriscape plants.

Acceptable Practices

Standard turfgrass lawns are the single largest consumer of water in the landscape. By reducing the amount of turf to provide only the area necessary for function and aesthetics, a corresponding reduction in water use can be effected. Selecting grass types that are adapted to the site and have low water demands will reduce both water use and

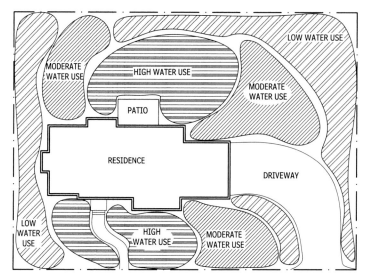

WATER USE DIAGRAM

Figure 7.88 Typical water use diagram.
Source: Hopper, *Landscape Architecture Graphic Standards.* Copyright John Wiley & Sons, Inc., 2007.

maintenance time. Examples of these grasses are shown with the list of potential plant choices at the end of this section.

A xeriscape landscape does not need to sacrifice beauty for less water use. Nor does the design need to include exclusively low-water plants. Grouping plants according to their water needs allows some areas of the site to feature higher water use and more intense plantings, while other zones can be low water use. Xeriscape plants are available in every plant type, from trees to shrubs to ground covers to perennials. The best example of a xeriscape plant for a particular region is one that is native to that region, where it has adapted to the available water and climate. As shown in Figure 7.89, a xeriscape design that follows the water zoning schematic can provide as much beauty and practicality as a traditional design.

Watering only those plants that need it and only when they need it is key to an efficient xeriscape. Drip irrigation emitters and bubblers place the water where it is needed without spraying unnecessary areas. Running the irrigation for longer periods on an as-needed basis encourages deeper root growth, which helps plants survive drier periods.

Applying mulches to planting areas helps to minimize evaporation, cool the soil, reduce weed growth, and slow erosion. The mulches can

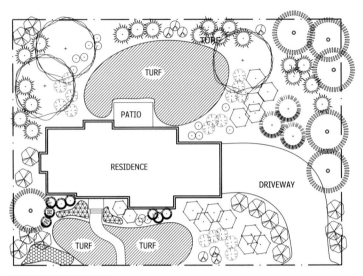

SCHEMATIC DESIGN BASE

Figure 7.89   Schematic design based on water use diagram.
Source: Hopper, *Landscape Architecture Graphic Standards.* Copyright John Wiley & Sons, Inc., 2007.

be organic, such as bark chips or pine straw, or inorganic, such as gravel or decorative rocks.

Generally, successful xeriscapes are lower maintenance than traditional landscapes. However, proper ongoing maintenance will help ensure a healthy, low-water landscape. This includes proper mowing height and frequency for lawns; thinning, as opposed to shearing, of shrubs; and controlling weeds and pests.

Plant Selection

The following lists contain a sampling of low-water-demanding plants for different regions of the United States. These are broad regions, however, and thus may not reflect the soils and climate of a particular site. Contacting the local native plant society or xeriscape council is advised.

Plants for the West Region

Trees

- Incense cedar — *Calocedrus decurrens*
- Goldenrain tree — *Koelreuteria paniculata*
- Pinyon pine — *Pinus edulis*

- Limber pine — *Pinus flexilis*
- Black locust — *Robinia pseudoacacia*

Shrubs

- Mountain mahogany — *Cercocarpus* species
- Apache plume — *Fallugia paradoxa*
- Junipers (many) — *Juniperus* species
- Sumac — *Rhus* species
- Blue mist spirea — *Caryopteris* x *clandonensis*

Ground Covers

- Kinnikinnick — *Arctostaphylos uva-ursi*
- Ice plant — *Lampranthus* species
- Rosemary — *Rosmarinus officinalis*

Perennials

- Yucca — *Yucca* species
- Iris (many) — *Iris* species
- Penstemon (many) — *Penstemon* species
- Sedum (many) — *Sedum* species
- Red-hot poker — *Kniphofia uvaria*

Turfgrasses:

- Blue grama grass — *Bouteloua gracilis*
- Buffalograss — *Buchloe dactyloides*
- Tall fescue hybrids — *Festuca* hybrids

Plants for the Southwest Region

Trees

- Acacia (many) — *Acacia* species
- Desert willow — *Chilopsis linearis*
- Olive — *Olea europaea*
- Velvet mesquite — *Prosopis velutina*
- Desert ironwood — *Olneya tesota*
- Afghan pine — *Pinus eldarica*

Shrubs

- Fernbush — *Chamaebatiaria millefolium*
- Cliffrose — *Cowania mexicana*
- Big sage — *Artemisia tridentata*

Ground covers

- Hardy iceplants — *Delosperma* species
- Yellow rockrose — *Helianthemum nummularium*

Perennials

- Mat daisy — *Anacyclus depressus*
- Poppy mallow — *Callirhoe involucrata*
- Sundrops — *Calylophus* species
- Chocolate flower — *Berlandiera lyrata*
- Penstemons (many) — *Penstemon* species

Accents

- Parry's century plant — *Agave parryi*
- Ocotillo — *Fouquieria splendens*
- Hedgehogs — *Echinocerus* species

Turfgrasses

- Blue grama grass — *Bouteloua gracilis*
- Buffalograss — *Buchloe dactyloides*

Plants for the Southeast Region

Trees

- Virginia pine — *Pinus virginiana*
- Loblolly pine — *Pinus taeda*
- Leyland cypress — *Cupressocyparis leylandii*
- Shumard oak — *Quercus shumardii*
- Live oak — *Quercus virginiana*

Shrubs

- Abelia — *Abelia* x *grandiflora*
- Japanese barberry — *Berberis thunbergii*
- Yaupon holly — *Ilex vomitoria*
- Southern waxmyrtle — *Myrica cerifera*
- Virginia sweetspire — *Itea virginica*
- Showy jasmine — *Jasminum floridum*
- Nandina — *Nandina domestica*
- Sweetshrub — *Calycanthus floridus*

Ground covers

- Wintercreeper euonymus — *Euonymus fortunei* 'Coloratus'
- St. John's wort — *Hypericum calycinum*
- Asiatic jasmine — *Trachelospermum asiaticum*
- Periwinkle — *Vinca minor* or *Vinca major*

Perennials

- Yarrow — *Achillea millefolium*
- Gaillardia — *Gaillardia* x *grandiflora*
- Red hot poker — *Kniphofia uvaria*

- Blue salvia — *Salvia farinacea*
- Sedum (many) — *Sedum* species

Turfgrasses

- Carpetgrass — *Axonopus affinis*
- Bermudagrass — *Cynodon dactylon* and hybrids
- Centipedegrass — *Eremochloa ophiuroides*
- Tall fescue — *Festuca arundinacea* hybrids
- St. Augustine grass — *Stenotaphrum sedundatum*

Plants for the Central Region

Trees

- Amur maple — *Acer ginnala*
- Choke cherry — *Prunus virginiana* 'Schubert'
- Western catalpa — *Catalpa speciosa*
- Western juniper — *Juniperus occidentalis* and *scopulorum*
- Hackberry — *Celtis occidentalis*
- Green ash — *Fraxinus pennsylvanica*
- Colorado spruce — *Picea pungens*

Shrubs

- Shadblow serviceberry — *Amelanchier canadensis*
- Butterfly bush — *Buddleia davidii*
- Silverberry — *Elaeagnus commutata*
- Mugo pine — *Pinus mugo*
- Potentilla — *Potentilla fruticosa*

Perennials

- Yarrow — *Achillea filipendulina*
- Purple coneflower — *Echinacea purpurea*
- Blanket flower — *Gaillardia* x *grandiflora*
- Gayfeather — *Liatris punctata*

Turfgrasses

- Blue grama grass — *Bouteloua gracilis*
- Buffalograss — *Buchloe dactyloides*
- Tall fescue — *Festuca arundinacea* hybrids

Plants for the Northeast Region

Trees

- Winter King hawthorn — *Crategus viridis* "Winter King"
- Pitch pine — *Pinus rigida*
- Eastern red cedar — *Juniperus virginiana*
- American holly — *Ilex opaca*

Shrubs

- Bayberry — *Myrica pensylvanica*
- Rose of Sharon — *Hibiscus syriacus*
- Winterberry — *Ilex verticillata*
- Butterfly bush — *Buddleia davidii*
- Bluebeard — *Caryopteris clandonensis*
- Sweet fern — *Comptonia peregrina*

Ground Covers

- Kinnikinnick — *Arctostaphylos uva-ursi*

Perennials

- New England aster — *Aster novae-angliae*
- Butterfly weed — *Asclepias tuberosa*
- Bird's foot violet — *Viola pedata*

Turfgrasses

- Little bluestem — *Andropogon scoparius*
- Indian grass — *Sorghastrum nutans*
- Tall fescue — *Festuca arundinacea* hybrids

References

ALSO IN THIS BOOK

See Chapter 1, "Soils," Chapter 4, "Trees," and Chapter 8, "Irrigation."

OTHER RESOURCES

Hawver, G. Influence of root restriction and drought stress on container grown trees: Impacts on plant morphology and physiology. Master's thesis. Cornell University, 1997.

Hopper, Leonard J. *Landscape Architectural Graphic Standards*. Hoboken, NJ: John Wiley & Sons, Inc., 2007.

International Society of Arboriculture. www.isa-arbor.com.

Trowbridge, Peter J. and Nina L. Bassuk. *Trees in the Urban Landscape*. Hoboken, NJ: John Wiley & Sons, Inc., 2004.

Urban, James. *Up by Roots*. Champaign, IL: International Society of Arboriculture, 2008.

Weiler, Susan, and Katrin Scholz-Barth. *Green Roof Systems*. Hoboken, NJ: John Wiley & Sons, Inc., 2009.

Part III

Irrigation

Chapter 8

Irrigation and Water Use Efficiency

Irrigation Systems

Irrigation Systems

Description

Overview

There are a number of different approaches to applying water efficiently to a landscape that minimize water usage and are cost-effective. Different approaches can be used in combination to meet the requirements of more complex landscape designs.

System Components

The system begins with a water source. In the case of a potable, municipal water supply, the irrigation system is afforded an inherently pressurized supply, and a pump would be needed only if pressure were deficient and needed to be boosted. If, as in Figure 8.1, the water

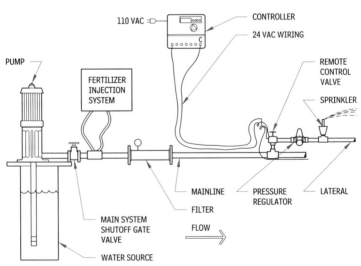

Figure 8.1 Overview of basic components of a pressurized irrigation system.
Source: Hopper, Landscape Architecture Graphic Standards. Copyright John Wiley & Sons, Inc., 2007.

source is a lake, canal, or other nonpressurized source, pressure is created using a pump.

▶ Also see "Water Source Alternatives," in the Assessing Site Conditions section of this chapter.

The next system component, continuing downstream in the overview shown in Figure 8.1, is a filter. Primary filtration with a screen or media (sand) filter is necessary with many surface water supplies and with most, if not all, drip irrigation systems.

Further downstream is the lateral valve, which, in this case, is a remote control valve automated by applying 24 volts AC to the solenoid using the controller. This valve is depicted as being installed in an angle configuration. Water flows from the mainline pipe, through the valve, and then out into the lateral.

The controller is programmed electronically to open and close the valve on selected days and at selected times. Controllers need one station for each remote control valve in the system, plus extra stations for future expansion.

Downstream of the remote control valve is a pressure regulator. A pressure regulator may be required, if the water pressure available does not match the water pressure required in the lateral.

Note that, as mentioned previously, the mainline pipe is the portion of the pipe network upstream of the remote control valve. The lateral pipe is the pipe network downstream of the remote control valve. Sprinklers, or other water emission devices, are located on the lateral pipe.

Backflow Prevention

Most landscape irrigation projects in the United States use potable, municipal water supplies. The water user is generally required to install, maintain, and periodically test a device, called a "backflow prevention device," that is designed to prevent any contaminated (and therefore nonpotable) water from flowing backward into the potable water system.

By definition, "backflow" is the undesirable reversal of the direction of flow of water or other substances into the distribution pipes of the potable water supply, from any source or sources, caused by backpressure and/or backsiphonage. "Backpressure" is backflow caused by a pump, elevated tank, boiler, or pressure "head" in a pipe, or any means that could create greater pressure within a piping system than that which exists within the potable water supply. "Backsiphonage" is the

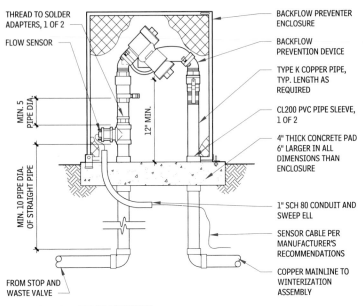

THREAD TO SOLDER ADAPTERS, 1 OF 2

FLOW SENSOR

MIN. 5 PIPE DIA.

MIN. 10 PIPE DIA. OF STRAIGHT PIPE

12" MIN.

FROM STOP AND WASTE VALVE

BACKFLOW PREVENTER ENCLOSURE

BACKFLOW PREVENTION DEVICE

TYPE K COPPER PIPE, TYP. LENGTH AS REQUIRED

CL200 PVC PIPE SLEEVE, 1 OF 2

4" THICK CONCRETE PAD 6" LARGER IN ALL DIMENSIONS THAN ENCLOSURE

1" SCH 80 CONDUIT AND SWEEP ELL

SENSOR CABLE PER MANUFACTURER'S RECOMMENDATIONS

COPPER MAINLINE TO WINTERIZATION ASSEMBLY

BACKFLOW PREVENTION ASSEMBLY

Figure 8.2   Backflow preventer.
Source: Hopper, Landscape Architecture Graphic Standards. Copyright John Wiley & Sons, Inc., 2007.

reverse flow of water, mixtures, or substances into the distribution pipes of a potable water supply system, caused by negative or subatmospheric pressure in the potable water supply.

A backflow prevention device (see Figure 8.2) is equipment or means designed to prevent backflow created by backpressure, backsiphonage, or backpressure and backsiphonage acting together.

Backflow prevention, under high hazard circumstances, may be accomplished with any of the following methods:

- An air gap.
- A reduced pressure principle backflow prevention assembly.
- A pressure vacuum breaker backflow prevention assembly.
- An atmospheric vacuum breaker backflow prevention assembly.

Each approach has specific applications, criteria, and requirements.

The reduced pressure principle device, or RP device, is composed of two internally loaded check valves with a mechanically independent, pressure-dependent relief valve between and below the check valves. The differential pressure relief valve is designed to maintain a pressure between the check valves of at least two pounds per square inch (PSI) lower than the upstream supply pressure. The RP device is intended to prevent either backpressure or backsiphonage. The device can be installed below sprinklers or other water emission devices, but the device must be installed above grade, or otherwise installed with suitable positive drainage, so that the relief valve is never submerged.

A pressure vacuum breaker device, or PVB device, consists of an internally loaded check valve and a loaded air inlet opening between two resilient-seated shutoff valves and test cocks (see Figure 8.3). The device is not intended to respond to backpressure and must therefore be located at least one foot above all sprinklers or other water emission devices.

An atmospheric vacuum breaker device, or AVB device, is composed of a float-operated air inlet valve, which admits air whenever the pressure in the unit drops to zero. The device is not intended to be pressurized continuously, so there can be no downstream valve of any type that would keep the unit under continuous pressure. In landscape irrigation, this requirement translates to one device for each lateral in the system, so, although one device is rather inexpensive, the total system cost can easily be high. When used, the device must be installed 6 inches above all sprinklers or other water emission devices.

As to equipment cost, the RP device is the most costly but also the most flexible in application. The PVB device is substantially lower in cost than the RP device, but must be installed at the high point in the

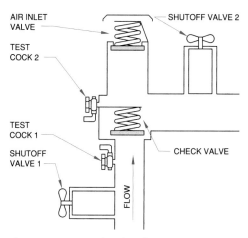

Figure 8.3   A pressure vacuum breaker diagram.
Source: Hopper, *Landscape Architecture Graphic Standards*. Copyright John Wiley & Sons, Inc., 2007.

irrigation system. The AVB is the least expensive of these three devices, but one must be installed on every lateral in the system, and the device must be 6 inches above grade. Because of the constraints noted, the AVB is seldom used with landscape irrigation systems.

Further, there are pressure loss differences to consider with these devices. An RP device experiences the highest pressure loss because of the manner in which the device functions. Most RP backflow devices have a loss of approximately 12 PSI. All other devices have a lesser loss, which is associated with the flow through the device. The pressure loss is higher at high flow rates and lower with low flow rates.

Selection of the appropriate backflow prevention device often takes some contemplative effort. For example, a designer might initially elect to use an RP device, but later choose to use a PVB in order to minimize pressure losses in the system and avoid a booster pump. Experience with the devices and iterations with alternatives for real projects are invaluable for the decision process.

Where freezing temperatures occur, the backflow prevention device must be protected. During winter months, the device must be insulated or heated, or the water removed from the device. Ideally, the backflow device is winterized with compressed air at the same time the entire irrigation system is winterized.

Assessing Site Conditions

The design of an irrigation system is dependent on many technical factors, covered later in this section, or in other sections of this book. From a technical point of view, the following parameters must be understood and evaluated before appropriate irrigation methods can be ascertained:

- Soil texture and profile
- Soil infiltration rate
- Water source
- Available flow and pressure
- Water quality
- Water cost
- Irrigated area
- Site grading and elevation changes over the site
- Plant material type, treatment, and placement
- Historical evapotranspiration rate and annual rainfall
- Construction budget

System Capacity

Whether an irrigation system is designed for an existing water supply system or a proposed project, its design capacity will depend on three factors:

- *Water pressure* — In an existing water supply, this can be determined easily by connecting a pressure gauge to an outside hose bib (closest to the meter, if there's more than one) and measuring the static water pressure in pounds per square foot (PSI).
- *Water volume* — If the existing system has a water meter, the size should be indicated on the water meter itself. If the water system is connected directly to the service line running from the main, the size of the service line will be used to calculate capacity.
- *Service line* — The line from the supply main to the project contributes to the calculation of water volume.

These three factors, in conjunction with any elevation-related pressure changes, pressure loss through the water meter or valves and friction loss through the pipes themselves, will be used to calculate the irrigation design capacity, in gallons per minute (GPM).

▶ **If the project is proposed, coordination with the engineer will be required to obtain this information.**

Approvals

Check with local authorities as to the requirements for the installation of an irrigation system and any permits that may be required. Different municipalities have varying requirements for the irrigation system components, particularly the type of backflow prevention system.

Utility Conflicts

As with any project that requires excavation, check with local utilities or the municipality's "one call center" to determine the location of any existing utilities, to avoid possible conflicts during the design phase and damage during construction.

Water Source Alternatives

Overview

The conservation and efficient use of all available water resources have become increasingly important. Effluent or wastewater supplies are often "there for the taking," and more golf courses and other large landscape projects are looking closely at reclaimed water—with envy, not trepidation.

The use of reclaimed effluent will increasingly be a viable approach for mitigating or, in some cases, solving water shortages.

In general, effluent sources are considered and evaluated because:

- They are probably less expensive.
- They may not be subject to the rigorous restrictions placed on potable supplies during a drought.
- The use of reclaimed effluent may be mandated by government entities.
- The use of effluent is generally viewed as an environmentally sound practice.
- Potable sources may be limited in quantity, restricted in practice, or increasing in cost.

From Potable to Effluent Water: Considerations

There may be very little involved in making the change from, say, potable water to reclaimed effluent. The newer irrigation systems may already have the sprinklers, valves, and other components that are suitable for effluent. Otherwise, consideration must be given to changing equipment, and this need often dictates a general upgrade in the irrigation system.

One complication can be the primary delivery system—the pipe system delivering water to the project. Although it may be more common in the future, very few locales currently have both potable and effluent delivery systems. The end user may be responsible for providing or extending the effluent delivery system to the project.

If the irrigation equipment is suitable, and if the flow and pressure from the effluent source are equal to or greater than the flow and pressure from the existing source, the physical switch can be as simple as disconnecting from one source and connecting to the other. The following are important considerations:

- Any cross-connection between the previous water supply and the effluent water supply must be corrected. A physical disconnect must be made and maintained.
- Permitting should not be overlooked. Depending on the project and the locale, state or local agencies will have application, permit, and annual reporting requirements that must be met.

- Certain water quality measurements, available from the effluent provider or made by a commercial laboratory, are needed to determine the suitability of any water for irrigation.
- The differences between irrigation components that are suitable for only potable water versus effluent water are not particularly dramatic.
- Some administrative agencies now require the use of color-coded components (valve box lids, pipe, quick coupler covers) in irrigation systems using effluent water. Purple is the required color. Additionally, valve boxes may need an advisory stamped into the lid, and warning tape may be required in the trench above pipe networks.

Acceptable Practices

Common Irrigation System Symbols

Figure 8.4, "Typical landscape irrigation legend," shows symbols that are commonly used in landscape irrigation design to depict system components. Note that most symbols represent an *assembly*. For example, a sprinkler symbol actually represents an assembly consisting of the fitting or fittings between the lateral pipe and the sprinkler, in addition to the sprinkler itself. Likewise, a valve assembly includes the valve box, gravel, wire connectors, and all the required fittings, in addition to the valve.

Overview of Valves and Valve Assemblies

Valves offer the primary means of hydraulic control in irrigation systems. They are used manually to close off the entire system or some portion of the system. They are used automatically, and operated from the programmed controller, to allow fully automated irrigation.

Consider valves from the start or point of connection (POC) of the irrigation system, working downstream along the mainline pipe.

The first valve may actually be the water purveyor's valve; it may require a special valve box key or valve key to fit and operate the valve itself. This valve is equipped in this way so that unauthorized persons cannot open or close it. Typically, this valve is used only by the water purveyor when service is required within its system or when the water bill has not been paid by the customer.

The next valve downstream is generally the primary shutoff valve for the entire system. A curb stop ball valve is generally used. It may be a stop and waste valve. This valve, being below the frost line, is the valve

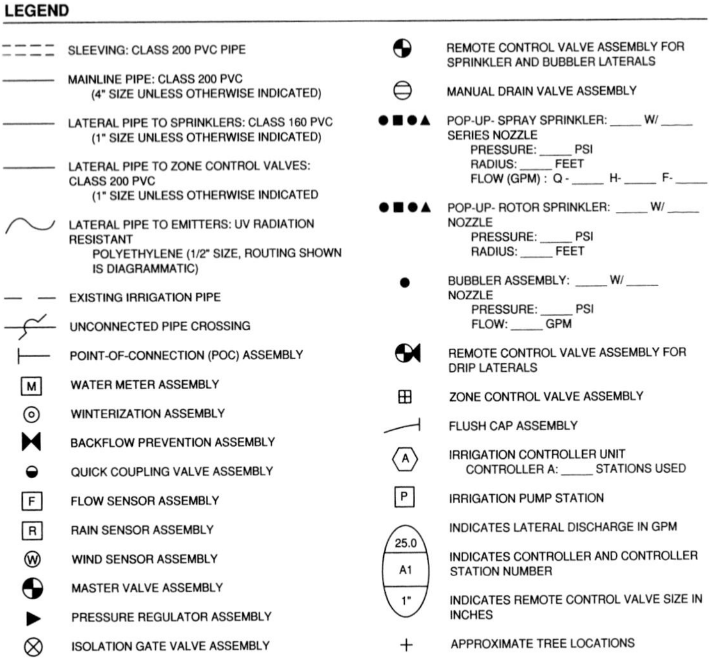

LEGEND

‒ ‒ ‒ ‒	SLEEVING: CLASS 200 PVC PIPE	⊕	REMOTE CONTROL VALVE ASSEMBLY FOR SPRINKLER AND BUBBLER LATERALS
———	MAINLINE PIPE: CLASS 200 PVC (4" SIZE UNLESS OTHERWISE INDICATED)	⊖	MANUAL DRAIN VALVE ASSEMBLY
———	LATERAL PIPE TO SPRINKLERS: CLASS 160 PVC (1" SIZE UNLESS OTHERWISE INDICATED)	●■●▲	POP-UP- SPRAY SPRINKLER: _____ W/ _____ SERIES NOZZLE PRESSURE: _____ PSI RADIUS: _____ FEET FLOW (GPM) : Q - _____ H- _____ F- _____
———	LATERAL PIPE TO ZONE CONTROL VALVES: CLASS 200 PVC (1" SIZE UNLESS OTHERWISE INDICATED	●■●▲	POP-UP- ROTOR SPRINKLER: _____ W/ _____ NOZZLE PRESSURE: _____ PSI RADIUS: _____ FEET
◠◡	LATERAL PIPE TO EMITTERS: UV RADIATION RESISTANT POLYETHYLENE (1/2" SIZE, ROUTING SHOWN IS DIAGRAMMATIC)	●	BUBBLER ASSEMBLY: _____ W/ _____ NOZZLE PRESSURE: _____ PSI FLOW: _____ GPM
— —	EXISTING IRRIGATION PIPE		
◞⌇	UNCONNECTED PIPE CROSSING	◀◘▶	REMOTE CONTROL VALVE ASSEMBLY FOR DRIP LATERALS
⊢	POINT-OF-CONNECTION (POC) ASSEMBLY	⊞	ZONE CONTROL VALVE ASSEMBLY
Ⓜ	WATER METER ASSEMBLY	⌐┤	FLUSH CAP ASSEMBLY
⊙	WINTERIZATION ASSEMBLY	Ⓐ	IRRIGATION CONTROLLER UNIT CONTROLLER A: _____ STATIONS USED
◢◣	BACKFLOW PREVENTION ASSEMBLY	P	IRRIGATION PUMP STATION
⊖	QUICK COUPLING VALVE ASSEMBLY	25.0	INDICATES LATERAL DISCHARGE IN GPM
F	FLOW SENSOR ASSEMBLY	A1	INDICATES CONTROLLER AND CONTROLLER STATION NUMBER
R	RAIN SENSOR ASSEMBLY		
Ⓦ	WIND SENSOR ASSEMBLY	1"	INDICATES REMOTE CONTROL VALVE SIZE IN INCHES
⊕	MASTER VALVE ASSEMBLY		
▶	PRESSURE REGULATOR ASSEMBLY	+	APPROXIMATE TREE LOCATIONS
⊗	ISOLATION GATE VALVE ASSEMBLY		

Figure 8.4   Typical landscape irrigation legend.
Source: Hopper, *Landscape Architecture Graphic Standards.* Copyright John Wiley & Sons, Inc., 2007.

that would be closed throughout the winter months when the irrigation system is winterized and not in use.

The next valve downstream may be a part of the backflow prevention assembly. Some backflow devices require upstream and downstream valves, adjacent to the device itself, for testing purposes. This valve can also be used to shut off the irrigation system for maintenance and, being above grade, it is easily accessed if the backflow assembly is not in an enclosure.

Isolation gate valves, such as that depicted in Figure 8.5, are generally the next valves in the system. It is not necessary that irrigation systems have isolation gate valves, but larger systems have them so that some portion of the irrigation main line can be closed off for maintenance purposes. These valves are most often manually actuated.

Continuing downstream on the main line, the next valve frequently encountered is the quick coupler valve (see Figure 8.6). Quick coupler valves are manually actuated and suitable for incidental water demands around the site. These valves can be added or removed over time.

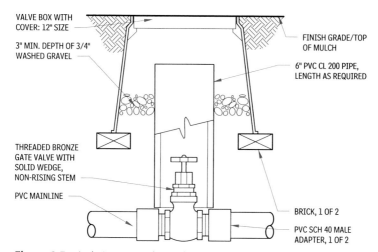

Figure 8.5   Isolation gate valve and valve box.
Source: Hopper, *Landscape Architecture Graphic Standards.* Copyright John Wiley & Sons, Inc., 2007.

Basically, the quick coupler valve is situated at any convenient location along the main line where incidental water may be required or desired.

Quick couplers come in ³/₄-inch, 1-inch, 1¹/₂-inch sizes and are available with different colored covers to indicate potable versus effluent water. Covers can have a lock if desired.

A key is used to open a quick coupler valve. The key usually has a swivel on the top so that a hose can be directed in a 360-degree arc

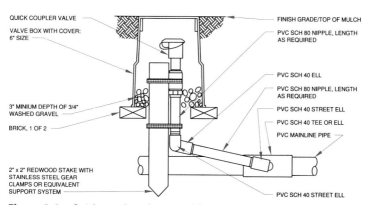

Figure 8.6   Quick coupler valve assembly.
Source: Hopper, *Landscape Architecture Graphic Standards.* Copyright John Wiley & Sons, Inc., 2007.

around the valve and not kink in the process. A manual valve on the key itself is desirable to allow for on-off operation without removing the key, and for controlling flow.

Quick couplers are often used near ball field infields to add water to the infield soil before play. They are often found near sidewalks or entryways to allow for washing of hard surfaces. Quick couplers may also be placed near perennial plantings to provide for incidental washing or watering of plants. Quick couplers have also been used to provide short-term water for establishment of dry land grasses or native plant materials.

The next valve in the system, one that is necessary in almost all irrigation systems, is the "lateral valve," which is also called a "remote control valve" when the system is automated (see Figure 8.7). Remote control valves are also referred to as "solenoid valves" and "automated electric valves"—all three terms are synonymous.

Some features of the remote control valve assembly are important. The valve itself can be installed in either a "globe" or "angle" configuration.

In a globe configuration, the inlet and outlet are more or less in line with one another. In an angle configuration, the inlet is on the bottom of the valve, and the outlet is on the side. Some valves offer either configuration, and a plug is installed in the inlet that is not used. Angle configurations experience less pressure loss because water passes through the valve in a less turbulent way.

All remote control valves should allow for flow control by virtue of the valve handle depicted on the top of the valve. Although some low-cost remote control valves are manufactured without a flow control, they should be avoided. Flow control allows for fine-tuning of the

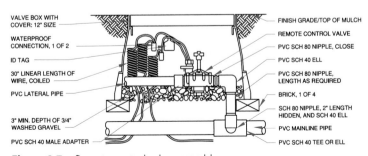

Figure 8.7   Remote control valve assembly.
Source: Hopper, *Landscape Architecture Graphic Standards.* Copyright John Wiley & Sons, Inc., 2007.

Figure 8.8 Valve installation. Valves are available with integral pressure vacuum breakers or a double check valve, where required by code, to protect against backflow. They can be controlled remotely or operated manually. Courtesy of Rain Bird Corporation.

lateral operating pressure by creating additional pressure loss across the valve. There is no easier or less expensive way to provide this flexibility. See Figure 8.8.

From the electrical perspective, note that the wires are connected by a waterproof connector and coiled to allow for wire expansion and maintenance. When excess wire is used in this way, the top of the valve, or bonnet, can be removed for maintenance without affecting the wire or the valve's solenoid.

Remote control valves, as well as other valves, should never be located in low spots in the landscape. Valve leakage, valve sticking, and mainline failure all result in excess water flowing to low spots, and valve boxes filled with water or even covered by standing water add substantially to maintenance problems.

Irrigation Methods and Components

There are numerous approaches to irrigating landscapes (see Table 8.1), which can be used singly or in combination, to minimize installed cost, minimize annual water applications, or otherwise match the differences and complexity of landscapes. The ideal system applies water efficiently, is easy to repair and maintain, and is operationally simple.

Table 8.1 Comparison of Landscape Irrigation Methods

	Sprinkler Irrigation	Bubbler Irrigation	Drip Irrigation
Basic concept	Sprinklers are patterned to fit the irregular shapes of the landscape and spaced to complement one another.	Bubblers are located in planting wells or gridded in shrub beds to irrigate level basins.	Emitters are located at each plant, and water drips slowly and directly to the root zone of each plant.
Precipitation rate	Medium to high	Medium to high	Very low to low
Slope considerations	Suitable for moderate slopes	Not suitable for slopes	Suitable for many sloped situations
Unit installed costs	Medium to high	Medium to high	Low to medium with shrub beds, high with turf grass
Turf application	Suitable	Not appropriate	Some line source products suitable for turf applications
Shrub bed application	Appropriate	Very appropriate	Very appropriate
Operating pressure	Medium to high	Low	Very low
Water quality considerations	Minor concerns	Minor concerns	Filtration required, as well as periodic lateral flushing for maintenance

Sprinkler Types

There are two broad categories of sprinklers used in landscape irrigation: pop-up spray sprinklers and pop-up rotor sprinklers. Pop-up sprays are generally suitable for small-radius applications and small or irregular areas. Pop-up rotors are suitable for large-radius applications and larger areas.

▶ **Large-area pop-up rotors (for areas 25′ diameter and larger) should not be installed on the same zone as small-area pop-up sprinklers (for areas 25′ by 25′ or less).**

The term "pop-up" implies, in both cases, that the top of the sprinkler is installed flush with the finished grade. When the irrigation system is not operating, only the sprinkler top can be seen from the surface. When a lateral valve opens, sprinklers on that lateral rise up for operation as the lateral pressurizes. When the lateral is fully pressurized, the sprinklers are fully popped up; sprinklers begin to function normally, rotate, and throw the distance specified.

The material cost of a single pop-up spray sprinkler is low compared to that of a pop-up rotor sprinkler. The installed unit cost of rotors, however, is lower than the installed unit cost of sprays. This is simply because a single rotor covers a dramatically bigger area than a spray sprinkler, and the associated trenching and pipe lengths are reduced. Even though lateral pipe size is greater for pipes serving rotor sprinklers, the total length of pipe can be dramatically lower. When the cost of the installed sprinklers and pipe is divided by the area of coverage, the installed unit cost of rotors is almost always less than the installed unit cost of sprays.

Sprinkler flow rates are expressed as gallons per minute (GPM). Sprinkler pressures are expressed in pounds per square inch (PSI). The operating pressure of a sprinkler is most often considered to be the pressure at the nozzle. Alternatively, the operating pressure can be noted as the pressure at the base of the sprinkler. The manufacturer should specify in its catalog where performance pressure is taken.

A device called a "pitot tube" (pronounced "pea-toe") can be used to measure pressure at the sprinkler nozzle under field conditions. A pitot tube is simply a small-diameter copper tube, gradually sweep curved to 90 degrees, and attached to a pressure gauge. The tube is inserted into the flow stream coming from the nozzle, approximately at the center of the stream, and held in position while a pressure is read off the gauge.

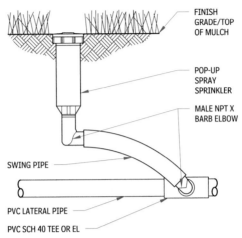

Figure 8.9 Pop-up sprinkler detail.
Source: Hopper, *Landscape Architecture Graphic Standards.* Copyright John Wiley & Sons, Inc., 2007.

Spray Sprinklers

Plastic pop-up spray sprinklers are very simple in mechanical action (see Figure 8.9). Water pressure causes the stem of the sprinkler to pop up, overcoming the resistance of an internal spring resisting the pressure and trying to pull the stem back down. The stem seals when it reaches the full-up position. At this time, under normal conditions, the nozzle reaches full operating pressure, and the sprinkler throws the specified distance and flows at the specified rate.

A pop-up spray sprinkler nozzle can usually be adjusted down about 30 percent, using the nozzle's adjustment screw. So a commonly available 10-foot nozzle can be reasonably adjusted down to 7 feet. Any greater adjustment than 30 percent of the effective radius may distort the pattern and result in poor application efficiency. For this reason, and because spray nozzles are not commonly available in an effective radius of less than 10 feet, the practical minimum width of turf that can be effectively irrigated using sprinklers is considered to be 7 feet.

Some special patterns to handle narrow rectangular turf areas are available, but nozzle performance is not as predictable or as uniform as that of quarter-, half-, or full-arc nozzles.

Characteristics of pop-up spray sprinklers include:

- Appropriate for small radius (7 to 15 feet), small areas (generally less than 45 feet in width), and irregular or curvilinear areas.
- No mechanical action except for riser pop-up caused by pressure in the sprinkler lateral. In plastic pop-up sprays, retraction is caused by

a stainless steel spring. In the older brass sprinklers, retraction is caused by the weight of the riser stem.

- Operating pressures: 15 to 45 PSI ± (relatively low).
- Nozzle arcs: quarter, half, and full (abbreviated Q, H, and F); three-quarter and one-third (3Q and 1Q) arcs are also possible. Specialty nozzles may be available, depending on manufacturer.
- Throw adjustment is accomplished (within limits) using a screw in the nozzle.
- Materials include plastic or brass or a combination thereof.
- Precipitation rates are 1 to 2.5 IPH (inches per hour) (i.e., relatively high).

High pop-up spray sprinklers can be set in shrub beds with the top above grade to achieve a higher functioning position. Twelve inches is the standard pop-up height for high pop-up sprinklers, but the top of the sprinkler body may be set somewhat above grade. Sprinklers can also be installed above grade on risers for shrub beds. See Figures 8.10 through 8.14.

Check valves may be desirable added features with pop-up sprays if there are elevation changes within the lateral. If elevation changes exist and there are no check valves in the sprinklers, water will drain through the sprinkler or sprinklers in the lowest part of the lateral, after the lateral valve is closed. A check valve prevents this action within certain specified limits.

Figure 8.10 Pop-up sprinkler head being connected to lateral.
Courtesy of Rain Bird Corporation.

Figure 8.11   Pop-up sprinkler head being set to the right height.
Courtesy of Rain Bird Corporation.

Figure 8.12   Pop-up sprinkler in action in a lawn area.
Courtesy of Rain Bird Corporation.

Figure 8.13 Pop-up sprinklers in shrub bed typically rise up 12" above grade.
Courtesy of Rain Bird Corporation.

Figure 8.14 Pop-up sprinklers are easily adjusted using a screwdriver.
Courtesy of Rain Bird Corporation.

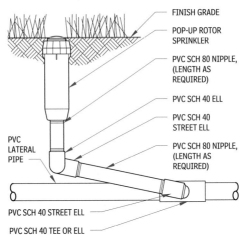

FINISH GRADE

POP-UP ROTOR SPRINKLER

PVC SCH 80 NIPPLE, (LENGTH AS REQUIRED)

PVC SCH 40 ELL

PVC SCH 40 STREET ELL

PVC SCH 80 NIPPLE, (LENGTH AS REQUIRED)

PVC LATERAL PIPE

PVC SCH 40 STREET ELL

PVC SCH 40 TEE OR ELL

Figure 8.15   Rotor sprinkler detail.

Source: Hopper, *Landscape Architecture Graphic Standards.* Copyright John Wiley & Sons, Inc., 2007.

Rotor Sprinklers

Rotor sprinklers can be further described by the mechanism that causes the sprinkler to rotate (see Figure 8.15). Impulse or impact sprinklers use a spring-loaded arm that strikes the water stream coming from the nozzle to cause rotation. A ball drive sprinkler uses centrifugal force and the impact forces from two stainless steel balls to cause sprinkler rotation. Piston drive sprinklers utilize a diaphragm and piston, which together move the sprinkler a few degrees each time the piston finishes a stroke. Gear drive sprinklers use flowing water and a series of intricate gears (similar to an automotive transmission) for rotation. See Figures 8.16 through 8.20.

Various drive mechanisms have differing susceptibility to poor water quality. Generally, impact sprinklers tend to exhibit the fewest problems under marginal (dirty) water conditions, followed by piston drives, ball drives, and gear drives, respectively.

Characteristics of rotor sprinklers include:

- Appropriate for large-radius (30 to 90 feet) applications, large areas (generally greater than 30 feet in width), and more regular landscape areas.
- Flowing water and a mechanical action, working together, cause rotation.
- Operating pressures are 40 to 90 PSI ± (relatively high).
- Nozzle arcs can be infinite arc adjustment in many sprinklers or fixed arcs in 15-degree increments.

Figure 8.16 Impact rotary sprinkler uses water flow to cause rotation.
Courtesy of Rain Bird Corporation.

Figure 8.17 Rotary nozzle is installed into sprinkler head body.
Courtesy of Rain Bird Corporation.

Figure 8.18 Close-up view of rotary nozzle. Nozzle arcs can be set for varying conditions.
Courtesy of Rain Bird Corporation.

Figure 8.19 Rotary nozzle view from top.
Courtesy of Rain Bird Corporation.

Figure 8.20   Rotary nozzles can cover wide areas.
Courtesy of Rain Bird Corporation.

- Radius of throw is adjustable in some sprinklers, but not all.
- Materials include plastic or brass or combinations thereof.
- Precipitation rates are 0.30 to 0.75 IPH (i.e., relatively low).

Many small projects, and most large projects, require both pop-up spray and pop-up rotor sprinklers to address different size and shape attributes in the landscape. From the designer's standpoint, the choice of the best sprinkler, whether rotor or spray, is based primarily on the dimensions of the area to be irrigated and the relative complexity of the shape. Many curvilinear shapes warrant short-radius pop-up sprays because they can be located so as to avoid overspray onto hard surfaces.

Features of Both Types of Sprinklers
Table 8.2 provides a detailed comparison of pop-up spray and pop-up rotor sprinklers.

Overview of Precipitation Rates
By definition, the "precipitation rate" for sprinklers is the rate at which overlapping sprinklers apply water. The concept is similar to measuring the rate at which rain falls, and the units are the same, as well. The common English units for precipitation rates are inches per hour (IPH).

Typically, quarter-arc sprinklers and half-arc sprinklers are grouped together on a lateral, and full-arcs are grouped together on a separate

Table 8.2 Comparison of Pop-Up Spray and Pop-Up Rotor Sprinklers

	Pop-Up Spray Sprinklers	Pop-Up Rotor Sprinklers
General description	Manufactured of plastic or brass (more commonly plastic) or a combination such as a plastic sprinkler body with a brass nozzle; no mechanical action except for riser pop-up as effected by lateral pressure, water throw adjustment via screw-in nozzle	Manufactured of plastic, metal, or some combination of plastic and metal; mechanical action (gears, pistons, levers, centrifugal force) causes rotation, water throw adjustment possible with many models
Radius of throw	Radius of approximately 7 to 15 feet; appropriate for small dimensions (<30 feet) smaller areas, and irregular areas	Radius of approximately 30 to 90 feet; appropriate for large dimensions, larger areas, and more regular areas
Operating pressure at the sprinkler nozzle	15 to 50 PSI (relatively low)	40 to 90 PSI (relatively high)
Precipitation rate	1 to 2.5 IPH (relatively high)	0.30 to 0.75 IPH (relatively low)
Approximate installed unit cost	(relatively high)	(relatively low)
Innovations in recent years	Matched precipitation rates (MPR), high pop-up models, pressure-compensating nozzles designed to achieve regulated pressures and constant sprinkler flows, check valves to minimize low sprinkler drainage	Built-in check valves to avoid low sprinkler drainage, small surface area and rubber covers for sports applications, high pop-up models, color-coded nozzle sets, increasingly lower precipitation rates to match low soil infiltration rates, and distribution rate curve improvement

lateral because of precipitation rate differences. Partial arcs of 180 degrees and less are often mixed together on laterals, for economy, even though the precipitation rate may vary somewhat.

In recent years, many manufacturers have begun to provide matched precipitation rate (MPR) sprinkler nozzles. With the MPR concept, nozzles are engineered and manufactured such that quarters, halves, and fulls all complement one another with flow rates proportioned to the arc. When the flow rates are proportional to the arc, precipitation rates can be identical or nearly identical.

Sprinkler Distribution Rate Curves

Ideally, sprinklers would apply water uniformly, like rain. But the basic pattern of a sprinkler is one that applies more water near the sprinkler and less and less water as you move farther from the sprinkler (see Figure 8.21). This is why sprinklers are spaced to complement each other. "Head-to-head" coverage, whereby one sprinkler throws to the next (see Figure 8.22), is generally good practice.

Figure 8.23 depicts a graphic concept of the effect of overlapping and complementing sprinklers. Sprinklers are often spaced at the effective radius recommended by the manufacturer. The DRC for each sprinkler is shown as a smooth curve. The actual depth of application, due to the combined effects of multiple sprinklers, is shown to have high points and low points. The desired minimum application is a flat horizontal line indicating the minimum amount of water that must be applied to keep the turf green and aesthetically appealing.

Figure 8.21   This sprinkler head is specially designed to deliver two sprays, with one directed to the area immediately around the spray head.
Courtesy of Rain Bird Corporation.

Figure 8.22 Sprinkler layout with overlapping head-to-head coverage.
Courtesy of Rain Bird Corporation.

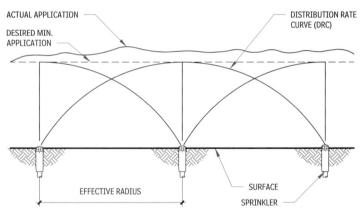

ACTUAL APPLICATION

DISTRIBUTION RATE
CURVE (DRC)

DESIRED MIN.
APPLICATION

EFFECTIVE RADIUS

SURFACE

SPRINKLER

Figure 8.23 Overlapping sprinklers complement each other.
Source: Hopper, *Landscape Architecture Graphic Standards.* Copyright John Wiley & Sons, Inc.,
2007.

The sprinkler spacing is generally the maximum spacing recommended by the manufacturer; however, spacing can be less than the maximum. Spacings less than maximum are necessary because actual site dimensions force the designer to close up the spacing to fit the project. Sprinkler spacing should not be stretched, but sprinklers can be closer together, and the actual spacing within a given area can vary. The spacing does not need to be constant between sprinklers.

Sprinkler Layout

The following rules are intended to provide some initial direction and assistance with sprinkler layout:

- Generally, lay in sprinklers around the perimeter of the landscaped area first, then lay sprinklers into the interior of the irregular shape.
- The sprinkler layout patterns should form equilateral triangles, squares, distorted triangles, and distorted squares. All the patterns mentioned are appropriate and can, and probably will, be mixed within the layout. See Figure 8.24.
- Pentagon shapes should be avoided. Pentagons generally indicate a problem—usually stretched sprinkler spacings or a sprinkler left out.
- Place sprinklers in all corners and other obtuse angles of the perimeter. (Today's water costs and public concern about water on hard surfaces dictate utilizing sprinklers in corners.)
- Consider wind. In practice, wind effects in small areas are often ignored. Prevailing wind should be considered on large, open turf areas such as parks and golf courses.
- It is preferable for the "flat" layout of the scaled irrigation drawing to show the actual number of sprinklers required, or somewhat more than might be required.

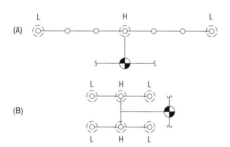

IDEAL LATERAL PIPE LAYOUT

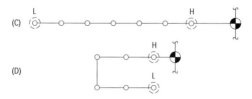

LATERAL PIPE LAYOUTS TO AVOID

Figure 8.24   Lateral layout alternatives.
Source: Hopper, *Landscape Architecture Graphic Standards.* Copyright John Wiley & Sons, Inc., 2007.

- Sprinkler overspray onto any hard surface should be minimized. Overspray wastes water and can also increase owner and designer liability.
- Spacing is manufacturer- and sprinkler nozzle–specific. (Maximum effective radius is provided in catalog performance data, and distribution rate curve data can be obtained from the manufacturer or from independent testing laboratories.)

Sprinkler Installation

Point of Connection

The point of connection should be near the water meter. The water supply should be turned off, the water supply tapped into in accordance with all applicable codes, and a gate valve shut-off installed. With the gate valve installed, the water supply can be turned on again.

Install a backflow preventer that meets all applicable codes. If the backflow preventer is installed in a location that may be exposed to freezing temperatures, consider installing a drain valve between the gate valve and backflow preventer to allow it to be drained in the winter.

Install a tee fitting (1" threaded) after the backflow preventer, to be used to connect an air compressor to blow out the irrigation system for winter. Install a threaded cap on the tee.

▶ If the point of connection is outside the building, valve boxes will need to be installed for easy access to all valves.

Main Line

The main line connects all valve manifolds to the point of connection. The main line is generally one pipe size larger than the largest lateral line. The mainline pipe run is usually marked out with spray paint. If there is existing sod, it is stripped with a flat shovel and, along with any removed soil, laid on a tarp set a couple of feet away from the trench line for later backfill and reinstallation. A trench is dug, by hand or with a trencher, at a depth that is in accordance with all applicable codes. See Figures 8.25 and 8.26.

If the main line needs to be installed under pavement, it may be possible to install the pipe without breaking up the pavement. For narrow widths such as sidewalks, a galvanized pipe with a cap threaded onto both ends can be hammered through the soil under the pavement. A water jet nozzle attached to a pipe can penetrate through the soil under the pavement. There are also horizontal augers that are specially designed for this purpose.

Figure 8.25 A trench is dug for installation of the main line and wires to be connected to valves.
Courtesy of National Lawn Sprinklers / Attilio Petroni.

Figure 8.26 This machine trenches for the pipe and lays the wires out for the valves, all at the same time.
Courtesy of National Lawn Sprinklers / Attilio Petroni.

The mainline pipe should be laid out along the trench and installed starting at the point of connection and working toward the last manifold. Pipes should be kept free of dirt and debris during installation.

▶ On large irrigation systems with multiple valve manifolds, installing isolation valves at each control valve manifold can provide desired flexibility if one specific area requires maintenance, without having to shut down the entire system.

Valve Manifolds

The valve manifolds are connected to the main line (see Figure 8.27), leaving adequate spacing between valves for any necessary maintenance. A capped pipe stub should be included for easy connection of future valves, should the system need to be expanded at some point. Valve boxes should be installed to provide easy access to the valves whenever needed (see Figure 8.28).

Figure 8.27   Valves installed between the main line and lateral lines.
Courtesy of Rain Bird Corporation.

Figure 8.28   Installation of a valve box provides easy access to the valves whenever needed.
Courtesy of Rain Bird Corporation.

Lateral Lines

The line connecting all the sprinkler heads to the zone valves should be marked out with spray paint, and, as with the main line, any existing sod should be removed and a tarp used to prevent existing sod from being damaged. Mark the location of the sprinkler heads with flags, and confirm that head-to-head coverage will be provided with the sprinkler heads specified.

The trenches for the lateral lines are cut in the same manner as for the main line, in accordance with all applicable codes (see Figure 8.29). The pipe for the lateral lines should be laid out alongside the trench and installed starting at the zone valve and working toward the last spray head. Pipes should be kept free of dirt and debris during installation.

Controller

The controller (see Figures 8.30 and 8.31) should be installed in an indoor location with easy access to an electrical outlet or source for

Figure 8.29 Machine trenches for lateral lines.
Courtesy of National Lawn Sprinklers / Attilio Petroni.

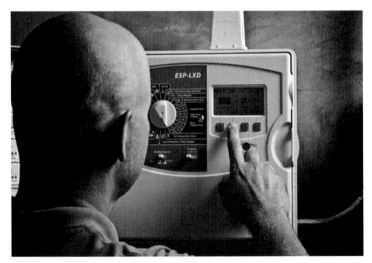

Figure 8.30 Programmable controllers can program watering days, times, duration, and a varying list of more complex factors for water efficiency.
Courtesy of Rain Bird Corporation.

Figure 8.31   Sensors connected to the controller can control watering times by factoring in sun exposure and periods of rain to maximize water efficiency. Courtesy of Rain Bird Corporation.

connection of the low-voltage transformer. Specially colored irrigation wires need to run from the controller to each of the zone valves. Each valve will need its own wire plus one common wire. The wires should be long enough to reach each of the valves. The wires should be connected to the valves with waterproof connectors. An expansion loop should be included at all changes in direction, to prevent pulling and stretching that could damage the wire.

▶ The wires connecting the controller to the zone valves can be run under the irrigation pipe, to prevent accidental damage from digging in the future.

Sprinkler Heads

The sprinkler heads can be installed at the required heights to the lateral pipes. The last head on the line should be left off, to allow the system to be flushed. With all the heads installed except for the last one on the line, the system should be turned on manually at the zone valve and the water checked to see that it is running clear and free of debris. After flushing the system, turn off the zone valve and install the last sprinkler head.

After installation of the last sprinkler head, the controller should be activated and the zone valve turned on from the controller, to ensure that the wires connecting the controller to the zone valve are connected properly. Any necessary adjustments for coverage can be made to the sprinkler heads at this time.

Backfill

After flushing, testing the system, and checking for any leaks, backfill the pipe trenches and reinstall any existing sod (if applicable). The trench and backfill should be free of any large stones that could damage the pipe or wire. The trench should be carefully backfilled and compacted in 4–6 inch lifts to prevent later settling. See Figures 8.32 and 8.33.

Sprinkler Laterals

A sprinkler lateral constitutes all of the pipe network and sprinklers that are brought together, by virtue of the pipes, and located downstream of the lateral valve. When the valve opens, the pipe gradually becomes pressurized and the sprinklers begin to function.

▶ Small laterals, having very few sprinklers, are desirable from the standpoint of management flexibility.

One technique to use when considering pipe routing is to think of yourself, the designer, as the ditching machine operator completing the excavation for the lateral you have designed. Wanting to complete the trenching work efficiently, you will consider an approach that will

Figure 8.32   Trenches are backfilled in lifts and compacted with a rammer.
Courtesy of National Lawn Sprinklers / Attilio Petroni.

Figure 8.33 The surface is restored and compacted with a roller.
Courtesy of National Lawn Sprinklers / Attilio Petroni.

minimize the number of "starts and stops," or the number of times you will have to stop, reposition your trenching machine, drop the digging chain boom, and start ditching again.

Another important consideration with lateral pipe routing is lateral hydraulics. As water flows through pipe and fittings, water pressure is lost as a result of friction with the pipe and fittings. The goal is to link sprinklers together with a pipe network that is as efficient as possible from both the installation and the hydraulic standpoints.

Sprinkler Zones

If the area to be irrigated exceeds the system design capacity, or if certain areas of the landscape have varying irrigation requirements, the irrigation system should be divided into zones. The division of the system into zones allows for specific portions of the landscape to be irrigated at different times, thereby staying within the design capacity of the system. It also allows specific areas of the landscape to receive more or less water as required.

Each zone requires its own control valve. Control valves from multiple zones can be grouped together in a valve manifold. Valve manifolds should be located close to the valves that are attached, in an accessible location for maintenance.

▶ Locate valve manifolds in a location that will not be sprayed if the irrigation system is activated manually.

Drip Irrigation

Drip irrigation is advantageous in numerous situations. A drip irrigation system can conserve water, reduce initial construction costs, and enhance plant growth.

Drip irrigation is also commonly referred to as "trickle" or "low-flow" irrigation. The basic concept of drip irrigation is to provide near-optimal soil moisture on a continuous basis while conserving water. It is a system that applies water directly to individual plants, as opposed to sprinkler systems, which irrigate all of the surface area. This is accomplished by relatively small-diameter lateral pipes with "emitters" attached, to supply each plant with water. Emitters are the key devices within the system, as their hydraulic design affords flow rates of $\frac{1}{2}$ to-2 gallons per hour. Note that these low flow rates, expressed as GPH rather than GPM, are basically different from pop-up spray sprinklers by a factor of 60.

With drip irrigation and the ability to select emitters of different flow rates and/or vary the number of emitters per plant, a flexibility becomes available to the irrigation designer that no other irrigation method affords. See Figures 8.34 through 8.36.

Figure 8.34   Driplines can be installed with emitters already in place at specified distances.
Courtesy of Rain Bird Corporation.

Figure 8.35 Driplines can have the emitter location installed on site by using a special tool that punctures the dripline and positions the emitter at a specific location where it is needed.
Courtesy of Rain Bird Corporation.

Figure 8.36 Dripline tubing is easily connected by various barbed connectors.
Courtesy of Rain Bird Corporation.

Landscaping is the arena where drip irrigation is experiencing the greatest growth. Drip irrigation has proved viable in landscapes because of the ability to save costly water while providing a growth advantage to the plants and reducing initial construction costs.

In landscapes, drip irrigation is most often used together with sprinkler irrigation, resulting in what is referred to as a combination sprinkler/drip irrigation system. Sprinklers irrigating turf grass offer the lowest cost per irrigated area, but drip irrigation offers numerous advantages over sprinklers on mulched shrub beds, trees, potted plants, and the like. It is particularly cost-effective where plant spacing exceeds 2.5 feet on centers.

Emitters

Emitters are the key component of the system. They are available in many sizes and shapes. Various emitters incorporate very different hydraulic methods to reduce pressure (or head) and create the 1- or 2-GPH flow. All emitters should incorporate a UV-inhibiting agent to prevent damage from solar radiation.

Emitters can be generally classified into two categories—point source and aerosol. A cross section through the two types of emitters, assuming that the emitter flow rate is equal, is illustrated in Figure 8.37.

A point source emitter drips water directly to the soil surface. The soil volume directly under the emitter may be saturated during system operation and immediately thereafter.

As implied by the name, the aerosol emitter throws water through the air for some distance before water contacts the soil surface. Unfortunately, aerosol emitters are not as predictable as sprinklers, and distribution rate curves are not readily available to describe their performance.

Within each category, both pressure-compensating and non-pressure-compensating emitters are available. In general, pressure-compensating emitters will be somewhat more expensive than non-pressure-compensating emitters, but pressure-compensating emitters offer the distinct advantage of tolerating significant changes in elevation without materially affecting emitter flow rate.

Emitter hose products have been available for many years. These products can be used in special landscape cases requiring that narrow turf strips be irrigated.

Guidelines to follow for proper emitter placement include:

- Balanced emitter configuration around the plant.
- An even number of emitters.

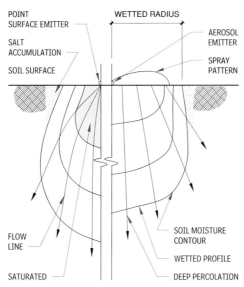

Figure 8.37 Contrast between point source and aerosol emitters having equal flow rates. Note: Point source emitters drip at 1 or 2 gallons per hour (GPH) to a point directly below the emitter. Aerosol emitters, sometimes called mini-sprinklers, throw water through the air for some distance before contacting the soil surface.
Source: Hopper, *Landscape Architecture Graphic Standards.* Copyright John Wiley & Sons, Inc., 2007.

- Emitters placed at or near the dripline of the tree and moved outward as the plant matures and the dripline expands.

Placement schemes are illustrated in Figures 8.38 through 8.42. The very flexible polyethylene or PVC hose used in landscapes lends itself to rather dramatic directional changes and circuitous pipe placement. In fact, the irrigation designer should not attempt to show the irrigation contractor every nuance of pipe placement in the design drawing, but should simply give an indication of routing and pipe quantity.

Drip Irrigation Advantages and Disadvantages
The advantages of drip irrigation include:

- Precise placement of water in the plant root zone.
- Reduced weed growth.
- Minimal (even negligible) evaporative losses.
- High application efficiency.
- Low flow rates relative to sprinkler irrigation (this implies smaller POC and lower plant investment fees, fewer valves, smaller controller, and less wire).

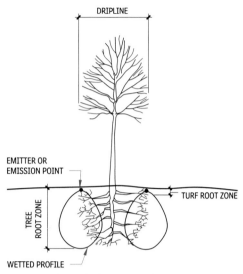

Figure 8.38   Section through drip-irrigated tree.
Source: Hopper, *Landscape Architecture Graphic Standards.* Copyright John Wiley & Sons, Inc., 2007.

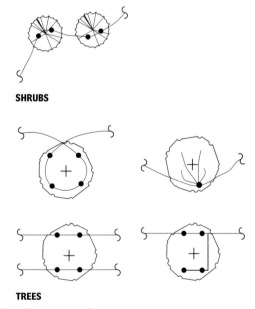

Figure 8.39   Pipe routing alternatives.
Source: Hopper, *Landscape Architecture Graphic Standards.* Copyright John Wiley & Sons, Inc., 2007.

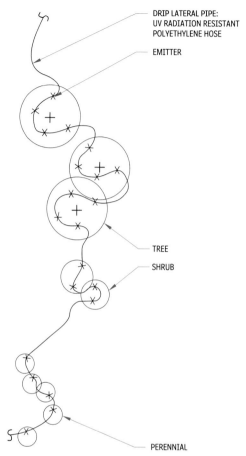

Figure 8.40 Pipe routing and emitter placement installation detail.
Source: Hopper, *Landscape Architecture Graphic Standards.* Copyright John Wiley & Sons, Inc., 2007.

- Evaporation and overland flow minimized.
- Lower installed unit cost than sprinklers (when stapled on the soil surface in shrub beds and hidden under mulch).
- No evidence of the irrigation system and, therefore, high vandal resistance.
- Favorable plant response (larger, healthier plant materials over time).
- Flexible operating hours, given possible irrigation during daytime hours, in high wind conditions, and with pedestrians present (a good way to expand the water window).
- Flexibility to add emitters if plants are added.
- Ability to introduce water-soluble fertilizers and chemicals into irrigation system with relative ease.

Figure 8.41 Distribution lines running from a multi-outlet manifold to a drip emitter.
Courtesy of Rain Bird Corporation.

Figure 8.42 Close-up of drip emitter.
Courtesy of Rain Bird Corporation.

Disadvantages of drip irrigation:

- Filtration required to prevent emitter clogging.
- Proper management more complex.
- Adaptation can be more involved than with sprinkler irrigation.
- First indication of maintenance problems (emitters clogged) may show up only after plants are stressed.

As compared to sprinkler irrigation, drip irrigation offers a rather unique opportunity. Sprinklers will apply a fairly uniform amount of water to the whole soil surface. Drip irrigation applies water only where it is needed, as dictated by an emitter. The quantity and flow rate of individual emitters irrigating plants that differ from one another in the plant pallet allow the irrigation designer to develop a scheme to provide different ratios of water to each plant species.

Drip Irrigation System Components

Typical drip irrigation system components, working downstream, are:

- Pump (or pressurized water source)
- Primary filter
- Fertilizer injector
- Primary pressure regulator
- Mainline pipe
- Remote control valve
- Secondary filtration
- Secondary pressure regulation
- Lateral manifold pipe
- Zone control valve
- Lateral pipe
- Emitters
- Flush plug

Figure 8.43 indicates how the drip lateral pipe is typically routed downstream of a zone control valve. A multi-outlet emitter is used on the tree, while two single-outlet emitters are used on each shrub. Note that the polyethylene lateral culminates at a flush plug. Flush plugs can be very simple and need not be installed in a valve box, but every lateral end should have a flush plug to facilitate periodic flushing to remove any suspended solids that have settled from moving water as the velocity drops.

Figure 8.44 shows a common approach for a remote control valve assembly used in drip irrigation. Working downstream in the detail, note the ball valve for maintenance, the wye filter for secondary filtration, the solenoid valve, and the pressure regulator. The ball valve and

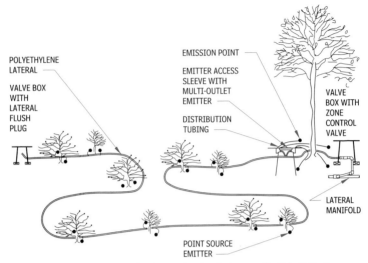

Figure 8.43 Zone control valve and polyethylene or flexible PVC pipe routing concept.
Source: Hopper, *Landscape Architecture Graphic Standards.* Copyright John Wiley & Sons, Inc., 2007.

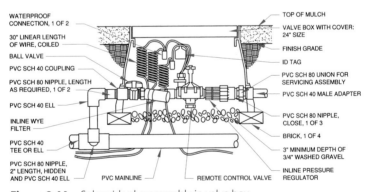

Figure 8.44 Solenoid valve assembly in valve box.
Source: Hopper, *Landscape Architecture Graphic Standards.* Copyright John Wiley & Sons, Inc., 2007.

the union, utilized together, allow the valve assembly to be removed for maintenance without the need to close other valves, which would disrupt operation of the whole system.

Zone control valves are used to isolate selected portions of the lateral for maintenance purposes. This concept consists of a manually actuated ball valve at the location where the lateral manifold stops, and upstream of the polyethylene or flexible PVC portion of the

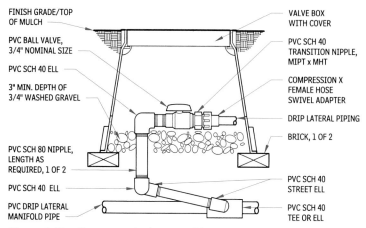

FINISH GRADE/TOP OF MULCH

PVC BALL VALVE, 3/4" NOMINAL SIZE

PVC SCH 40 ELL

3" MIN. DEPTH OF 3/4" WASHED GRAVEL

PVC SCH 80 NIPPLE, LENGTH AS REQUIRED, 1 OF 2

PVC SCH 40 ELL

PVC DRIP LATERAL MANIFOLD PIPE

VALVE BOX WITH COVER

PVC SCH 40 TRANSITION NIPPLE, MIPT x MHT

COMPRESSION X FEMALE HOSE SWIVEL ADAPTER

DRIP LATERAL PIPING

BRICK, 1 OF 2

PVC SCH 40 STREET ELL

PVC SCH 40 TEE OR ELL

Figure 8.45   Zone control valve assembly.
Source: Hopper, *Landscape Architecture Graphic Standards.* Copyright John Wiley & Sons, Inc., 2007.

lateral. Figure 8.45 shows the ball valve installed on a conventional swing joint to ensure that the valve and valve box can be easily set to final grade.

A fixed, in-line pressure regulator can be added downstream of the ball valve to further control lateral operating pressure. This approach is desirable on slopes. If primary pressure control for the lateral is accomplished at the top of the slope, secondary pressure regulation can occur downslope to overcome pressure increases due to elevation.

Although ball valves are not generally suitable for flow regulation, they can be used to fine-tune lateral flows at points downstream of pressure regulators. In addition, zone control valves are desirable when maintenance might normally interfere with lateral operation, as the zone control valve can be closed temporarily during repairs on a portion of the lateral. See Figures 8.46 and 8.47.

Installation

Installation of many drip irrigation system components is identical to that of sprinklers. There is no difference for backflow devices, main line, and mainline components. Differences in other parts of the system tend to be concerned with the lateral itself.

The lateral manifold is usually installed at a burial depth of 8 to 14 inches. Polyethylene or flexible PVC lateral pipe is often installed on the soil surface but protected under mulch and staked at 6- to 10-foot intervals with wire stakes. See Figures 8.48 through 8.53.

Figure 8.46   Zone control valves are connected to control flow to the lateral lines.
Courtesy of Rain Bird Corporation.

Figure 8.47   Multi-outlet emission devices allow multiple distribution line connections. They can control flow independently from each port and contain filters.
Courtesy of Rain Bird Corporation.

Figure 8.48   Lateral lines are connected to the main line.
Courtesy of Rain Bird Corporation.

Figure 8.49   Multi-port emission devices are connected to laterals.
Courtesy of Rain Bird Corporation.

Figure 8.50   Driplines are run from the multi-outlet to where they are needed on the site.
Courtesy of Rain Bird Corporation.

Figure 8.51   Drip emitter being installed.
Courtesy of Rain Bird Corporation.

Figure 8.52 Drip emitter installed in planting bed.
Courtesy of Rain Bird Corporation.

Figure 8.53 Mister head installed in drip emitter system.
Courtesy of Rain Bird Corporation.

Management Considerations

With drip irrigation, light but frequent irrigations are usually applied, which presents a favorable soil moisture environment. When the system is properly managed for climatic and soil conditions, the plant root zone is seldom saturated or dry; most plants respond very favorably.

Under proper irrigation system management, drip irrigation saves water because only the plant's root zone is supplied with water, and little water is lost to deep percolation, weed consumption, or soil surface evaporation.

A primary disadvantage of drip irrigation is that the small passages required of all emitters make the emitter susceptible to clogging. Therefore, the potential for clogging must be addressed at the design stage, and maintenance practices to prevent clogging must be followed after construction.

Clogging is caused by particles in the water, biological growth, precipitation of chemicals, or some combination of these causes. The prevention of clogging is first addressed through filtration. Pumps should have an intake screen. POCs should have primary filtration, which can take several forms. A device known as a "centrifugal separator" is appropriate for suspended high-density solids, such as sand, in the water. Centrifugal separators should be followed by a screen filter. Algae and other organic contaminants in the water are best removed by a medium such as a sand filter. Any filter must be backflushed, as contaminants cause excessive pressure loss across the filter. Backflushing can be automated or accomplished by manually opening the flush valve if the flushing cycle is not required too frequently.

Winterization

In freezing climates, when pipe is not installed below the frost line, water must be drained or otherwise emptied of water during the winter. The common approach to irrigation system winterization is a function of personal preferences and acceptance in the region.

If pipes are installed on a grade, drain valves can be installed at low points in the system. Figure 8.54 shows a concept for draining water from low points in the pipe. A sump must be provided and filled with gravel to receive the considerable volume of water held in the pipe.

Some disadvantages of drain valves include:

- Susceptibility to valve clogging (resulting in a slow, imperceptible leak).

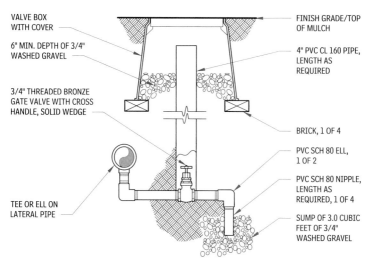

Figure 8.54 Winterization drain valve assembly.
Source: Hopper, *Landscape Architecture Graphic Standards.* Copyright John Wiley & Sons, Inc., 2007.

- Possibility of valve failure.
- Costly assembly, inclusive of piping, fittings, the valve, and a valve box.
- Unit installed cost of the irrigation system goes up when the irrigation contractor must grade trenches and pipes to drain.

If a particular project has many elevation changes and an undulating terrain, numerous drain valves must be used, and the cost can be quite high. On the other hand, some projects have a uniform grade, and a few correctly located drain valves can provide winterization at rather low cost.

An alternative that is quite common in many areas is to winterize the piping system using an air compressor to displace the water with air. Remote control valves will function under air pressure just as well as with water pressure. After the primary shutoff valve is closed, a compressor is connected at or near the water source. When mainline pressure is sufficient, a lateral is opened and water is forced out through the emission devices on the lateral. Generally, a lateral at a low elevation is winterized first and water is pushed out of the main line, through the remote control valve, and out from the lateral through the sprinklers.

Care should be taken, when winterizing with compressed air, to avoid causing harmful surges of water or air, to keep air velocity low to avoid heating of system components, and to keep pressures well below the pressure rating of pipe, fittings, and components. In most cases, air pressure should not exceed 50 to 60 PSI, and the output pressure regulator on the air compressor should be adjusted accordingly.

Control Systems

Most landscape irrigation systems are automated by using electrically or hydraulically actuated valves. Almost all new systems utilize electric valves because the latest solid-state controllers provide so many desirable features and value for the cost—features that simply cannot be provided in an electromechanical hydraulic controller.

The term "independent irrigation controller" is applied to controllers that are completely separate from (and independent of) other controllers. In other words, there is no "feedback" or communication link between these controllers, as there can be with centralized irrigation control.

The controller is an electronic device, which, in its most basic form, is an electronic calendar and clock housed in a suitable enclosure for protection from the elements. A low-voltage output (24 volts AC) is provided, as programmed, to certain "posts" or "stations" within the controller; valves open, and stay open, when voltage is applied.

Controllers are powered by 110 volts AC. Valves are opened by 24 V AC. Most remote control valves are "normally closed," meaning that the valve is closed until the solenoid is actuated by 24 V AC. A "normally open" remote control valve remains open until the solenoid is actuated.

The pedestal-type controller enclosure is generally bolted to a concrete pad. Sweep elbows in the pad protect the incoming power wire, as well as the low-voltage wires to the valves. Controllers can be wall-mounted in a garage, pump house, or maintenance building.

The basic features of any independent irrigation controller are to provide the time of day, a day-of-the-week calendar, the ability to change the time setting on each station, and a means of physically connecting stations to valve wiring.

Other features that are important in controllers include:

- Multiple programs so that sprinklers, drip emitters, bubblers, and outdoor lighting can be on completely separate operating programs.

- Extended, flexible calendars that adapt to every-third-day schedules or other imposed restrictions that are local-area-specific.
- Nonvolatile memory, which holds the time settings and program in the event of 110 V AC power loss.
- Easy adaptability to rain, freeze, or moisture sensors.

Some controllers allow every station to be programmed independently of other stations; some irrigation managers consider this feature to be quite important. Programming such a controller can be more complex and time-consuming, but the flexibility may be worth it.

Rising water and power costs demand increased attention to sound management of landscape water. Large projects, such as school or park districts, functioning under one management group should be particularly alert to their water management strategy (see Figure 8.55). Centralized irrigation control is not only an appropriate tool for improving water management, but also the means for accomplishing other objectives at the same time.

There are many central control systems to choose from; the user base is very large and geographically diverse, with hundreds of systems

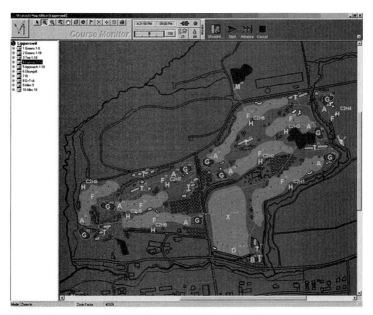

Figure 8.55 Central control systems working through a computer can provide improved water usage for large sites.
Courtesy of Rain Bird Corporation.

throughout the country. Basic technical capabilities, reliability, and cost-effectiveness have been demonstrated repeatedly to the satisfaction of even the most skeptical.

Irrigation System Management

With water rates and public awareness of wasted water increasing, irrigation managers are becoming more concerned with annual water use, system operating constraints, and total annual irrigation costs. Good irrigation managers recognize that the greatest potential for reducing water costs is implementation of a strategy to match irrigation applications to landscape water requirements. This process is known as "irrigation scheduling." To implement an irrigation scheduling program, irrigation managers must have local and current evapotranspiration rate and rainfall data, and they must employ a number of tools, some remedial, to assist in their efforts.

The evapotranspiration (ET) rate, the combined loss of water from soils by evaporation and plant transpiration, has become something of a household word in some areas because of the frequent exposure to the term on television or in the newspaper. Homeowners, and, more importantly, turf managers understand that knowing the seasonal and day-to-day variation in ET is key to proper irrigation. ET is generally expressed as inches per day (IPD). "Potential evapotranspiration," by definition, is the ET rate of the unstressed plant material.

The ideal management or irrigation scheduling program should come as close as possible to providing the precise amount of water required over a given time period. Important factors in an irrigation scheduling program include ET_0, rainfall, and soil moisture storage.

Many irrigation scheduling techniques and decisions are related to soil texture. The textural name of a soil is based on the relative percentages of sand, silt, and clay.

Figure 8.56 shows how field capacity and wilting point tend to change as a function of soil texture. "Field capacity" is the soil moisture content immediately after wetting. The "wilting point," or "wilting coefficient," is defined as the soil moisture content below which plants will wilt permanently. Wilting point is generally taken to be the lower limit of available water, although it is dependent on the plant involved as well.

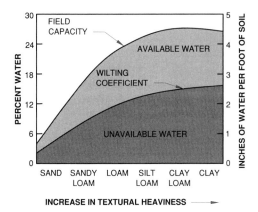

Figure 8.56 Relationship between key soil moisture parameters and soil texture.
Source: Hopper, *Landscape Architecture Graphic Standards.* Copyright John Wiley & Sons, Inc., 2007.

Soil Infiltration Rate

It is very important to match the sprinkler application rate to the soil infiltration rate. Infiltration rates are expressed as inches per hour (IPH), just as with sprinkler application rates. Even with an existing landscape and irrigation system, it is desirable to measure the infiltration rate to help determine maximum run times and the need for programmed repeats.

Practices to Avoid

- Do not overlook requirements for approvals and permits. This is particularly important if effluent water is being considered for irrigation purposes.
- Avoid damage to existing utilities; check for their locations and avoid potential conflicts in the design.
- Avoid locating remote control valves, as well as other valves, in low spots in the landscape. Valve leakage, valve sticking, and mainline failure all result in excess water flowing to low spots, and valve boxes filled with water or even covered by standing water add substantially to maintenance problems.
- Avoid overspray onto hard surfaces. Overspray wastes water and can also increase owner and designer liability. Locate sprinklers in all corners and use short-radius pop-up sprays for controlled water applications in tight spaces.

References

ALSO IN THIS BOOK

See Chapter 1, "Soils."

OTHER RESOURCES

Hopper, Leonard J. *Landscape Architectural Graphic Standards*. Hoboken, NJ: John Wiley & Sons, Inc., 2007.

Index